The Lockean Commonwealth

I0792484

The Lockean Commonwealth

Ross J. Corbett

State University of New York Press

Cover art: *The Battle of La Hogue*, by Benjamin West (c. 1778, oil on canvas), Andrew W. Mellon Fund; image courtesy of the Board of Trustees, National Gallery of Art, Washington.

Published by
State University of New York Press, Albany

© 2009 State University of New York

All rights reserved

Printed in the United States of America

No part of this book may be used or reproduced in any manner whatsoever without written permission. No part of this book may be stored in a retrieval system or transmitted in any form or by any means including electronic, electrostatic, magnetic tape, mechanical, photocopying, recording, or otherwise without the prior permission in writing of the publisher.

For information, contact State University of New York Press, Albany, NY
www.sunypress.edu

Production by Marilyn P. Semerad
Marketing by Michael Campochiaro

Library of Congress Cataloging-in-Publication Data
Corbett, Ross J., 1977–
The Lockean commonwealth / Ross J. Corbett.
p. cm.
Includes bibliographical references and index.
ISBN 978-1-4384-2791-1 (hc : alk. paper) 978-1-4384-2792-8 (pb : alk.)
1. Locke, John, 1632–1704. Two treatises of government I. Title.
JC153.L853.C37 2009
320—dc22

2008051868

10 9 8 7 6 5 4 3 2 1

Contents

Acknowledgments

This book has benefitted from the insightful comments of a number of people over the years. I am especially grateful to Thomas Pangle, Clifford Orwin, and Melissa Williams, who shepherded it from a confused and tentative idea about James Madison and Thomas Jefferson, and only incidentally about John Locke, into a passable dissertation. I would also like to thank H. Don Forbes and Nathan Tarcov for their further comments and suggestions on my dissertation. My entire dissertation committee has given me wonderful support and encouragement in revising and augmenting the ideas that are in this book, and in prodding me to publish it in a timely manner. Peter Josephson and Benjamin Kleinerman provided invaluable help in tightening some of the arguments I make and in persuading me that I did not need to write a book twice as long as this one.

While writing this book I received generous support from the Political Theory Project at Brown University. The PTP provided an intellectually stimulating atmosphere and the opportunity to teach some of the best undergraduates around, in addition to the financial resources to spend a good deal of time on research. Its associated Political Theory Workshop provided much needed feedback on a part of this book and in general was a source of valuable debate. I would also like to thank the Jepson School of Leadership Studies at the University of Richmond for the support it provided through the Jablin Dissertation Award.

A portion of chapter 3 previously appeared as "The Extraconstitutionality of Lockean Prerogative," by Ross J. Corbett, *The Review of Politics* 68, no. 3 (Summer 2006): 428–48, which is reprinted with the permission of Cambridge University Press.

The cover image is from Benjamin West's *The Battle of La Hogue*, © 1778. Image courtesy of the Board of Trustees, National Gallery of Art, Washington, DC.

Finally, I would like to acknowledge the support of my Mom, Dad, and two brothers. One deficiency of academic freedom is that it does not include the freedom to live where one wishes.

Notes Regarding the Texts

In quoting and referring to the *Two Treatises of Government*, I have used the edition in the Cambridge Texts in the History of Political Thought edited by Peter Laslett (1960, repr. Cambridge: Cambridge University Press, 1988), corrected at points in light of arguments made by Richard Cox and Nathan Tarcov; see Cox (ed.), *Second Treatise of Government*, by John Locke (Wheeling, IL: Harlan Davidson, 1982); Nathan Tarcov, *Locke's Education for Liberty* (Chicago: University of Chicago Press, 1984), 229–30, 253–54. For the *Essay Concerning Human Understanding*, I have used Peter Nidditch's abbreviated edition (Oxford: Oxford University Press, 1979). *An Essay on Toleration* is reprinted in John Locke, *Political Writings*, ed. Mark Goldie (Cambridge: Cambridge University Press, 1999): 134–59. For *The Reasonableness of Christianity*, I have used the Gateway edition, edited by George W. Ewing (Washington, DC: Regnery Gateway, 1965). I have retained Locke's capitalization, punctuation, and italicization as they appear in the above editions, except where noted or at the beginning of a sentence. I have also reversed the italicization of the Preface to *Two Treatises of Government*.

For the *Letter Concerning Toleration*, I have used J. W. Gough's translation of the Latin text as edited by Raymond Klibansky in *Epistola de Tolerantia—A Letter on Toleration* (Oxford: Clarendon Press, 1968). I have opted for this translation over William Popple's due to dissatisfaction with the latter; I have silently amended Gough's translation at points to render it more literal. Because the Gough/Klibansky book is out of print, I have also given the page number corresponding to Popple's translation in James Tully's edition of *A Letter Concerning Toleration* (Indianapolis: Hackett Publishing, 1983).

For the *Second Letter Concerning Toleration*, *A Third Letter for Toleration*, and *A Paraphrase and Notes on the Epistles of St. Paul*, I consulted the *Works of John Locke in Nine Volumes*, 12th ed. (London: Rivington, 1824; repr. Online Library of Liberty [oll.libertyfund.org]). These works are in volumes five and seven of that compilation.

I do not frequently refer to Locke's *Questions Concerning the Law of Nature* (or *Essays on the Law of Nature*). Von Leyden, presuming that Locke intended his unpublished manuscript to consist of essays, does not number those entries which consist only of a title; this can introduce some confusion as numerous interpreters will speak of, say, Locke's fifth query, which in von Leyden's edition is presented as the fourth. See John Locke, *Essays on the Law of Nature and Associated Writings*, ed. W. von Leyden (1954; repr. Oxford: Clarendon Press, 1988); cf. J. W. Gough, *John Locke's Political Philosophy*, revised ed., (Oxford: Oxford University Press, 1956), 12–17; John W. Yolton, "Locke on the Law of Nature," *The Philosophical Review* 67, no. 4 (October 1958): 477–98; and Leo Strauss, *What is Political Philosophy? and Other Studies* (1959; repr. Chicago: University of Chicago Press, 1988), 197–220. For a criticism of von Leyden's text on this point, see Robert Horwitz's introduction to *Questions Concerning the Law of Nature*, by John Locke, ed. and trans. Robert Horwitz, Jenny Strauss Clay, and Diskin Clay (Ithaca, NY: Cornell University Press, 1990), esp. 45ff.

Most of the seventeenth-century texts to which I refer are available at Early English Books Online, eebo.chadwyck.com. When giving their publication information, I refer to this website as EEBO and give the appropriate short title catalogue information (*STC* for that of Pollard and Redgrave, *Wing* for that of Donald Wing), e.g., Samuel Rutherford, *Lex Rex: The Law and the Prince* (London, 1644; EEBO, Wing R2386).

Parenthetical citations refer to Locke's works, abbreviated as follows:

ET — *An Essay on Toleration*, cited by page in Goldie (e.g., ET 140).

LCT — *A Letter Concerning Toleration,* cited by page in Gough [page in Tully] (e.g., LCT 117 [44]); I use this format even when I am quoting or otherwise referring to Popple's translation.

2LCT — *A Second Letter Concerning Toleration*, cited by page in vol. V, 1824 *Works of John Locke in Nine Volumes* (e.g., 2LCT 116).

NL — *Questions Concerning the Law of Nature*, cited by essay number and folio page number in Horwitz, et al. (e.g., NL IV 37).

TT — *Two Treatises of Government*, cited by first or second treatise and section (e.g., TT II 21).

ECHU — *An Essay Concerning Human Understanding*, cited by book, chapter, and section (e.g., ECHU I.3.5).

RC — *The Reasonableness of Christianity*, cited by section in Ewing (e.g., RC 245).

Introduction

In November of 1688, William of Orange landed in England with a substantial force of infantry and cavalry. The English king, James II, had been anticipating his son-in-law's attack for some time, and had already defeated a nephew's attempt to drive him from the throne three years earlier. In the end, however, William's invasion resembled a triumphal parade more than a military confrontation. James fled as his armies dissolved, leaving England in a delicate situation. A Convention Parliament was assembled to decide just what had happened, at least from a legal point of view. Had James II *abdicated* the throne in leaving the country? If so, why did this not make his newborn son king? Or did it? Or if his son were also to be excluded from the throne, on whatever pretext, was William the new king (he was descended from Charles I on his mother's side)? Or was his wife Mary instead a sovereign queen, being James II's eldest daughter? Was Parliament going to *decide* these issues, or simply *recognize* the legitimate heir to the throne? The answers to these questions would in effect constitute a declaration of which principles were at the root of the English system of government.

We can view what came to be known among Whig historians as the Glorious Revolution as a continuation of the imperfectly resolved Civil War. But this means, therefore, that we must recognize that it was just as ambiguous in its causes. The struggle between Catholicism and the Protestant Reformation, and between factions within the Reformation, was entangled with struggles between Parliament and the Crown, the House of Commons and the House of Lords, court and country lords. William emphasized that he was a Protestant; others, that he had the support of the people, from whom all rightful authority flows.

For a number of reasons, therefore, William's victory had to be consolidated. James II had found support in Ireland and Scotland, as did his son and grandson after him; the suppression of this Jacobitism played a major role in the ruin of those two countries. Beyond the consolidation of the *military* victory, however, was the matter of the political victory. This was not simply a question of discrediting Jacobitism in the public mind, but of establishing the nature of the alternative to counter-revolution. What sort of government did England have? What was the character of the revolution?

What followed was a barrage of pamphlets, tracts, and treatises. This was nothing new in England. There had been a push to exclude James II from the line of succession while his older brother, Charles II, was still on the throne, and the resulting Exclusion Crisis prompted a flurry of pamphleteering all its own. It is a testament to the diffusion of political power that partisans sought to influence men without speaking to them, or that the ambitious thought the opinions of the merely literate important—just a generation earlier, treatises had served an entirely private and local purpose.[1]

Most of what was written makes for tedious, uninspiring reading. It was no doubt different for those embroiled in the political contests of the time, just as most of the political commentary that is published today will thankfully be a magnet for some library's dust and mold tomorrow. Historians alone seem interested in wading through the piles of material, assembling them into critical editions, and then (what is strangest of all) reading them. And, to my knowledge, the intrepid historians who subject themselves to this tedium do not claim to find anything interesting about the perennial questions of politics. Indeed, some return from the archives to declare that there can be *nothing* of permanent or enduring interest if anyone, anywhere, at any time found what they just read interesting.

An exception to this near-universal disregard is John Locke's *Two Treatises of Government*, or at least the *Second Treatise*. In fact, I suspect that there continues to be a market for Robert Filmer's and Richard Hooker's works primarily because of the enduring popularity of Locke's. Once, when I was visiting a new doctor for a physical exam, we got to talking and I told him that I was writing a book about Locke. "Get out!" he exclaimed. It turns out that he had an intense interest in Lockean philosophy and was delighted to have the opportunity to discuss it with one of his patients. Not every physician is part of a philosophically inclined reading group, of course, but I cannot help but wonder if I would have received the same level of care had I been working on George Lawson or William Lloyd. Locke is frequently dry, but he is not irrelevant to our concerns.

It might be objected that we find Locke interesting because we misread him, or read more into the text than what he put there. I grant that it would be absurd to deny the influence of chance on what we find relevant. The *Two Treatises* receives a hearing because of its reputation, and Whig historians had an incentive to claim the great philosopher of *An Essay Concerning Human Understanding* as an intellectual forebear.[2] We might legitimately wonder whether the *Treatises* would still be among the required readings in any survey of the history of political thought worth an undergraduate student's tuition if Locke had not finally acknowledged authorship in a codicil to his will. But we should not be overawed by the differences the accidents of history can make. The *Two Treatises* was still being plagiarized by the anonymous author of the *Political Aphorisms* while Locke was very nearly ending friendships over the suggestion that he had indeed composed it.[3]

The *Two Treatises* comes to sight as the only thing written surrounding the Glorious Revolution worth reading. Yet it was not written in support of the Glorious Revolution. It certainly supports *a* revolution on the basis of the arguments it contains, but Locke appears to have composed the bulk of it in 1681–82, or even as early as 1679. He fled England in 1683 under a cloud of suspicion regarding the alleged Rye House Plot, and his fellow partisans had a hand in convincing the Duke of Monmouth to launch his ill-fated rebellion in 1685. Locke's conclusion certainly sounds like a call to arms. Yet it is not as though Locke published his treatises *before* any of the great upheavals of his day. It wasn't waiting for the Duke of Monmouth when he landed on the shores of Lyme Regis. It didn't play John the Baptist to William of Orange's redemptive invasion. Its part in the most immediate political struggles was not one of incitement to action. The timing of its publication suggests that it was always intended to be an argument that reconciled its readers to a *fait accompli* or, at most, to fight against a counter-revolution.[4]

But this was not its only purpose. After all, had that been enough, Locke might well have written something like William Lloyd's *Discourse of God's Ways of Disposing of Kingdoms*, which argued that the success of William III's invasion proved that James II had lost God's mandate to rule. Lloyd presents a bizarre argument, one bordering on the absurd, that boils down to the assertion that might is right because God rules the universe. Yet if his preface can be believed, the new king and queen were quite pleased when they heard his little sermon and directed him to publish it. The divine right of kings, as Locke had suggested in regard to Filmer, can support usurpers just as well as established inheritors of the crown (cf. TT I 121). And when you consider that a usurper must gain God's favor individually, while a Rehoboam may rule only because of his grandfather's particular merit, divine right might seem to actually favor the usurper's claim. Not surprisingly, Locke did not attempt this route. The particular principle that convinced the English people to accept William III was of decisive importance. The *Two Treatises* presents an account of government that is not tied to any particular revolution but is instead intended to "co-opt," as it were, *any* revolution.

Men do not by and large undertake earthshaking revolutions out of a calculation of narrow self-interest. They do so because they believe that their cause is just. A divination of what would be to our more material advantage may unconsciously guide our arguments about justice, but it does not supplant them. Even criminals tend to believe that they are the victims of some injustice or another that absolves them from guilt.

Yet there are always so many justifications to choose from! Perhaps Charles II had actually married Lucy Walter while in exile, making the Duke of Monmouth the legitimate heir to the throne in preference to his uncle James. Perhaps the divine right of kings applies only to kings who are faithfully Protestant. Perhaps it is the king-in-Parliament that is sovereign, and so any king who attempts to rule without Parliament in fact commits treason against the sovereign. These are only some of the justifications that were floated.

Accepting the first alternative would require either clear rules of succession as a matter of English law, together with an account of why that law must be respected over the kings' declarations, or similarly clear rules as a matter of natural law. The second would require an elaboration of what it means to be a Christian commonwealth. The third would require some sort of explanation for why Parliament was not simply the king's council; hidden within this justification is an appeal to historical accident or the right of the nobility.

The *Two Treatises* by and large privileges the claims of Parliament over the king, insofar as the presentation of the English constitution is that of the Whigs. Yet these claims gain what potency they have from the people's consent, not from Parliament's rights or its members' dignities. Locke is studiously ambiguous regarding the ultimate source of his political convictions, be it secular or Socinian or Protestant, yet he cannot seriously be accused of having intended the *Two Treatises* to be justified more by the *Reasonableness of Christianity* than by his *Letter Concerning Toleration*. And while he hints that the English people are so far from abolishing the monarchy that even in revolution they generally look to the deposed's line for a replacement, he never suggests that they would have to.

Locke does not attempt to support the Glorious Revolution on the basis of legitimate descent since that would encourage the perception that a legitimate heir *could* rule as he liked. He does not derive its goodness from an arrangement of biblical verses because that would support the principle of theocracy. And he ignores the arguments from law and history since that would make pettifoggery an authority before which common sense must bow. Locke's purpose in writing the *Two Treatises* was to influence how the people perceived a revolution that would have just happened, and to do so in order to direct the sort of government that would rule afterward.

We may safely say, then, that the *real* revolution was to take place after Locke had justified whatever events pushed one or the other Stuart brothers from the throne. The military campaigns or assassinations would get the name of the "revolution"; Locke wanted the substance of it for himself.

Locke's justification for revolution was the revolution that mattered. He published his justification, when he published it, in order to bring about the Lockean commonwealth.

In this book I am going to try to retell a somewhat familiar story about John Locke and his *Two Treatises of Government*. Before the final page is turned, a new, more radical, and significantly more interesting Locke will be available for criticism or acceptance. My focus is on the political doctrine that is presented, primarily in the second of the two treatises. That is, what I am revising is our understanding of the conclusion of Locke's reasoning, not so much our understanding of his somewhat obscured premises. At present, there is a great deal of discussion on questions like, Was Locke a Hobbesian? and How entirely wedded to the medieval natural law tradition was he? It is assumed that we know pretty much where he gets to, even if Locke scholars retire to separate intellectual ghettos when it comes to where he started from. But it is precisely the political doctrine that I think needs revisiting. The standard view of it does not adequately address what he says about prerogative. The failure to make prerogative the center of analysis distorts the image we have of the Lockean commonwealth, the kind of society that Locke sought to bring about with his book. The commonwealth appears too stable, too legalistic; it is interesting to look at only when it is broken. This image is unsustainable once the problem of prerogative is taken into view. Prerogative requires of us a reorientation. What is important to Locke, or what appears to us to be important to Locke, shifts. His concerns seem different. He seems more preoccupied with what preoccupies us.

I argue that Locke speaks to a particularly pressing and uncomfortable issue, namely, the problem of unlawful executive action. He addresses the possibility that the public safety and comfort might not always be achievable by strictly legal means, and that ambition might tempt a leader to claim that this is the case even when it is not. There are many who feel that the war on terrorism has brought about one of these possibilities or the other. Ascertaining the truth of the matter is a difficult enough challenge in itself. The greater difficulty arises, however, when we move beyond the question of fact—i.e., whether it is a concern for the public good that has motivated certain presidential decisions or rather a contempt for our Constitution's system of checks and balances—and ask how we should address either possibility should it prove to be the case. Our liberal principles demand that we not allow our government to proceed unlawfully. But as the good of the people—our good—lies at the heart of liberalism, our principles also demand that we permit it to act for that good in whatever mode necessary. It is the reconciliation of these competing principles which forms the uncomfortable problem of unlawful executive action.

What would it mean for prerogative to be central to Locke's political system? Prerogative is extralegal. Locke's point, then, is not simply to agitate for the supremacy of Parliament. Prerogative is extraconstitutional. Locke is not, then, strictly a constitutionalist. Rather, Locke is an ambivalent friend of legalism, of a disposition at once both necessary to communal life and dangerous. He is consequently also a close-cutting critic of that disposition. The tendency to look to the law in deliberations about what is to be done must be encouraged for there to be lawful governance, but it is wise only insofar as the law is a good guide to prudent action. The centrality of prerogative means that for Locke the insufficiency of the politics of law is the central problem of political practice.

In considering Locke's political doctrine through the lens of a conflict between the public good and the strict rule of laws, I am aware that I break from the approach taken by many interpreters. Some argue that the operative tension is instead one between consent and reason.[5] This difference results largely from my goals in this study. The relationship of consent and reason becomes problematic only once we move beyond Locke's political rhetoric and instead interrogate its foundations. On the surface, however, Locke conceals any difficulties that might arise from how he argues for his political doctrine, whereas the tension between legalism and necessity is plainly visible in his presentation. My contribution is to show that it is in fact a fundamental core of his presentation.

Part of what I will argue is that considerations regarding prerogative are employed by Locke to move his readers, and not just his more discerning readers, away from a focus on questions of authority, or the suspension of one's private judgment in favor of obedience to obligatory commands and guidelines. Put another way, the style of political theory attributed to Locke by Greg Forster, Ruth Grant, Kirstie McClure, A. John Simmons, and Alex Tuckness, among others, is instead what Locke attempts to move his readers away from.[6] Still, as political authority comes about only by consent, and as only reasonable consent can generate that authority, and as it is reasonable to accept as authoritative only those actions clearly undertaken pursuant to a general law made for the public good by those entrusted by the community to do so—for these reasons, this shift toward an emphasis on the public good, and the assertion that this good can be safeguarded only by a sometimes extralegal prudence, might seem to be an unusually exposed element of the ubiquitous debate between consent and reason.

Locke's antinomy of authority/law and the public good/prudence does not perfectly track that between consent and reason, however. Because the people must judge prerogative, for example, reason never competes with consent as a basis for authority.[7] Moreover, Locke's antinomy is set up by his having already declared that irrational acts of consent do not count, i.e., there can be no authority established by consent that puts those consenting to it in a worse condition than they were in before.

Locke may indeed intend to direct his best readers' attention to the problems raised by the peculiar character of his assault on absolute monarchy, but such subtleties are not a part of the public political doctrine which I am dealing with here. One may conceal or reveal esoterically the grounds of one's counsel, but one cannot dissemble regarding what one actually advises, at least if one wishes to be heeded. This is not to say, however, that I take the *Two Treatises* to be as demonstrative in nature as it might at first glance appear to be. Locke's public doctrine has a rhetorical purpose, and it contains a movement away from established ways of thinking about politics and toward Locke's own way. Locke revises his statements.

According to the now-standard account of the *Two Treatises*, the text we have was intended to be a manifesto of sorts. Locke was called upon to express the views of the more radical Whigs that had clustered around his friend and employer, Anthony Ashley-Cooper, the 1st Earl of Shaftesbury. For years they had opposed what they saw as the increasingly dictatorial stance adopted by Charles II with regard to the powers of Parliament—a stance that in their mind was either supported by the Catholic religion or was intended to foster and promote it without parliamentary meddling. When it became apparent that Charles's openly Catholic brother, James, would inherent the throne, Shaftesbury's party sought to enact a law that would exclude him from the line of succession. Charles said that they couldn't do that, and dissolved Parliament. Parliamentarians objected that he couldn't do that. Parliament mysteriously remained dissolved.

The *Two Treatises*, we are told, grew out of these conflicts. At some point, Shaftesbury's party became convinced that the ambition of the Stuart kings to rule in their own right, like the king in France, could not be checked through simply conventional means. The idea began to circulate that the king may have to be unseated. A general framework developed to argue—discreetly, of course—for that end, much of it borrowed from the contests surrounding the Civil War and the Commonwealth. Government exists by the consent of the governed, for example. Another common theme was that, just as the people have rights which others must respect or else be sanctioned by a court, so too do they have *natural* rights which the king must respect. The Parliament, as the legislature, is supreme over the king, who is just an executive of its will, went another. Locke was charged with crafting these rhetorically powerful slogans into a manifesto that would more or less make sense. There is some dispute as to whether he limited himself to this task, and I do not think he did. In any case, once William, Prince of Orange, invaded from the Netherlands and drove James II into exile, and once it was clear that a Convention Parliament would decide issues surrounding the Crown, Locke published the *Two Treatises of Government.*

The standard account of what Locke produced goes something like this. From the natural equality of every human being, it is apparent that no one has the right to command another's obedience. Life without government, however, exposes one to criminal violence. The law of nature condemns the depravations of unjust men, of course, but that law is ineffectual. What is needed is a government that makes it effective, but that does not itself violate it. The people, therefore, come together and consent to the creation of a government that will rule them according to law, not the whim of its chief magistrate. The legislative power must be distinct from the executive, and the latter must be entirely subordinate to the former. Should anyone in the government violate the principle of legislative supremacy, they have abdicated their authority and may be opposed by the people. In short, there can be no argument against what the Parliament does, or what the people do in support of Parliament.

The influence of this standard account can be seen in the scholars noted above, as well as in Carl Schmitt's assault on Locke's politics. I will discuss Schmitt at greater length in chapter 6, yet I will note here that he refers to Locke's statements regarding prerogative as proof that Locke's theoretical project was doomed to failure. Many contemporary "Lockeans" do not so much rebut Schmitt's reading of the *Two Treatises* as stubbornly defend the errors he attributes to Locke. This seems, at best, an impolitic way of defending liberal government.

But what if this accepted story about the *Two Treatises* were somehow deficient? What if it actually focused on the window dressing to the exclusion of Locke's view? Prerogative is not some undiscovered chapter, a piece of the Lockean apocrypha. Scholars of the American presidency, for example, pay it great attention, albeit with mixed results. When Locke scholars take notice of prerogative, however, they tend to try to tack it on to this now-familiar story. The result is about as satisfying as the Christian elements in the *Beowulf* epic. We are denied the easy shortcut of saying that the *Two Treatises* was written by two or more people, however. If Locke was torn—if he was both poet and interpolating scribe, in this analogy—then should not this tension loom large in our understanding of what he wrote?

Locke's purpose was not to fashion an account of political authority out of whole cloth. There were certain well established tropes which he could not avoid using without rendering the *Two Treatises* irrelevant and failing in his effort to direct the course of English politics. Locke does not emerge from those statements which mirror or imitate what had been said in various radical pamphlets surrounding the Exclusion Crisis, the Rye House Plot, the Monmouth Rebellion, and finally William's success. Rather, it is the systemization of these statements, their synthesis, that forms Locke's original contribution, and in which his mind can best be seen. Attentiveness to how he fits the pieces together, however, reveals a mind concerned with issues very different from political authority. In other words, the standard account of Locke focuses on what he could not have failed to say, rather than on what he chose to say. For a number of reasons, Locke chose his words very carefully.

Let us begin at the surface of the standard account. The king is to be ruled by law. His possession of a power above and beyond the law, therefore, would undermine this goal, and some scholars as a result have attempted to force prerogative into a purely legal framework, or at least subordinated it to Parliament. The motivation for doing so, however, is that the doctrine of prerogative as Locke plainly states it stands against the strict subordination of the executive to the law—it contradicts what we *know* about Locke's purposes. Except—why do we know this to have been Locke's purpose? Why would Locke argue for the subordination of government to *law*?

In a grand rhetorical reversal, Locke presents the right of revolution as nothing more than defending oneself against a criminal, as the support rather than the overthrow of the existing legal order (cf. TT II 226). Yet every criminal knows that it is not the *law* that stands in between him and his activity. It is the police. And they don't do that so much with a badge as with billy clubs. The whole point of revolution is that law cannot be relied upon to bring about good government. It is the threat of revolution which gives teeth to the threats of those who press Parliament's rights against the king's encroachments. As it is these encroachments, and not the battle against them, that constitute the true nature of rebellion, the people's possession of a right of revolution, and their awareness of it, constitutes "*the best fence against Rebellion*" (TT II 226).

So at first glance it appears that prerogative undermines Locke's society governed by laws, but this is misleading. The Lockean commonwealth is not sustained by laws but rather by the people's spirited vigilance. How then would prerogative undermine this? How would extralegal action be an anomaly in a community regulated by the deterrent of legitimate military opposition?

Prerogative is no longer so anomalous. Locke concludes his discussion of prerogative with how to control abuses of that power. Should any question of prerogative arise between an executive and a legislature that depends on him for its meeting, he says, there can be no judge on earth. The same is true for any conflict between the legislature and the people. In every case where there is disagreement over the rightness of an extralegal government act, there remains only what Locke calls the "appeal to Heaven." Whatever else may be said about that appeal, it is not an institutional solution, and most of the time (if not every time) it is nothing more than a military solution. That is, Locke ends his thematic treatment of prerogative the same way that he ends the *Two Treatises* as a whole.

Where is the constitution in what is left, then? Where is the law in Locke's system, if everything hinges on popular revolution? I will address this question at greater length in chapter 5, but I hope to have suggested that the rule of law plays a far lesser role in the Lockean commonwealth than the standard account would lead one to believe. It does play an important role, but mainly as a tripwire, a sort of dummy's guide to identifying tyranny.

We may compare what Locke says with how Robert Ferguson supported the revolution. Ferguson, in 1689, published *A Brief Justification of the Prince of Orange's Descent into England.*[8] And we see that it touches upon a number of familiar themes. It may be that government is ordained and instituted by God, Ferguson concedes, but the significance of this is limited to the fact that rulers are obliged to respect the laws of nature and what is vouchsafed by plain revelation. Beyond that, all government power results from explicit grants by the people, who can place what limits on it they wish. No ruler can claim any authority beyond these grants, for everyone was equally master of his property and liberty before they compacted to establish a government. Force and conquest can provide no title to rule until the people give their consent, either tacitly or explicitly. Nonresistance is a doctrine incompatible with the preservation of liberty. Any transgression of the laws is an immediate abdication of the right to rule and restores the people to the state of their primitive freedom. The real traitors, the real rebels, are those who violate the constitution in this way, not those who oppose them.

Ferguson was also a supporter of Shaftesbury's party, and like Locke fled to the Netherlands on suspicion surrounding the Rye House Plot (though, unlike Locke, he returned to England to aid the Monmouth Rebellion, after which he fled again). Not surprisingly, Ferguson's *Brief Justification* reads a lot like what certain historians tell us to find in Locke's *Two Treatises.*[9]

But note what is absent: there is no prerogative in Ferguson's description of legitimate government. He not only omits it, but he flatly denies that any such thing could legitimately be claimed in England. He goes so far as to declare it *treason* to suggest that any king or magistrate possesses more power than was explicitly granted to him by the constitution.[10] "'Tis upon this account affirmed by an English King, That he can do no wrong, because he can do nothing but what the Law impowers him. For though he hath all things Subjected to his Authority, while he acts according to Law, yet there is nothing left to his Arbitrary Will."[11] Two pages later, Ferguson says that there isn't even anything left to the king's discretion, let alone arbitrary will. It is instead Parliament where all questions of policy and government are decided. Ferguson represents a line of argument that suggests James II unkinged himself because he broke the law or because he did not recognize the supremacy of Parliament (which amounts to the same thing).

The principle Locke advances is not simply that of his party. Ferguson remarks that he will not consider government in general except insofar as is absolutely necessary. Six and a half pages later, he is done. Most of his forty-page tract deals with English history and law, various transgressions of James II, and the Convention Parliament's right to offer the crown to the Prince of Orange. Locke, by contrast, attacks Filmer and then does nothing but give general considerations of government. He does not mention James II or Charles II at all. One would almost never know from the text that there was a revolution underway, Locke's slapdash preface aside. And while Robert Ferguson mentions in passing that there is a condition of primitive freedom which precedes the agreement to form a government, John Locke provides extensive presentations of the state of nature, the law of nature, property, the family, the purposes of government in general, and what it means for government to be dissolved. Ferguson argues for a policy. Locke advances an entire stance toward politics.

I am suggesting that the rhetoric that Locke was compelled to employ was one of legalism, but that the essence of his teaching is anti-legalistic. Schmitt's criticism of liberalism would have been much easier had it been Ferguson who had achieved Locke's stature (however unlikely Ferguson's lack of subtlety made this). Locke had to speak in terms of law. He would have been irredeemably irrelevant had he not. The whole question was one of the king's rights, Parliament's rights, the people's rights, etc., and one cannot speak of rights without conjuring images of law. It was to be expected that the majority of the Whigs followed Hugo Grotius, a Dutch jurist, in attempting to explain their opposition to the Stuarts.[12] Yet my argument is that Locke saw the prevailing rhetoric of his day as a hindrance, as something which obscured the real issue. He, and the more astute of his political comrades, would have to have realized this as soon as Shaftesbury's party moved away from legislative attempts at exclusion and toward actual revolution. The securing of rights is not done by magnae cartae, petitions of right, or Coke's rulings in court, but rather by the threat and application of force. The most important right, therefore, is the one that Blackstone later remarked could never be recognized by any legal order, namely, the right to declare the legal order dissolved and oppose all who deny its dissolution.[13]

That the people possessed this right was denied, and even many who supported the revolution balked when called upon to declare that they had actually *unseated* James II, rather than simply driven him into exile. There was the danger that William might have been allowed only to rule as regent, leaving the country in an awkward position should James or his son attempt to return. There was also the question of whether William would accept so limited a title. This uncomfortable situation could hardly be resolved if the people had no right to resolve it. Locke addresses himself to this problem. His immediate purpose was to persuade his countrymen that they did have a right to drive out James II and to declare him king no more. He presents the right of revolution as a matter of common sense. He therefore intimates that the problem in England was that its people lacked common sense.

And here lies the crux of the argument. Here the importance of prerogative comes to the fore. Consider what were *not* redressable problems in England in the seventeenth century, according to Locke. The problem was not that her kings sought tyranny. That was of course a problem, but there really wasn't anything that could be done about that. Reminding rulers of their duties is a bit like celebrating diet and exercise in order to combat obesity.

The problem also was not that the kings could persuasively claim to possess certain powers which they then went on to misuse. I should say that again because it forms part of the core of my thesis. It is also contentious. It is where I think that the standard account of Locke's *Two Treatises* gets things wrong. To repeat, the problem was not the recognized powers of the Crown. The problem was not that the king could convoke and dissolve Parliament. The problem was not even that the king could suspend the operation of the laws. Rather, it was that the people did not acknowledge that they had as much a right as the king to judge whether he had abused these prerogatives; they were obedient subjects, not engaged citizens. And convincing them that they should remain obedient subjects, but of the *law*, would not just result in a somewhat servile society but an ineffectual one to boot.

Let me say a bit more about this. The months and years following the revolution saw the Bill of Rights (1689), the Triennial Act (1694), the Act of Settlement (1701), the Act of Union (1707), etc. Each of these increased the power of the English Parliament. Its power over the purse was reaffirmed, as were certain legal protections for the subject from the Crown. For example, Coke's conclusion in *Prohibitions del Roy*,[14] namely, that the king could not sit in judgment of any case, was written into the law of England, nor could the king subvert the judiciary by the simple step of just establishing his own courts. Parliament had to meet every year, with an election every three, and was responsible for setting the line of the king's succession. Scotland, its Parliament absorbed into the English, now jointly styled the Parliament of Great Britain, could not cause trouble by selecting a different king.

These are legal reforms. They are important to the extent that the law is important. I do not wish to be taken to demean the significance of this. Behavioralist accounts of the U.S. Constitution ran into trouble insofar as they disparaged the importance of the text in determining and making sense of behavior. Yet they were correct to note that something more than the text is necessary for understanding the American regime, and in this they share Locke's insight into the efficacy of law. What is crucial is not the structures and activities that the constitution demands, but those that will be enforced. In a democracy it is the structures and activities that will be enforced by the people. What is most important, then, is the stance toward politics adopted by the people.

Politics, Locke tells us, is a human affair. There is no divinely ordained government. It was created by human beings, and created to serve their temporal ends of survival and material well-being. Human beings, moreover, *had* to create governments. God's care for individuals does not extend to this world, if what Locke says about the state of nature, property, and the appeal to Heaven are any guide. We are free, therefore, to guide our politics by reason alone. We must watch the government, and this requires that the governors rule by settled, standing laws. Yet these same governors cannot rule only by law, for prudence cannot be reduced to an algorithm. We both need and cannot have the strict rule of laws.

To put the point bluntly, the problem that Locke faces is this: Secular government can exist only if secular government is somehow justified. There can be no separation of church and state unless the state can convince human beings to support it without the aid of divine inducements. What was believed both religiously and politically, however, prevented the acceptance of this. The purpose of the *Two Treatises of Government*—the purpose which makes it what it is, rather than Ferguson's *Brief Justification*, Lloyd's *Discourse*, or even the anonymous *Political Aphorisms*—is the presentation of a secular account of government. It is this idiosyncratic goal that accounts for what J. G. A. Pocock sees as Locke's being "isolated from the Whig-Tory debate, as this actually proceeded, by the ancient-constitution premise on the one hand and by the *de facto* premise on the other."[15] Locke's purpose was to nudge his countrymen closer to believing this secular account and thereby take a step away from subjection and toward citizenship. As a secular government must serve secular ends, which for Locke are materialistic ends, Locke could not long avoid the ambiguous nature of legalism. For a commonwealth like Locke's, the problems which necessitate prerogative and the danger of prerogative constitute the central problems of politics.

This book begins with a discussion of Locke's state of nature. He presents his account of government as answering the defects of this state, and so we cannot understand the rhetoric he employs in discussing political society and the rule of law (chapter 2), the necessity of prerogative (chapter 3), and what it means for government to be dissolved (chapter 4) without first obtaining a deep appreciation for the condition of man without government, too.

Chapter 2 explores the rule of law. The initial reaction to the state of nature is to establish the kind of authority whose absence defines that state. Locke asks how this might arise from consent and what constraints this sets upon the resulting authority. The theoretical problem that must be addressed if men are to escape from the state of nature is how individuals may take obligations upon themselves such that they no longer exercise their private judgment. In establishing limited government as the alternative to absolutism, Locke must address why these obligations can be accepted only so long as the government is lawful.

Prerogative, the subject of chapter 3, however, is occasioned by the inability of law to secure the public good. The main cause of legalism's political failure is what Locke calls the flux of things. But this failure, whatever its cause, means that from within a Lockean understanding the establishment of authority is an insufficient answer to the problem of politics. Put at its starkest, the elimination of states of nature is an insufficient answer to the problem of politics.

The turn away from authority and obligation as the sole touchstone of political legitimacy, moreover, complicates the question of revolution. This is especially significant because Locke is universally considered to be a theorist of revolution. The simple command, favored by many interpreters of Locke, to resist those who exceed their authority can no longer be Locke's message, for prerogative is exercised without authority in the strict sense. This complication is taken up in chapter 4.

Chapter 5 attempts to give a coherent account of what Locke is trying to do in the *Two Treatises*, drawing together the insights of the previous four chapters. The Lockean commonwealth is a mixture of authority and private judgment and so cannot be captured by a constitution that clarifies to whom and under what circumstances the commonwealth's members are obligated. It instead requires a popular diffusion of something like Locke's doctrine; it represents an outlook more than a constitution. This outlook, moreover, carries with it problems of its own.

Several questions remain about the Lockean commonwealth, however. Why should authority and obligation not be the central questions of political theory, for example, especially as Locke's more manifestly theological opponents and comrades took their cues from the fact that the Bible is more unequivocal about a duty to obey the rulers now on earth than about profiting and avoiding suffering? Why does the conflict between the need for the rule of law and the inability of rule by law to provide for the public good form the core of Locke's political theory? An answer to these questions is presented in chapter 6: Locke's politics are secular, pursing secular goals justified by secular reasons. This is seen clearly in that work of Locke's that is both undeniably political and theological in content, the *Letter Concerning Toleration.*

Chapter 1

The Condition of Man without Government

Government for Locke is ministerial. It exists to meet certain ends, and these ends are antecedent to the existence of government. In order to determine what these ends are, we must look at man without government and see what he lacks. Locke therefore introduces us to the state of nature, a state of freedom, equality, and peace. Paradoxically, such a condition is not to be endured. Instead, it is the thoroughly undesirable state from which all rational men flee and establish political society. This is certainly a startling conclusion given Locke's initial depiction. What he did not emphasize when he first introduced the state of nature was that it was a condition wherein each had a *right* to these things. These rights do not secure themselves. The state of nature is a description of man's obligations and powers according to which life ought to be free and peaceful. In practice, however, a world without political restraints upon this natural liberty is one of slavery and war. Or rather, it can easily degenerate into one. The state of war is far more prevalent where government is lacking, but it is not so ubiquitous as to make the two states identical.

Locke is quite clear about what constitutes the state of nature. It is in fact the first thing he deals with in the *Second Treatise.* It is a state of perfect freedom wherein each man may do as he wishes with himself and his possessions "without asking leave, or depending upon the Will of any other Man" (TT II 4). True, a man is restricted in this by "the bounds of the Law of Nature," but this is a small, a very small, constraint on his actions: live and let live, especially when the former takes precedence over the latter, is hardly a demanding moral code. Along with this perfect freedom comes equality. This equality may have its foundation in the fact that men are "born to all the same advantages of Nature, and the use of the same faculties," but the character of this equality is one of "Power and Jurisdiction," "no one having more than another" (TT II 4). There is no natural subordination of one human being to another, and thus all are equal. The freedom is freedom from natural obligations to another, i.e., jurisdictional equality. This equality and perfect freedom, then, are simply two aspects of the same thesis: a total and complete lack of hierarchy. Hierarchy, or obligation to another's will, is the result of convention, not nature.

If all have equal power and jurisdiction, then there is no common superior on earth. This aspect of the state of nature is so much more important than the degree of a man's freedom that Locke almost entirely forgets about the latter and instead focuses on the absence of any recognized judge as *the* defining characteristic of the state of nature.[1] "*Want of a common Judge with Authority, puts all Men in a State of Nature*" (TT II 19); "those who have no such common Appeal, I mean on Earth, are still in the state of Nature" (TT II 87); "where-ever there are any number of Men, however associated, that have no such decisive power to appeal to, there they are still *in the state of Nature*" (TT II 89); etc. It should be noted that by someone to judge, Locke also means someone to enforce judgment, i.e., someone with a "decisive power to appeal to." A judge common to two parties must be more powerful than either party.

I should pause here and discuss an objection to my identifying the absence of a recognized judge as the necessary and sufficient condition of a state of nature. A. John Simmons disagrees, positing that this is not the definition of the state of nature: it might be a sufficient condition, but it is not a necessary one.[2] This is because, he says, men may have a common judge in the state of nature, e.g., an absolute monarch. For him, a tyrant is a "common judge *without* authority." He therefore focuses more on the first quotation in the preceding paragraph than on the latter two. Seeing as the authority of the common judge is an essential feature in its definition for Locke, however, Simmons' objection does not seem appropriate. There can be no common judge without authority; if one lacks authority, one is not a judge.

So all men are free in the state of nature, and all power and jurisdiction are shared equally. Yet they are free to follow the law of nature, and the possession of jurisdiction suggests that there is some law to enforce. The definition of the state of nature is a formal one describing the legal relations between persons; it does not provide much of an idea of how those relations work themselves out in practice. Obviously, they will work differently in an anarchic state of nature than in one characterized by an absolute monarch. Locke chooses to begin with the former. He describes a state of nature devoid of any claimant to political power; it is the actual functioning of that state that Locke found important for justifying political society. It is with this in mind that we turn to the law of nature.

The Law of Nature

Perhaps no aspect of Locke's thought has attracted more attention, and been the source of more controversy, than what he says about the law of nature. I wish to avoid most of these controversies for now. Instead, I would like to focus on some of the more obvious facets of the law which operates in the state of nature. The enforcement of this law—natural executive power—is a kind of attempt to address the problems which will ultimately require a political solution, and the failure of this natural "government" is crucial for the demands placed upon actual government.[3]

The law of nature is reason (TT II 6), the "measure God has set to the actions of men for their mutual security" (TT II 8), the "common Rule and Measure God hath given to Mankind" (TT II 11) to be the "Rule betwixt Man and Man" (TT II 172). Locke can rely upon Scripture as evidence of the law of nature (cf. TT II 11), but it is the same whether one cites reason or revelation (TT II 25). It is the "Voice of Reason confirmed by inspiration" (TT II 31). "God and Reason" command man (TT II 32), his duties laid on him by "God and Nature (TT II 60, II 168), or the "Law of God and Nature" (TT II 66, II 195). It is "plain and intelligible to all rational Creatures" (TT II 124), an "Eternal Rule to all Men" and a declaration of "the Will of God," trumping every "Humane Sanction" (TT II 135). Whatever the relation between the natural faculty of reason and the divine activity of commandment in Locke's presentation, the content of the law of nature is treated as transparent to unassisted reason (cf. ECHU I.3.13).

As the law of reason, the law of nature "obliges every one" (TT II 6). How does it do so? Locke does not tell us directly in the *Two Treatises*. What Locke silently relies upon in the *Treatises* is precisely what he suggests in the *Essay Concerning Human Understanding*: reason arrives at the law of nature by applying itself to its experiences, i.e., to those things which Providence has ordered (cf. ECHU II.1.2–9, II.7.1–6, II.12.1–5, II.20.1–3, II.22, etc.; NL V). He does say in the *Two Treatises* that one must study the law of nature; it does not speak unbidden (TT II 6, II 12, II 124). It seems strange, then, that it should oblige everyone, the penalty for deviance being death or slavery (TT II 8, II 23), as if lack of study made one a criminal. After all, such lack of study might make one unwittingly commit crimes against the law of nature. It is, however, plainer than positive laws (TT II 12, II 124), and ignorance is no excuse in positive law. The poor student, then, may be treated as a lion or tiger (TT II 11).

It is not knowledge of the law of nature but the mere possession of reason, then, that counts for sufficient promulgation (TT II 57, II 63). It is the bare capacity of knowing the law that puts one under that law and makes one free under that law (TT II 58). Unpromulgated laws are not binding, and so children are not under the law of reason (TT II 57), nor are those who suffer from "defects that may happen out of the ordinary course of Nature" (TT II 60). Not to consult reason is, then, a capital crime; it is *the* crime, as far as Locke is concerned. Fools are not only to be pitied, but also punished. The prescriptive command upon which the entire law of nature is based is "be rational."[4] When Locke turns to explaining how men do evil in the *Essay Concerning Human Understanding*, he elevates the error that lies behind such actions to a moral level: "by a too hasty choice of his own making, he has imposed on himself wrong measures of good and evil" (ECHU III.21.56). To reason rightly is presented as not only profitable but also or primarily obligatory. Locke does not provide the source of this injunction.

The law of nature is amenable to so much rational scrutiny, in fact, that its content may actually change as circumstances change. Let us see one way in which this works. By nature, men have a duty to all mankind. They are part of one community, and the oneness of this community is presented as the source of man's natural law obligations: "sharing all in one Community of Nature, there cannot be supposed any such *Subordination* among us, that may Authorize us to destroy one another, as if we were made for one anothers uses, as the inferior ranks of Creatures are for ours" (TT II 6). Yet the essence of political society is the agreement to form a separate community, distinct from all mankind (TT II 211), and in agreeing to join this particular community each individual renounces his right to do whatever he thinks fit for the preservation of the rest of mankind (TT II 128).

Moreover, the individual does not entrust this right to society. Rather, society is empowered to act only for the good of the society, i.e., of the members of that society, not for the good of the rest of mankind (TT II 88, II 131, II 134, II 159). This is precisely as cold as it sounds. Society has no right to employ the force of its members to any end other than the benefit of its members. Ruth Grant is far too optimistic in suggesting that the good of one's society can conflict with the good of mankind only if one's society is unjust, especially given the fact that competition is reasonable when resources are scarce.[5] One has a duty to all of mankind and therefore a right to act on that duty. In joining political society, one alienates this right. But society has neither the right nor the duty to preserve all of mankind; its sole concern is its members. To whom has the individual alienated his right? It seems that it just disappears into thin air. And to say that I have a duty toward you but, sorry, I have no right to act on that duty, is just an underhanded way of saying that I have no duty at all. One may, then, *renounce* one's natural law obligation to all mankind. And one may do so because it is *reasonable* to do so: it is required for the escape from the state of nature.[6]

Reason teaches several things, the first being the right of self-preservation. Being possessed of "the desire, strong desire of Preserving his Life and Being," "the first and strongest desire God planted in Men, wrought into the very Principles of their Nature," each man's reason could not but assure him that he had a right to act on it (TT I 86, I 88). He knows that he *must* have a right to it, for his desire for it is just that powerful. Desire may not be the basis of right, but it is the only basis we have for knowing what is right: it must be the basis of what we say is right. The content of what human beings may know about good and evil comes from reflection upon pleasures and pains (ECHU II.20). Self-preservation is a "Fundamental, Sacred, and unalterable Law" (TT II 149). Linked with this is a prohibition on harming others, for "being all equal and independent, no one ought to harm another in his Life, Health, Liberty, or Possessions" (TT II 6). This proscription is based on the equality and independence of each, i.e., on being in the state of nature, and does not yet suggest a positive duty toward others. It is essentially a doctrine of noninterference.

There is, however, some form of positive duty that operates in the state of nature, and it is linked to self-preservation. "Every one as he is *bound to preserve himself*, and not to quit his Station wilfully; so by the like reason when his own Preservation comes not in competition, ought he, as much as he can, *to preserve the rest of Mankind*" (TT II 6). Each man is bound to preserve himself; from this follows the obligation of preserving others.[7] While this is broader than the prohibition on harm, it is not a sacrificial duty: when one's preservation is not entirely secure, e.g., when one joins in seeking reparations for an aggrieved party, it is a right, not a duty (cf. TT II 10, II 11). In the normal operation of the state of nature, it seems limited to charity, others having a claim upon one's surplus (TT I 41–42).[8] So, for example, a father may claim his child's goods if he needs them (TT I 90), even though children have a right of inheritance (TT I 88–89).[9] The only way the punishment of him who lets his possessions spoil makes sense is if he *actively* denied his neighbors access to his surplus: the goods would have rotted anyway, whether they were in his possession or not, so how could he have done them any harm unless their rotting in his possession denied them to others (cf. TT II 37)?[10] A just conqueror may not take full reparations if such would starve the innocent wife and children of the vanquished criminal, but this limitation operates only so long as the conqueror does not need such reparations for his own survival (TT II 183). One still has a right, however, to stand in common defense in the state of nature, even if this right is not yet a duty. When one is not at risk, on the other hand, one has a *duty* to aid others.

This positive duty toward others, however, might be better described as a duty toward one's community. As discussed above, this community changes. When Locke first states this duty toward others, it is a duty toward the rest of Mankind. By the law of nature, each individual "and all the rest of *Mankind are one Community*, make up one Society distinct from all other Creatures" (TT II 128). After men form distinct commonwealths, however, every articulation of the law of nature states that the duty is to "all the Members of that Society" (TT II 88), "of every person in it" (TT II 134), and to "*all* the Members of the Society" (TT II 159).

One aspect of this right or duty to preserve one's community, here understood as all of mankind, has tremendous implications for political life—man's natural power to execute the law of nature. While explaining that refraining from harming others includes respecting their "Liberty, Health, Limb, [and] Goods," Locke mentions as an aside that this restraint need not prevent one from doing "Justice on an Offender" (TT II 6). It turns out that this aside is far more significant than the general prohibition in which it is initially contained: as Patrick Coby notes, the right to preserve mankind is in fact a license to kill, so much so that the right to preserve oneself and the rest of mankind becomes the right to preserve oneself and punish offenders (cf. TT II 6 with II 87).[11] It is with this shift that the state of nature becomes unbearable, for now vengefulness acquires a claim to rationality. At present, however, it is sufficient to note that there is an executive power of the law of nature.

But why is this the case? What principle guides one to this conclusion? After all, that there should be a natural power to execute the law of nature is not immediately obvious. Indeed, an equally good case can be made that no such right exists. All power and jurisdiction in the state of nature is reciprocal, "no one having more than another" (TT II 4). One might, however, take this to mean that *no one* may punish another; all are equally *free* from the coercive adjudication of others. And indeed, Locke suggests that this conclusion is intuitive; the existence of such a power seems or actually is "strange" (TT II 9, II 13). He even implies, while leaving himself some room for escape, in his *Second Letter Concerning Toleration*, that there is no such power (2LCT 112–3). Why, then, does this equality mean that men are equally *endowed* with a right to punish, rather than equally *bereft* of such a right?

Locke initially suggests that he has biblical support for this. Against almost all common sense, he cites the words of a fratricidal Cain as evidence that "the great Law of Nature, *Who so sheddeth Mans Blood, by Man shall his Blood be shed*, . . . [was] writ in the Hearts of all Mankind" (TT II 11). Now this raises even more problems that it solves, for it seems that it is possible to be ignorant of the law "for want of study" (TT II 124); Locke devotes a chapter of the *Essay Concerning Human Understanding* to arguing that there are no innate practical principles (ECHU I.3); a parallel discussion in the *Questions Concerning the Law of Nature* concludes, "there exists no such inscription of the law of nature in our hearts" (NL IV 37); and Locke later argues that the passage from Paul's epistle to the Romans often cited in favor of an inscribed law of nature says nothing of the kind (Rom. 2:14–15; RC 19).[12] Yet, this wrinkle aside, Locke must surely have been aware that God corrects Cain in the very verse after the lamentation which he quotes: "And the LORD said unto him, Therefore whosoever slayeth Cain, vengeance shall be taken on him sevenfold" (Gen. 4:15).

Let us try to save Locke, here. Perhaps he took this as a one-time grant of clemency on God's part rather than a repudiation of Cain's understanding of justice. This is precisely how Martin Luther took this passage, for example.[13] Luther, of course, did not claim that Cain had the penalty due to murderers written upon his heart: rather, he concluded from Cain's knowledge of that penalty that Adam must have told him, meaning that God must have told Adam. Locke must have reason to believe, therefore, that either God did not tell Adam or Adam Cain that a murderer may be killed by anyone who meets him. Such a command, after all, would remove man's executive power from the law of nature and place it within the law of revelation.

Whatever the case, accepting that what we have here is a one-time grant of clemency, let us look at the general rule that would still stand. Locke says that this "great Law of Nature, *Who so sheddeth Mans Blood, by Man shall his Blood be shed*," is grounded upon man's "*Right of Self-preservation*," and "*the Right he has of Preserving all Mankind*;" the criminal, "having renounced Reason, . . . may be destroyed as a *Lyon* or a *Tyger*, one of those wild Savage Beasts, with whom Men can have no Society nor Security" (TT II 11). The verse Locke cites reads, "Whoso sheddeth man's blood, by man shall his blood be shed: for in the image of God made he man" (Gen. 9:4). To say nothing of the fact that this is one of those positive commandments given to Noah after the deluge, like the permission to eat meat (cf. TT I 39),[14] Locke at the very least has a peculiar understanding of the reason behind the "great Law of Nature" which he reads five chapters back into Cain's despair. Locke cannot claim Luther as his authority for this peculiar understanding.

Scriptural errors or improprieties aside,[15] let us not miss a peculiarity of the argument here. Locke appeals to necessity rather than a taut argument from the basis of right.[16] The law of nature serves a purpose, and that purpose cannot be served by denying each man the right to enforce it. Even the law of nature is a means to an end. "For the *Law of Nature* would, as all other Laws that concern Men in this World, be in vain, if there were no body that in the State of Nature, had a *Power to Execute* that Law, and thereby preserve the innocent and restrain offenders" (TT II 7). "Where the Laws cannot be executed, it is all one as if there were no Laws" (TT II 219). "Law will have no force if there is no punishment" (NL VII 76). The fact that there is no natural superiority in jurisdiction, however, means only that "if any one in the State of Nature may punish another, for any evil he has done, every one may do so" (TT II 7). It is only when it is considered that no nonhuman agent effectively enforces the law of nature that every human gains that power. The lack of impediment to that power becomes a positive right to it once necessity is considered. "For in that *State of perfect Equality*, where naturally there is no superiority or jurisdiction of one, over another, what any may do in Prosecution of that Law, every one must needs have a Right to do" (TT II 7).[17]

The above argument, and that in the section that follows it (TT II 8), is not airtight: it will still "seem a very strange Doctrine to some Men" (TT II 9). Locke must counter this objection. He here leaves off talking about rights entirely and turns solely to political necessity. This doctrine, he says, ought not seem strange to anyone who would found governments on consent, for it articulates nothing but the power employed by princes and states in the punishment of aliens: such power must be natural, for they have no contractual authority over aliens.[18] Of course, one could counter that this in no way proves that princes and states are *right* when they punish aliens. After all, to take the way things are as the way things should be would grant to fathers the right of eating their children (TT I 57) and "the practice of the strong and powerful, how universal soever it may be, is seldom the rule of Right" (TT II 180). As a practical matter, however, we must grant that princes and states are correct in punishing aliens if we are to avoid the anarchy that would result from basing government on consent but leaving it powerless to redress (rather than defend against) injuries inflicted on its subjects by aliens. And if princes have this power, then everyone must have had this power in the state of nature. Locke's response to the "some Men" to whom this doctrine *seems* very strange reveals something about them. They must accept equality in the state of nature and see the power of princes and states as arising from consent; they may also, Locke assumes, be convinced by appeals to political necessity alone. If this were not the case, his arguments here would not be persuasive to his hypothetical audience.

Locke almost immediately summons up another objection. Now, however, man's natural executive power actually *is* a "strange Doctrine" (TT II 13).[19] Now, it appears to act *against* political necessity by fostering anarchy. The first time it was called a strange doctrine (TT II 9), it was defended as true because it prevented disorder and confusion in the treatment of aliens; now it is assailed since disorder and confusion will follow precisely if it *is* true. All the arguments for it on the basis of right (TT II 7–8, II 10–12) have not convinced Locke's objector. The sole basis of his assent or dissent is whether the doctrine conforms to the ends of the law of nature—the increase, peace, and preservation of mankind (TT I 59, II 7, II 182)—not whether it conforms to what Locke says are the bases of the law of nature. Is Locke's law of nature a salutary teaching for the cause of peace or not, his objector asks? Might not some other teaching conduce to peace more, one that does not lead to disorder and confusion, and must we not instead call *that* true? Locke's objector asks if all this does not necessitate, and thereby validate, a doctrine of divine right (TT II 13). Locke replies by conceding that civil government is the answer, i.e., that the law of nature is actually inadequate for preserving mankind. He continues, however, by attacking absolute monarchy, regardless of its justifying doctrine, as being more inconvenient than civil government, or even anarchy. And as Locke's strange doctrine is necessary for a nonabsolutist, civil government, it stands as true.

This seems an appropriate place to note that natural executive power is not the only doctrine that Locke calls strange, or says will seem strange at first, and that he deals with all of them in the same manner. The first strange doctrine belongs to Filmer (TT I 80), or is deciphered from Filmer's convoluted statements into "plain *English*" by Locke, and states that "Regal and Supreme Power is properly and truly his, who can by any Means seize upon it: and if this be, to be *properly a King*, I wonder how he came to think of, or where he will find, an Usurper" (TT I 79). And while Locke tells his reader to examine carefully Filmer's doctrine of usurpation, attempting to make it "intelligible" (TT Pref.), the only argument he himself musters against government being a consequence "of Force and Violence . . . where the strongest carries it" is that such a thesis would "lay a Foundation for perpetual Disorder and Mischief, Tumult, Sedition and Rebellion" (TT II 1). The third and final strange doctrine puts limits on the rights of conquest (TT II 180), but this doctrine will only seem strange. Locke's doctrine of resistance to unjust conquerors, usurpers, and tyrants will actually yield a better peace in the world than a doctrine of passivity: to preach up the latter is to promote a peace "which consists only in Violence and Rapine; and which is to be maintain'd only for the benefit of Robbers and Oppressors," "an admirable Peace betwixt the Mighty and the Mean" where the Lamb, "without resistance," yields "his Throat to be torn by the imperious Wolf" (TT II 228). The law of nature "willeth the Peace and *Preservation of all Mankind*" (TT II 7), and its content, strange as it might seem at first, must be determined by that light. We might wonder whether it is coincidence that each "strange" doctrine involves a case where Locke might seem to break from Hobbes and is assessed on Hobbesian grounds.

The law of nature needs an enforcer, and so "*every Man hath a Right to punish the Offender, and be Executioner of the Law of Nature*" (TT II 8). The means of this enforcement is war. One cannot enforce the Law of Peace peaceably. "They who by any Injustice offended, will seldom fail, where they are able, by force to make good their Injustice" (TT II 126), "since 'tis easily to be imagined, that he who was so unjust as to do his Brother an Injury, will scarce be so just as to condemn himself for it" (TT II 13). Moreover, this is not simply due to the utter viciousness of the criminal: one is not obligated to endure the absolute dominion of another, one's welfare being dependent entirely upon their will, even if such dominion is just (TT II 23). Criminals simply are not obligated to submit to just punishment. Reason might have a claim to authority under the sign of the law of nature, but the reasonable do not. Considering the severity of the crime, and the absoluteness of the punishment it may require, the law of nature would even *prohibit* the criminal from surrendering. He most certainly does not *gain* a right denied to innocents by his crime, namely, the right to put himself under the absolute authority of another (TT II 23).[20] The punishment of serious offenders is therefore "dangerous, and frequently destructive, to those who attempt it" (TT II 126).

Still, it may be preferable, considering the circumstances, to risk such danger rather than to suffer the criminal to live. In violating the law of nature, the criminal "becomes degenerate, and declares himself to quit the Principles of Human Nature" (TT II 10); he may be "destroyed as a *Lyon* or a *Tyger*, one of those wild Savage Beasts, with whom Men can have no Society nor Security" (TT II 11). He revolts "from his own kind to that of Beasts by making Force which is theirs, to be his rule of right" (TT II 172). Those who make might their right declare war on all mankind (TT II 11). It may be more dangerous to live among such beasts than to do something about it. Reason does not, after all, demand inaction in the face of every danger. Locke says nothing about these criminals' having been created in the image of God, nor their victims'—the reason the Bible gives for the verse Locke cites in support of this principle (cf. Gen. 9:6; TT II 11).

The right that any man has over such beasts is not, however, any "Absolute or Arbitrary Power" (TT II 8). A man is free, but not free to behave arbitrarily. In this case, Locke means that one is not free to violate the law of nature. "*Freedom of Nature* is to be under no other restraint but the Law of Nature" (TT II 22). To act arbitrarily, then, is to act irrationally.[21] The executioner may do what "calm reason and conscience dictates," but may not "use a Criminal, when he has got him in his hands, according to the passionate heats, or boundless extravagancy of his own Will" (TT II 8). He may not act out of a spirit of wrathful vengeance, but rather may do only "so much as may serve for *Reparation* and *Restraint*" (TT II 8).

The right of reparation springs from the right of self-preservation, while the right of restraining the criminal from future transgressions springs from the right to preserve all mankind (TT II 11). It may involve both disarming the criminal and deterring others (TT II 8), which disarmament, "*to secure* Men from the attempts of a Criminal," may involve killing him (TT II 11). Death may be the appropriate penalty even if the crime did not rise to the level of murder (TT II 12). The fact that he is "to deter others from doing the like

Injury . . . by the Example of the punishment that attends it" (TT II 11) means that, depending on the viciousness of the intended *audience*, such death need not be painless; the magistrate's sword is "for a *Terror to Evil Doers*" (TT I 92). To act arbitrarily is to act against the law of nature, i.e., to act irrationally; this does not mean that one cannot act bloodily.

Inconveniences of the State of Nature

The state of nature is governed by an enforced law, a law which is plain and intelligible to all rational creatures, one that preserves the innocent in the enjoyment of their properties, grants children the protection they need until they reach such an age whereat they can shift for themselves, and punishes those who cannot abide by the possession of their just share with penalties suited to the purpose. It is also "unsafe and uneasie" (TT II 131), "full of fears and continual dangers" (TT II 123), "an ill condition" (TT II 127) wherein one is "exposed to all the Misery and Inconveniences that a Man can fear from one [who is] corrupted with Flattery, and armed with Power" (TT II 91[22]), and "therefore not to be endured" (TT II 13). Government is "hardly to be avoided amongst Men that live together" (TT II 105; cf. TT II 74). The state of nature is defined juridically but described anthropologically. We must somehow reconcile these two views of the state of nature.[23]

A. John Simmons has claimed that Locke got himself into needless trouble by describing this state of nature, since many possible social conditions, ranging from idyllic peace to absolutist tyranny to something resembling Hobbesian brutality, are possible under his definition.[24] True, but the same can be said for Hobbes, for it is only when his definition is joined with his account of human nature that it acquires its frightening aspects.[25] It is, therefore, reasonable to join Locke's scattered account of human nature to his definition and see how it leads to precisely that awful state from which he says men flee into political society.

To start, let us examine how well the law of nature is enforced. Locke points us to "three defects" (TT II 131). The first is the absence of "an *establish'd*, settled, known *Law*, received and allowed by common consent to be the Standard of Right and Wrong" (TT II 124). The problem is not that the law of nature does not exist, or that men do not accept that it exists, but that they quarrel over its content, "being biassed by their Interest, as well as ignorant for want of study of it." Men do in fact guide their lives by a moral code, but that code is born of selfishness and stupidity: they mistake their own mindless will for the Law of Reason.

Even if, however, the law of nature were inscribed upon the hearts of men, there would still be criminal violence. This is due to the second defect.

"In the State of Nature there wants *a known and indifferent Judge*, with Authority to determine all differences according to the established Law" (TT II 125). Everyone in the state of nature is judge in his own case. Indeed, this equality of power and jurisdiction, here called a defect, is the defining characteristic of the state of nature.[26] Self-love makes men partial to themselves and to their friends, while ill nature, passion, and revenge carry them too far in punishing those whom they have judged to have wronged them (TT II 13, II 125).

This lack of an impartial judge is so great that the state of nature runs the risk of becoming a war of all against all. The crime of murder, or any violent act which begins the state of war, is so heinous that through it one declares war on all mankind (TT II 11, II 16–18). The punishment for such an act is death (TT II 12). It is once Locke reveals this facet of his doctrine of natural executive power that it is assailed on the grounds of peace (TT II 13).

There are two parts to the objection: one, the problem of determining guilt, and two, the problem of determining proportionality in punishment. Neither problem, however, is caused by reason's being insufficient to know the law of nature and so be the standard for judging both of these. Rather, self-love, ill nature, passion, and revenge pervert one's application of the law. This objection could have been raised earlier, but it is only now that such misapplication can lead to widespread violence: it is only now that Locke mentions that men may declare war on all mankind. Carrying out a sentence of death on one who is innocent must be treated as murder if it stems from partiality rather than an honest mistake, and so be a declaration of war on all mankind. Moreover, punishing one with death who, though a criminal, does not deserve it, is actually to commit murder, and so to once again declare war on all mankind if it stems from ill nature, passion, or revenge.[27] We must certainly wonder what proportion of mankind in the state of nature would go through life without so declaring war on the rest of mankind, and hence the objection.

Let us suppose, however, that not everyone in the state of nature is as irrational as the partial judges just described. Even individuals who have studied the law of nature and apply it justly cannot remedy the above two defects: "In the state of Nature there often wants *Power* to back and support the Sentence when right, and to *give* it due *Execution*" (TT II 126). Those who judge rightly have "ordinarily but [their] own single strength," and so lack "force enough to defend [themselves] from Injuries, or to punish Delinquents" (TT II 136). This leads to a more pervasive problem than the overzealous prosecution discussed above: craven noninterference. The desire to preserve others is not primary or even secondary by nature (cf. TT I 88), and men are negligent in correcting the wrongs done to others (TT II 125). The inconveniences of the state of nature stem from "the irregular and uncertain exercise of the Power every Man has of punishing the transgressions of others" (TT II 127). Moreover, the danger that such enforcement exposes one to makes this inaction reasonable (TT II 126): one is obligated to help others only when one's own preservation is not at stake (TT II 6). This is, of course, not such a problem if men, when standing together, possess such an overwhelming force that the criminal cannot possibly defeat all of them, and is unlikely to be able to harm any *particular* one of them. The real problem comes when such an overwhelming force is not to be had by the rational. Let us then turn from the structural problems of the state of nature to the nature of man, or rather, to the nature of most men.

The "Principles of Human Nature" demand that one follow "the right Rule of Reason" (TT II 10). This should not be taken, however, as an assertion on Locke's part that man is by nature rational. Rather, any individual that does not live according to reason is "degenerate," a "noxious Creature." More than this, the "corruption, and vitiousness of degenerate Men" is so widespread that large numbers of men must quit the "great and natural Community" of men and "by positive agreements combine into smaller and divided associations" (TT II 128). Nor is this problem caused by a minority whose crimes cause tribulations out of proportion to their numbers: the "greater part" of mankind are "no strict Observers of Equity and Justice" (TT II 123). Most men in fact act irrationally.

It has been suggested that this viciousness is not natural to man but is rather the result of the tacit agreement to the use of money.[28] One can, of course, point to certain of Locke's statements to support this view. Meager possessions leave little cause for conflicts with one's rulers, for example (TT II 107). There could be "little room for Quarrels or Contentions about Property" when land was so plentiful that no one could enclose so much that another was harmed by it (TT II 31). Were each man to own only so much land as is necessary to provide for himself and his family, Locke assures us, there would still be more than enough land for everyone to have his share (TT II 36). In the absence of money, it is simply senseless to cultivate more land than one can use (TT II 28, II 48–49, II 51). The presence of such free land, however, is incompatible with the use of money (TT II 45), and as things now stand, Locke continues, the scarcity of land is such that nothing can compensate for its loss (TT II 184).

Money may certainly have had an effect on the state of nature, but its impact has been overstated. Even after the invention of money, there can be little room for quarrel (TT II 39, II 51; money having been introduced at II 36). Rather, it is covetousness and ambition that are the problem (TT

II 107). Nor is it the case that money allows for such opulence as to reveal man's natural covetousness, it having been hidden before; money is far from the root cause of the evil. The various tribes in America choose kings in order to lead them in war (TT II 102, II 108), even though they have few possessions (TT II 41), no money (TT II 108), and are out of the reach of conquering empires (TT II 105). Men in society are naturally wary of those outside of it (TT II 107). Yet what is there to fear from others? It turns out that there *is* something to dispute over before the advent of money. Men might not fear their king yet, but even in this primitive state they need a king to protect themselves from each other and from others altogether. Money corrupts politics, not the state of nature. Even penniless men cannot live without government; the corruption of money means only that men cannot live under kings.[29]

Mankind ought to be part of one community by nature, distinct from all other creatures (TT II 128). In this view, man is distinguished by his use of reason, just as the inferior species are by their lack thereof (TT II 172). But this community must disband in favor of more particular societies precisely because men do not, in fact, respect the law of nature, i.e., do not act rationally, and so indeed appear as if they were subhuman. They fail to exhibit the defining characteristic of humanity—not a minority, but most men. Locke goes even further than this. It is not just that most men are like beasts, with whom there can be no security or society, degenerate through their abandonment of reason, but that man is potentially more vicious than any lion, tiger, wolf, or any other creature which Locke says may doubtlessly be destroyed. Man is the most vicious of predators.[30] He is capable of the "most unnatural Murder," a "Cruelty" unknown in the "Dens of Lions and Nurseries of Wolves" (TT I 56). The "busie mind of Man" can "carry him to a Brutality below the level of Beasts, when he quits his reason, which places him almost equal to Angels." It is this characteristically human propensity—to have a busy mind without being rational—that makes mankind so dangerous. "Custom" and "Fashion" take over only where folly or craft leave off (cf. TT I 58). It is with such men that the rational individual in the state of nature must contend.

The state of nature has yet a further inconvenience, in addition to poor enforcement of the natural law and the general degeneracy of men. Men do, it turns out, have a common judge in their dealings with each other in that state, though it is not a judge on earth. Man's common judge is in Heaven. This is the final judge, one to which man may appeal for redress of wrongs. Indeed, it is the only appeal left open to men where there is no judge on earth (TT II 20, II 168); it is the only appeal when one is in the state of war

(TT II 21, II 242). The appeal to Heaven is an appeal to arms, all that is left to one in the state of war. This same imagery—God's judgment as the war's outcome—had been used four years earlier, in the *Declaration of James Duke of Monmouth* in his unsuccessful bid to unseat his uncle, James II:

> And Wee make our appeale unto *God*, . . . and above all our dependance & trust is upon the *Lord of hosts*, in whose name Wee goe forth, & to whom wee commit our cause, and referr the dicision betwixt us & our Enemies in the *Day of Battle. Now let us play the men, for our People, & for the Cities of our God, and the Lord do that which seemeth good unto him.*[31]

As Locke puts it, "In all States and Conditions the true remedy of *Force* without Authority, is to oppose *Force* to it" (TT II 155); patience and humility cannot save a life (TT II 228). Jephthah "leads out his Army to Battle" (TT II 21; cf. TT II 176, II 221).[32]

When men have no common judge on earth, their only judge is in Heaven. If Heaven is, as Locke repeatedly says it is, the judge of right (TT II 21, II 241), it is the judge of the law of nature, of the law of reason. And if, as Locke also states, there is no hand of munificent Providence to be found in the judgment of Heaven[33]—if Heaven, as judge of a law that concerns men in this world and whose judgment must also then be of this world (TT II 7), does not judge *by that law*, i.e., does not judge by reason, but rather *by force alone*—the sole possible conclusion is that the law of reason is judged by an irrational judge.

Heaven is the only judge common to men in the state of nature, but it is not a competent judge. Might is not right; robbers, pirates, and conquerors gain no right of empire by their dominion (TT II 175). But this is, in the state of nature, impossible to prove. The only judge says otherwise. All natural, i.e., rational, rights and relationships are absent in practice. One who has lost the war is judged to justly be a slave. An unjust conqueror is one who is later deposed. There is nothing in Locke of Richard Hooker's sanguine assurance that "conquerors by just and lawful wars do hold their power over such multitudes as a thing descending unto them, divine providence itself so disposing. For it is God who giveth victory in the day of war."[34] The rule of force does not operate only at the extremes of the state of nature; rather, in that state every least difference is likely to end in the state of war, with both sides appealing to Heaven (TT II 21).

To call such a state "inconvenient" is perhaps something of an understatement on Locke's part. Under the stewardship of Heaven, the state of nature is perverse. The absurdity of its "moral judgments" would be laughable were it not cause for lament. The outcome of every appeal to Heaven is determined solely by one's "procedural maneuvering" in its "courtroom"—the case before it is important only for initiating the proceedings, not for its "merits." If one views this spectacle in the belief that there is some standard of judgment other than might, then the terms *just* and *unjust*, *right* and *wrong*, are applied indiscriminately. We might feel the temptation to ascribe more to the appeal to Heaven than what Locke explicitly says about it. There is something unseemly about the suggestion that justice in the state of nature is simply blind, and so we might interpret some sort of divine support, however little, into Locke's account. The alternative to justice's blindness is its dementia.

Seeing the inconveniences of Locke's state of nature, one is tempted to recall to mind Hobbes's description of that state. It is, however, in at least one respect even worse. Hobbes, beginning from the passions of man, finds that rational individuals in the state of nature will lead lives that are nasty, brutish, and short. Each individual, recognizing that all are equally capable of killing, and so must all be taken to be equally wise as well, looks to his own passions and finds that *being* killed is the worst evil that can befall him. Recognizing this, he abandons all pretense to lofty moral codes and looks out for himself. Hobbes's war of all against all is among rational, or mostly rational, individuals.[35]

Locke's state of nature might, then, seem better than Hobbes's.[36] After all, he suggests that rational individuals can live together in peace; the whole rhetorical point of the law of nature, of the discussion of property, and of the family, is to show that rational individuals can indeed live together in peace.[37] Just because rational individuals can do so, however, does not mean that Locke's state of nature is peaceful. Rational individuals do not predominate; their rationality does not determine how the state of nature actually functions. Locke's state of war is between the rational few and the vast majority of men who live like beasts, the latter also warring among themselves. And so one might believe that the state of nature is unbearable because men are ignorant of the existence of the law of nature.

But this is not actually the case. In fact, when acknowledged by those heedless of reason, the law of nature increases, rather than reduces, the violence. Locke does not argue for the existence of such a law—he does not have to. Men recognize that there is a standard of right conduct that applies universally. In fact, they insist upon it. They just do not understand that its content is not defined such as to always place them in the right, no matter what they do. They might of course claim such an understanding, but they betray themselves whenever they are called upon to judge between themselves and another. Men also recognize that this universal standard is a permission to kill, and to do so brutally, if it will deter future aggression; they just do not understand that it includes a permission to kill the *guilty*, and that there is a difference between deterrence and wrath, displeasure and guilt. Locke omits any discussion of Hobbes's reasons for war, namely, diffidence, competition, and glory; Locke mentions "Self-love," "Ill Nature," "Passion," "Revenge," and "the partiality and violence of Men" (TT II 13, II 125). The problem is the moral indignation of those who, in the eyes of the law of nature, are criminals, raging against those who would defend their rights against their rapacity. The problem is the misapplication of justice, its being used largely to justify injustice. Man's understanding of the law of nature is just as demented as Heaven's.

This is not, however, a war of all against all. Locke assures us of this fact, "however some Men have confounded" the state of nature and that of war (TT II 19). One begins the state of war by "declaring by Word or Action, not a passionate and hasty, but a sedate setled Design, upon another Mans Life" (TT II 16). Even though murderers declare war on all mankind (TT II 11), this need not make everyone a murderer. Hobbes, however, does say that his state of nature is a state of war. How is this possible if it is Locke's that is actually the more terrible state?

Let us look at Hobbes's definition of war:

> For WAR consisteth not in battle only, or the act of fighting, but in a tract of time wherein the will to contend by battle is sufficiently known. And therefore, the notion of *time* is to be considered in the nature of war, as it is in the nature of weather. For as the nature of foul weather lieth not in a shower or two of rain, but in an inclination thereto of many days together, so the nature of war consisteth not in actual fighting, but in the known disposition thereto during all the time there is no assurance to the contrary.[38]

Hobbes confounded the state of war with the state of nature because he misdefined war: this seems to be Locke's rebuttal. To extend the analogy to weather, war is not to be measured by the inclination to foul weather, but in that tract of time wherein it is actually raining (and, since the state of war continues in the state of nature, in all times subsequent to the falling of rain). Fearful men are not at war simply because they are fearful, says Locke. The state of nature, after all, is "full of fears and continual dangers" (TT II 123). It is just not full of war.[39] Which is to say, war is ubiquitous according to Hobbes's definition; according to Locke's, it is just widespread.

The Rule of Reason

Whatever its origin—Locke is steadfast in affirming that it is the work of Providence—the world need not be hospitable to human beings. It is not visibly governed by reason, but rather by force; such force may or may not favor the more just, i.e., more rational, individual. This is the experience upon which reason works.[40] The law of nature, then, stands as reason's response to Providence; it is an attempt to make the world rational, accepting that such a project requires the *enforcement* of reason. Reason might work by persuasion, but the rule of reason requires an element of compulsion.

In its most benign form, such compulsion is directed against the Earth, forcing it to yield up more than the miserable penury which providence leaves to men (TT II 32, II 35). In the state of nature, such compulsion is directed against the more vicious beasts—and against men who degrade themselves to that level. The law of nature represents man's attempt to overcome providence, if perhaps in obedience to the source of that providence, but it is ultimately a flawed attempt. Vicious and degenerate men are so much the norm in an atomized state of nature that a defused enforcement of justice fails to control them; the problem is so widespread that adherence to the law of nature does not even solve the problem of penury. God has made it necessary for men to join political society (TT II 77). This is the conclusion reason comes to after examining the experience of the state of nature.

Reason also comes to the remedy. Men will institute governments which rule according to positive law, forsaking the direct rule of the law of nature. But, as the experience of tyranny teaches men, even this is not enough to escape the rule of force; such positive laws must be judged by the law of nature. Men cannot wholly forsake the law of nature, at least as a standard of judgment. And as the situation in which a man finds himself is different from either the brute or the ideal states of nature, the law of nature, in its very content, may subtly alter, as well. This is simply to recognize that what one should do, how one should behave, is always a question of what should be done in this or that context. Such alterations have already been discussed.

The law of nature is an imperfect attempt to establish the rule of reason. Political society—not just any coming together that is called political, but *Locke's* political society—is a more perfect attempt to establish the rule of reason. Still, the law of nature does not unequivocally command the entrance into political society, or rather into any particular political society. One might say that Locke, with Hobbes, believed that the law of nature commands one to seek peace where it can be had.[41] There is, however, significantly more discretion in this command in Locke: fewer forms of organization count as political society. This discretion appears most in deciding whether a given agreement will actually result in political society. In Hobbes, one might say, one must jump at the first contract that is offered; not so in Locke. The exit from the state of nature is not to be presumed. Something positive is needed. Something other than raw compulsion is needed. This is what consent provides.

Consent is the only way to leave the state of nature and establish some form of the rule of reason, to the extent that such is possible. Locke argues that, historically, all government had its genesis in the consent of the governed (TT II 102, II 103). Every society for which we have records of its founding had its beginning in some form of contract (TT II 101), and the continued rule of fathers as kings upon the adulthood of their children is possible only by the tacit consent of those same children (TT II 74). A political anthropology, even one so obviously fictional as this one, however, is insufficient to justify what ought to occur.

Consent is needed because it is the only way to give the recognized judge any power beyond that of Heaven, i.e., beyond the rule of beasts. Since the creation and continuance of society is based on consent, there could conceivably be an element of reason involved; as such, society may be justified rather than simply described.[42] Men support this judge by ceding to it their individual force, it is true, but as a practical matter that umpire cannot then use that force to compel them to exercise it according to his decisions. Men must agree to obey. Yet that judge must, in order to be judge, have a privileged position: men must be *obligated* to obey. To have a judge rule by compelling the recognition of his legitimacy is not to establish the rule of reason or anything like it; such would be tyranny, not a form of political society at all. To establish political society, then, men must be obligated to comply by something other than force. Obligation is effective only if the individual himself actually feels obligated. This can be accomplished, to the extent that it can be accomplished, only by his consent, as will be discussed in the next chapter.

Chapter 2

The Rule of Law

Political society is the opposite of the state of nature. The essence of the latter lies in the absence of a common judge on earth, while the former is defined by the presence of one (TT II 87). We come to a better understanding of what it means to have government by thinking about life without it, but it is political society that is conceptually prior. That is, the state of nature is defined *against* political society: it is a negative abstraction from a concrete image. There are power relationships in the state of nature, just as there are in political society; compulsion, law, friendship and enmity, among other things, are common to both. What the state of nature reveals, however, is the connection between government and legitimacy. A common judge on earth is a commonly *recognized* judge on earth—*this* is what we mean by government. Brigands plunder; rulers tax. The difference seems almost intuitive; articulating the difference has proven less tractable. And yet most people maintain that there is a difference. Locke has "never yet found any one so great a Patron of Anarchy as to affirm" the opposite, that "the State of Nature and Civil Society are one and the same thing" (TT II 94).

The above follows from the definitions of each state: each is essentially a description of how human beings are to relate to each other. When considered in this juridical respect, the state of nature is conceptually posterior to civil society. Yet Locke does not limit himself to juridical considerations, nor do these tell us why we should prefer the latter over the former. Of equal importance are the practices of men whose relations are defined by the lack of government. It is the actual functioning of the state of nature that makes political society necessary. The practices of government, as a result, are determined by the inconveniences of its absence. That is, the state of nature becomes the die with which political society is struck; the latter becomes posterior to the former.

This reversal in priorities is of course perfectly reasonable: the state of nature is employed as a thought experiment with which we acquire a critical distance from politics. It must, therefore, both rely upon and inform our perceptions about government, legitimacy, etc. Yet this results in two somewhat distinct accounts of political society. On the one hand, it is the presence of a common judge on earth that is juridically distinct from a local strongman, i.e., one to whom men are obligated; its essence is authority. On the other hand, however, political society is something that remedies the inconveniences of the state of nature (which a strongman but concentrates in his own person; cf. TT II 94, II 176); authority, as opposed to utility, is inessential.

Our immediate impression is that these accounts need not be at odds with one another. They may well be two separate demands, but this does not mean that we cannot satisfy both. Indeed, it would strike us as odd if a true normative political theory were bad for those who adhered to it. Even if one could have obligations only to the rule of law, the latter could conceivably still function as a government. This is to say that there is nothing in this account so far that stops one from adopting a position of "legalism," or the belief that legitimacy is reducible to legality in a just commonwealth.

An excellent analysis of legalism is provided by Judith Shklar, who defines it as "the ethical attitude that holds moral conduct to be a matter of rule following, and moral relationships to consist of duties and rights determined by rules."[1] I do not intend here to repeat Shklar's achievement or to follow her analysis in every detail. I do, however, have to say some things about legalism as I understand it.

Legalism is both a disposition and a doctrine. As a disposition, it renders certain opinions, certain statements, intuitively more plausible than others. One can possess a legalistic disposition without insisting upon every aspect of the legalistic doctrine. That doctrine, on the other hand, is much the same as that stated by Shklar. It can, however, be narrowed to simply a political aspect: morality as a whole may be too nuanced for the algorithmic application of rules, but political legitimacy may demand that everything be done in accordance with narrowly-tailored laws. Long experience with such a doctrine, even one so narrow as its political manifestation, can foster the legalistic disposition. Shklar notes that lawyers and judges, people whose profession compels them to adopt legalistic blinders, effortlessly become inclined to a legalistic view of all moral conduct.

Returning to Locke, then, there is nothing in the argument so far that prevents one from adopting the position of legalism. Political legitimacy seems to require that we adopt the legalist doctrine, while the actual obedience of the members of the community seems to require that they disinhibit and indeed celebrate that aspect of human nature which is responsible for the legalist disposition.

Yet Locke is not a legalist, Carl Schmitt's influential accusation to the contrary notwithstanding.[2] Locke does not think the rule of law adequate to all the demands of political life. Chapter 14 of the *Second Treatise*, "Of Prerogative," is all about this inadequacy. The demands of the social compact, taken to their logical extreme, conflict with the demands of necessity, and yet *both* seem to have moral standing. Something has to give.

At the same time, however, the *Two Treatises of Government* is not tragic. Nor still is it a *reductio ad absurdum* of political life, meant to convince its readers to transcend politics and its futility. Locke does not, that is, present us with two irreconcilable duties or desires. He does see himself as having solved the political problem. The good result is to take precedence over the imperatives generated by moral abstractions. The rule of law, after all, is but a means. If the problem is posed abstractly, it is insoluble; good, concrete results, on the other hand, can be achieved. This requires that government be more than political society: government is not always authoritative.[3]

Before Locke can convince men to accept his solution, however, he must make them see the problem the same way he does. Before he can suggest prerogative as a supplement to the rule of law, he must reveal the deficiencies of the rule of law. If he is to defend his corrective from the charge that it betrays everything upon which legitimate government is founded, he must give an account of legitimate government. That is, if he is going to say that extralegal action is justified *in the same way* that the legal state is justified, he must say *why* the legal state is justified. He must argue for the rule of law before he can transcend it. He must appear to be a legalist. As Michael Zuckert describes the procedure typical of the *Two Treatises*, "Locke does not begin by calling attention to his ultimate destination."[4]

This chapter, then, will analyze Locke's arguments for legislative supremacy, or the rule of law. Obviously, considering that this book does not end here, I do not believe the arguments presented in this chapter to be Locke's final word.

Individual Consent and Majority Rule

What does it mean to have a common judge on earth with the authority to decide controversies? We feel intuitively that it is more than the mere ability to enforce its judgments, though that too is necessary. Rather, this judge must be *legitimate*. It must be *right* to compel obedience, and those who defy its commands must be morally corrupt. The essence of political society, then, is inextricably tied up with obligation, i.e., with the surrender of private judgment. It is to have a will external to oneself, to have even one's mind ruled by another. It is, in short, to lack a right to disobedience. Only within political society is there authority, one man over another. It is the opposite of the state of nature.

Where there is a common judge on earth, there and only there exists political society. Said another way, obligation forms the essence of political power. A slave is not obligated to obey his master: should the latter be unable to threaten him with death, he may do as he pleases.[5] A member of the commonwealth, on the other hand, is obligated to obey the speed limit even when it is not enforced. Again, there is a difference between handing over one's wallet and paying one's taxes. But obligation is essential to political society for another reason: the community must be able to call upon its members to enforce the law and repel invasions. It is not enough that they refrain from doing what they normally would, i.e., that they obey the law. They must also do things that they would normally avoid. They must answer the call of duty.

Locke mentions two powers that men possess in the state of nature, at least when he is discussing obligations (TT II 128–30). The first is to do whatever they see fit in order to preserve themselves and the rest of mankind, i.e., to obey the law of nature in what way seems best to them. The second is to punish violations of that law, again, as they themselves judge it to be best. Both of these are surrendered. The first power is given up "to be regulated by the Laws made by the Society, so far forth as the preservation of himself, and the rest of that Society shall require" (TT II 129). It is relinquished, then, only insofar as it is not dangerous to do so: society determines how best to preserve each, but it does not say how much "preservation" each is entitled to. (Or rather, if all cannot be saved, those to be sacrificed are not duty-bound to go peacefully.)

The second, however, is "wholly" given up, and each member "engages his natural force . . . to assist the Executive Power of the Society, as the Law thereof shall require" (TT II 130). If we are attentive to the wording of this surrender, it becomes apparent that this obligation must be unconditional. It must be binding even up to the death of the citizen, if need be. That is, the duty to *serve* is not limited by what is necessary for self-preservation. It is limited by reciprocity: this duty "is not only necessary, but just; since the other Members of the Society do the like" (TT II 130).

The need for effective government requires at least some citizens who are willing to die, believing that others would do the same for them. But how does this make sense? How does such preemptive gratitude ("he *would* have done the same for me") square with the state of nature? There, I am reasonably afraid that he might kill me to save his own life (if, say, we are both starving and there is only food enough for one), but now, in society, I have become so confident that he would die for me that I will die for him? Government is needed precisely because such sentiments cannot be relied upon. Yet if that government is to be distinct from the state of nature, it cannot compel such sacrifices. Nor can the community rely on a sense of nobility if it is to remain faithful to the lessons of the state of nature: self-preservation rightfully trumps philanthropy.

There are no natural self-sacrificial obligations. That is, society cannot say that what it requires is only an apparent sacrifice, that self-abnegation in service to the good of others is actually the highest good. Some citizens must actively make the choice to do what no rational person would willingly choose to do, and must do so without being irrational.[6] This seems impossible.

The solution, then, is to have them not choose at all, i.e., for them to surrender the right of choosing. Their will must be formed by someone other than themselves. This is, in fact, what it means to have a common judge. It is the mindset necessary for the fullest cultivation of legalism. In the state of nature, one is empowered to decide for oneself whether another is a criminal; when a court of competent jurisdiction finds a man not guilty, however, the good subject is not supposed to treat him like one deserving of punishment. Second guessing and dissension are incompatible with authority: they instead indicate that one does not hold the pronouncement in question to be authoritative. It is only by "all private judgement of every particular Member being excluded, [that] the Community comes to be Umpire" (TT II 87).

The question of how to make men enforce society's judgments, then, is altered. It is no longer a matter of convincing them to do what they judge to be bad, but rather of convincing them not to judge at all. The lack of any natural hierarchy, however, means that this cannot be the result of simple submission. That is, the point is not to persuade men that they are not competent to judge for themselves. One submits to experts or to God, for example, because they are in fact better, because one is simply not their equal. In a way, such submission requires only that one recognize the truth, namely, that one does not have the discernment one supposed oneself to have, as it were. The natural equality of men, however, means that one must instead surrender, give up, alienate this judgment, i.e., that one did at some point assert some claim to possess it. What could possibly motivate a man to do so was discussed in the last chapter. The issue of how this is accomplished, however, requires some explanation on Locke's part. Really, what does it mean to surrender one's own "will"?

Locke's solution is sensible only if one accepts a doctrine of representation. That is, one must hold the acts of society to have the force of the individual's own judgments: it is, as it were, he himself that orders himself to obey the law (TT II 88–89, II 129). He has consented to society, and so he is internally dependent upon it. Moreover, as the "legislative" is spoken of as synonymous with society (TT II 89), and the laws are the will of society (TT II 151), this dependency means that the laws simply are his own will. It is impossible, therefore, that his will should be contrary to the law unless he contradicts himself, i.e., unless he behaves irrationally and therefore criminally. One considers only the rule. One blocks out all considerations that do not comport with legalism.

So, the essence of society is the existence of a relationship of authority and obligation. Because there is no natural hierarchy, moreover, this authority and these obligations can arise only from the consent of each individual. We can say, therefore, that any individual who has not alienated his will in this manner does not enjoy a political relationship with his neighbors. This is the sort of consent that is important when discussing obligation, the law, political society, etc.

It is clear, however, that Locke does not always use *consent* in this fashion. Tacit consent, for example, brings no new obligations. Rather, it is simply the acknowledgment of those obligations that are incumbent upon one who does not wish to begin a state of war; it does not even make one a member of the commonwealth (TT II 122). In a real sense, such consent serves only to signal one's peaceable intentions.[7] This is not the sort of consent that I am interested in, for political society (in the Lockean sense) cannot be founded on it. Every people, after all, has *submitted* to those that rule them: consensual government demands a bit more (cf. TT II 186). Consent, in this strong sense, then, differs from assent, permission, acquiescence, etc.[8]

If society is to be effective in remedying those ills incident to the state of nature, it must move as a single body; moreover, as there can be only one supreme power, someone must be in charge (TT II 96, II 149). There must be rulers and ruled, even if the former are more numerous than the latter. The obligation faithfully to obey the rulers is not, however, an obligation *to* them. Rather, "every Man, by consenting with others to make one Body Politick under one Government, puts himself under an Obligation *to every one of that Society*,[9] to submit to the determination of the *majority*" (TT II 97). Otherwise,

> this *original Compact* . . . would signify nothing, and be no Compact, if he be left free, and under no other ties, than he was in before in the State of Nature. For what appearance would there be of any Compact? What new Engagement if he were no farther tied by any Decrees of the Society, than he himself thought fit, *and did actually consent to*?[10] (TT II 97)

That is, there could be no society if one actually had to consent to every act.

That passage should be read again. Locke's choice of words is startling. Could he really have just said that about government and consent? Yet it is inescapably true that he did. He is, moreover, entirely right to have done so. He has just revealed a tension in the very conception of political society. It is not the state of nature because it is not the rule of force, i.e., it is justified by the consent of the governed. Yet it is this same legitimacy which authorizes it to command contrary to the consent of the governed. Consent may require more than bare acquiescence, but it surely cannot do without it. A government is legitimate if *we want it* to compel us to do things we do not want to do.

Of course, Locke has already argued how this is logically possible, namely, though representation. Political society may be paradoxical, but being contrary to common opinion is hardly grounds for a rebuttal. The fault lies, one might argue, in our opinions, not in the thing. It should cease to be paradoxical as soon as we accept that "Truth and keeping of Faith belongs to Men, as Men, and not [just] as Members of Society" (TT II 14). Only this imperative-stated-as-fact can counter the charge that Locke has failed to bind men's consciences with his dogma. Without it, there is no reason why acts contrary to the law must be contrary to one's own will: one could simply have changed one's mind concerning the benefits of a particular community in light of new evidence, namely, that membership in that community is not in fact beneficial. How does one contradict oneself, how does one act irrationally, by changing one's mind? The survival of the commonwealth, however, depends on a prohibition on second thoughts precisely when they seem the most reasonable. Consent may never be withdrawn once given; it is with this thought that the *Two Treatises* ends (TT II 243; cf. II 119–22).[11] The political relationship established by consent might be destroyed by someone else's perfidious actions, or some things may be asked of one to which no consent could have been given, but one is never free to dissolve that relationship on one's own judgment. The needs of the community dovetail nicely into what it means to be human. Man may not be a political animal in the Aristotelean sense, but he is well-suited for political life.

This is, of course, a very tidy little theory. Thomas Hobbes says essentially the same thing in the *Leviathan*, yet he says that it breaks down, that obligations cease, whenever one's life is in danger, i.e., precisely when society must rely on obligations the most. In the end, the sovereign cannot rely on "representation" anywhere that one might want it to function: compulsion is a constant facet of his commonwealth.[12] And what Locke says along the same lines certainly sits oddly alongside his natural law doctrine: in both he speaks of judgment, reason, etc., but these words seem to mean different things depending on the discussion at hand. It is with this in mind that we turn to Locke's account of how far, and to whom, one can be obligated on account of "representation."

The Principle of Majority Rule

Society comprises those who have consented to its authority. This consent must be unanimous. All involved must agree that they will become one body, possessed of a single will. The decision of how this will is to be articulated is then left to the majority. Its authorization to establish the frame of government did not, however, exist in the absence of this common declaration of one will, i.e., in the state of nature. We might then wonder why the constitution does not also require unanimous consent or why government itself should not require unanimity, for that matter. It is clear enough a wonder that Locke responds to it. And it is in this context that he argues that such a requirement would make political society no different from the state of nature (TT II 97).[13]

Yet the ultimate justification, the one that seals the deal, as it were, is that it would be impractical. The problem is not just one of actually assembling everyone together at once, but "the variety of Opinions, and contrariety of Interests, which unavoidably happen in all Collections of Men" (TT II 98). Because not everyone's interests may be satisfactorily reconciled, the whole cannot rule itself. We may add to this that even their just or reasonable interests may be incompatible, for Locke does not suggest that this is due to any moral deficiency.

A part must therefore be permitted to rule the whole. The majority is empowered as a practical matter. It is also empowered in order to distinguish political society from the state of nature. That is, democracy of a sort recommends itself in response to both demands which the state of nature makes upon any political theory.

The majority is not, however, empowered absolutely. There are limits to what the greater number may demand of the lesser. Exactly what these are will have to wait until later when we look at legislative supremacy, but the reason why there must be limits can be addressed now. Consent, once given, cannot be withdrawn; this, we shall see, is worlds apart from anything like popular sovereignty. The font of all legitimate authority need not be all-powerful: it need only possess all power that is legitimate before delegating it to others.

It has been suggested, however, that Locke sees no limits to the majority's authority. If we rely on what Locke says (esp. TT II 95ff.), according to Willmoore Kendall,[14] the majority can do no wrong because it is the judge of right. "[Any] decision other than that of the majority is in some definable sense ethically wrong. . . . [A] decision comes to be right the moment it marshals majority support behind it, and ceases to be right the moment the 'marginal' deliberator switches sides and reduces the erstwhile majority to a minority."[15] Fortunately for the rest of us, however, Kendall finds in Locke a "latent premise" that "a 'safe' majority of men (thus the 'average' man) are rational and just."[16]

Locke states the opposite of this to be the case (though not too loudly—he is, after all, advocating popular government). The "greater part" of mankind are "no strict Observers of Equity and Justice" (TT II 123). Kendall does make note of similar passages, saying that Locke "was quite capable of arguing the contrary when it served his purpose."[17] Indeed, it would seem that Locke lays it on rather thick whenever the contrary serves his purpose:

> Thus far [i.e., to beget children for the sole purpose of eating them] can the busie mind of Man carry him to a Brutality below the level of Beasts, when he quits his reason, which places him almost equal to Angels. Nor can it be otherwise in a Creature, whose thoughts are more than the Sands, and wider than the Ocean, where fancy and passion must needs run him into strange courses, if reason, which is his only Star and compass, be not that he steers by. The imagination is always restless and suggests variety of thoughts, and the will, reason being laid aside, is ready for every extravagant project; and in this State, he that goes farthest out of the way, is thought fittest to lead, and is sure of most followers: And when Fashion hath once Established, what Folly or craft began, Custom makes it Sacred, and 'twill be thought impudence or madness, to contradict or question it. (TT I 58)

Locke must have taken no small pleasure in suggesting that, in the great marketplace of ideas, it is the most bizarre, the most outlandish doctrines that find the readiest approbation. He continues, however, making it plain that this is not applicable only to the few, or in some unfortunate intellectual climes.

> He that will impartially survey the Nations of the World, will find so much of their Governments, Religions, and Manners brought in and continued amongst them by these means, that he will have but little Reverence for the Practices which are in use and credit amongst Men, and will have Reason to think, that the Woods and Forests, where the irrational untaught Inhabitants keep right by following Nature, are fitter to give us Rules, than Cities and Palaces, where those that call themselves Civil and Rational, go out of their way, by the Authority of Example. (TT I 58)

It seems that it was very much to Locke's purpose to impugn the moral judgments of the majority of men. "What form of viciousness would be not only permitted, but necessary, if the example of the majority were to give us law? Into what shame, iniquity, and into what a variety of crimes would the law of nature lead us, if we were to follow the path taken by the majority?" (NL VII 66).

Kendall derives his "latent premise" from the requirements of Locke's argument: he concludes that it must form the basis of his theory because, without it, his majoritarianism collapses into incoherence. Yet were this premise true, Locke's entire stated justification for government would fall apart. Political society was established precisely because the majority of human beings could not be trusted with the authority that Kendall grants them here. So it seems that we must abandon Kendall's majoritarian Locke instead.

Of course, given the facts related in the section of the *First Treatise* just quoted at length, the dissolute corruption of civilized man might cause one to suspect some sort of moral purity among savage peoples.[18] Indeed, considering that our worst natures are made real as a result of tradition and the law of custom, this suspicion is even reasonable in Locke's view. That man might be thought of as a "fallen" race, however, does not mean that he was somehow "good" before. Great falls need not be from great heights. They can also be into deep chasms. When Locke actually gets around to describing what men were/would be like without government, without even *customary* obligations to bind their consciences, they are not the sort of people one would want as neighbors. Locke is certain that most people in that state would want to leave it, not that they would themselves live lives of justice or humanity. A majoritarian Locke is one for whom the state of nature is meaningless except as a rhetorically serviceable ploy.

It would be surprising, then, to discover that Locke was so radical a democrat. But *why* isn't the majority's will simply authoritative? How can we be sure that we have not sold ourselves into political slavery to the numerically stronger? Locke may have rendered obligation such as to bind absolutely, but it turns out, there are limits to the obligations one can accept in the first place.

The Limits of Consent and Compulsion

Locke repeatedly says that there are some things to which no rational creature can be supposed to have consented. To constitute societies which immediately dissolve, for example, would be irrational, and so we should not assume that any such constitution actually took place (TT II 98). The same applies to surrendering one's equality, liberty, and natural executive power to the legislative power except insofar as it is to one's benefit (TT II 131, II 137) and, when free, to putting oneself into subjection to another for one's own harm (TT II 164).

Locke's qualifications for what constitutes a rational creature are rather lenient. The reason of which Locke speaks is purely instrumental in character, it existing only for the "best advantages of Life, and convenience" (TT II 26). So, for example, parental power can be exercised only until the children

> come to the use of Reason, or a state of Knowledge, wherein they may be supposed capable to understand that Rule, whether it be the Law of Nature, or the municipal Law of the Country they are to govern themselves by: Capable, I say, to know it, as well as several others, who live, as Free-men, under that Law. (TT II 170)[19]

The state of knowledge sufficient to govern themselves as well as other free-men is not an alternative to the use of reason—this is not the meaning of "or" in this passage—but is rather the definition of reason, as it is defined here. It is a political definition of reason. The use of reason, then, is relative to the community; it is a commonsense notion, rather than the abstract definitions of reason Locke elsewhere provides.[20] One need only not have put oneself into a worse state in order to satisfy this test (TT II 131, II 164); where one has not better preserved one's life, liberty, and estate, there we cannot presume consent.

Yet this does not express the full extent of Locke's limitations regarding consent: the fact that we cannot presume others to have acted does not deprive them of a right to act. Locke, however, repeatedly states that consent is in truth impossible under some conditions. His arguments seem almost obvious. "No body can give more Power than he has himself" (TT II 23). Any supposed consent that grants powers which no man has, or even which the individual in question does not have, is *prima facie* invalid. As A. John Simmons points out, this is not a matter of these rights' being "inalienable," for that would suggest that the individual possessed such rights but could not transfer them to another. Rather, these rights simply are not held at all.[21] No one has absolute, arbitrary power over oneself (TT II 23, II 135), nor does any society of men have this power over themselves (TT II 149). "God and Nature" never allow a man "to neglect his own preservation" (TT II 168). No one possesses the right to wage an unjust war (TT II 179). Thus, no one has the power to cede these rights to others, and so no person possessed of authority by contract can claim these rights (TT II 23, II 135, II 137, II 149, II 168, II 179). This does not simply prohibit the presumption of consent but even prohibits the acceptance of an express token of purported consent in these matters.

This assertion is clearly useful in vilifying claimants to absolute and arbitrary power. Kings may not gain their rightful authority from God, but the unnamed Hobbes suggested that they could get it as a result of some sort of agreement. This is countered by Locke's claim that it is impossible that anyone might consent to the creation of arbitrary power. In order to unpack this claim, we must ask what he means by "arbitrary power."

Attacks on the Stuart kings often accused them of establishing (or attempting to establish) an "arbitrary government." And "arbitrary" was really just the opposite of "legitimate." So, for example, an early pamphlet entitled *Of the Fundamental Laws, or Politick Constitution of this Kingdom* claimed that a king's unlawful acts would be arbitrary, but not those of Parliament; the latter could be good, and so could not be "arbitrary."[22] Locke's usage is more nuanced. On the surface, therefore, it appears contradictory.

He seems to have two definitions, one that is appropriate to the state of nature, one to political society, but he does not restrict his usage so conveniently (e.g., he uses the natural definition when speaking of society, and vice versa). In political society, arbitrary power is that which is exercised against the law of the land, or is not bound by law at all. Naturally arbitrary power, on the other hand, is that which is exercised against the law of nature, i.e., against reason.[23]

These two seemingly different definitions are, however, but aspects of a more general concept.[24] An arbitrary act is one that is forbidden by the law one is under. In the state of nature, one is under the law of nature: it would be an arbitrary act to violate it. Positive laws, on the other hand, are to govern political society, and so behavior not countenanced by them is also arbitrary. As the "Obligations of the Law of Nature, cease not in Society, but only in many Cases are drawn closer" (TT II 135), Locke continues to use the natural definition in political contexts: there one is under two laws, as it were. More importantly, Locke would prohibit his fellow Englishmen from consenting to a governor who is arbitrary in either sense. (How this is so will be addressed in the next section, when I deal with the limits on legislative power. It will be important to the discussion of prerogative that the above applies only to what one may consent to: it is only naturally arbitrary power that one is forbidden to wield.)

The implications of this should be clear: if no one may consent to arbitrary power, then the majority cannot wield arbitrary power as a matter of contract. As there is no natural right of majority rule—this is what man's natural freedom and equality demonstrate—the majority can have no claim whatsoever to arbitrary power. The basis of Locke's thought is not majority sovereignty, or popular sovereignty, or what have you. The word *sovereign* is all-but absent from the *Second Treatise*. The idea of any sovereign whatsoever is an anathema to government by consent.

There are two explanations for why Locke avoided the word *sovereign* when discussing his own political theory.[25] Richard Cox argued that this absence is merely rhetorical: "sovereignty" carried certain connotations which Locke wished to avoid, but his "supream power" does not differ in any significant manner from a sovereign ruler.[26] And there is some warrant for this interpretation. Robert Filmer, for example, uses both terms interchangeably. Locke does not do so, however, and it seems better to interpret his decision to eschew the language of "sovereignty" as an indication that the "supream power" in society is not sovereign.[27]

The question turns on what Locke understood by "sovereign." The word's only appearance in the *Second Treatise* indicates that God has not appointed one (TT II 4), which hardly sheds much light on what one is. In the *First Treatise*, however, Locke unmistakably uses it as a synonym for an "Absolute King" (cf. TT I 131).[28] And in this he tacitly follows Filmer: the latter's assertions that the king is sovereign were made in order to counter the authority of Parliament. Sovereign authority answers to no one.

For Filmer, debates regarding sovereignty boil down to a question of whose will is to govern absolutely. In the preface to *The Anarchy of a Limited or Mixed Monarchy*, he says that there must always be, in every society, an arbitrary power; the only question is who gets to wield it. Further on, he states that "'Absolute monarchy,' saith he [i.e., Hunton], 'is when the sovereign is so fully in one, that it hath no limits or bounds under God but his own will,'" to which Filmer responds, "It may peradventure make some doubt that there is no other sort but only that which he calls absolute."[29]

This is in turn Filmer's echo of Jean Bodin, whom he calls "the greatest modern politician."[30] The latter's sovereign does not need to answer to anyone for the content of his will, except God. "We may thus conclude that the first mark of sovereignty is to give law to all in general and in particular," he says. "But," he continues, "this is not sufficient. We have to add 'without the consent of any other, whether greater, equal, or below him.'"[31] As he had remarked earlier, "No matter how much power they have, if they are bound to the laws, jurisdiction, and command of someone else, they are not sovereign."[32]

So Richard Cox was correct in a sense: the word *sovereign* did carry certain connotations which Locke sought to avoid. It represented an approach to politics which he wished to confute. As Locke paraphrases Filmer's appropriation of Bodin's doctrine, sovereignty provides "an Absolute, Arbitrary, Unlimited, and Unlimitable Power, over the Lives, Liberties, and Estates of his . . . Subjects, . . . his unbounded Will [being] their Law" (TT I 9).

And this is precisely the problem: a sovereign grants rights—he is not bound by them. He alone, for some abstruse reason, is permitted to be judge in his own case (TT II 13, II 90). He therefore stands in a state of nature in relation to his subjects, yet his subjects are supposed to owe him obedience all the same. The cause of this, moreover, the source of their "obligation" to his will, is simply that he commands a multitude (TT II 13, II 91). "Might is right" is the law of beasts, and it is the only thing to which a sovereign can reliably appeal. Numbers do not change the fundamental character of the thing (cf. TT II 176, II 201). Sovereign oligarchs or majorities are not preferable to monarchs: each claims that an action is prohibited or commanded simply because it so wills things. An "Absolute King" is one species of sovereign, while legitimate government, no matter how organized, must be of a different genus entirely.

The problem of sovereignty is arbitrary power. It is more than this, however: it is arbitrary power that insists upon its own legitimacy. It is not enough that the subjects be abused, but they must further acclaim it to be by the will of God (as with divine right theorists) or even of their own doing (as with Hobbesian representation). This can be stated another way. Sovereign authority is premised on coercion, but it demands that men treat it as if it were not: it compels recognition. Its claim is that men are somehow obligated to it. That is, it desires obedience even when compulsion is lacking. It desires the inward devotion of its slaves. The fact that there exist justifications for sovereignty which counsel submission serves only to show that it is instead consent which forms the true original of government (cf. TT I 43, II 186).[33] Sovereigns of all stripes in effect demand that men consent to their arbitrary power, even if only because an ineffable God commands it. Yet this would require that men consent to their own destruction, or at least that they relinquish all moral claims to prevent it, and this is manifestly impossible, Locke says. Thus, there can be no obligation to sovereignty. Sovereign authority is a fraud, its somber proponents deluded about the nature of power: no one's will can be unlimited and illimitable unless the people are confused into accepting it. Legitimate, i.e., rational, choice-worthy government must operate according to what Locke will call legislative supremacy, or the rule of law. If monarchists differ from democrats only in where they think sovereignty should be lodged, then political society can be neither monarchic nor democratic.

But now something curious has happened: all sacrificial obligation whatsoever seems to disappear. Sovereignty is refuted because no one possesses the power to neglect his own preservation and so cannot consent to it. Yet this is precisely the species of obligation that political society requires, namely, citizens who render aid to the execution of the laws and the defense of the community without regard for their own lives. Compared with this, the obligation to pay one's taxes pales into insignificance. Consent does not seem capable of generating or occasioning self-sacrificial duties. And indeed it is not. On Locke's own account, there can be no obligation to sacrifice oneself.

Here we are at an impasse. The society which Locke has described requires the impossible. To be legitimate, its authority must be the result of consent; to be effectual, it must possess an authority which consent cannot provide. Locke's sneaky insertion of an absolute obligation to keep one's promises cannot resolve this when the problem is that the binding promise cannot be made in the first place (cf. TT II 14).[34] It has become morally attractive to base obligation upon consent because doing so recognizes the dignity of the individual,[35] yet the *raison d'être* of such theories is ultimately to justify destroying the individual. They tell society that it need not feel guilty about compelling him to do what he does not want to, for he *chose* this. A mantra of consent is needed in order to rationalize compulsion. Considering the number of intelligent people who believe this circle to have been squared, we cannot assume that Locke was aware of this failing in the argument.

At the same time, however, we cannot assume that it was not intentional on Locke's part. The rule of law is not his final word on political legitimacy; he argues so forcefully for it partly in order to make serious readers see its flaws the way he does. The obligations to the law form a part of this account. Eventually he justifies prerogative because it works but does not make obedience to lawless acts obligatory. That is, he reverses himself. He splits legitimacy from authority. His personal thoughts on the matter may rest satisfied with effectiveness; his talk of duties may be rhetorical or pedagogical. I strongly suspect it is. This would, at any rate, resolve the incongruence between the sort of rationality which discloses the law of nature and the rationality that is invoked in the doctrine of representation.

A perfect proof or disproof of this is, however, impossible. The text simply contradicts itself, and so some statements must be discounted. If we want to have Locke be deadly serious about moral obligation, then we must overlook the categorical statements regarding what one may consent to. The alternative (which I prefer) is to suggest that the lack of any "escape clause" in §130 is either an oversight or intentionally misleading. I shall proceed according to the latter assumption.

It has been noted that Locke did not intend to provide an account of moral obligation.[36] Nor was one really needed: the success of a revolution depends on convincing men that their supposed obligations to the previous regime are null, not that there is such a thing as obligation in the first place. In almost every context, the latter belief can be assumed (even if it goes by a different name). John T. Scott notes that Locke's "sovereignless state" requires a "shared language of obligation," a dominant discourse that allows the commonwealth to function; he does not attempt to show how obligation actually arises from consent.[37] Locke assumes that enough people will experience the pull of duty for the community to work; he relies on the nobility of spirit which finds no support in his moral theory.[38] His goal is to redirect their sense of duty; obedience is owed, not to James II and his heirs, but to whomever the people choose as their ruler.

Locke's account of obligation serves to ease society's conscience, not to bind the individual's.[39] It provides the former with a moral justification for sacrificing its parts to protect the whole (or rather the rest): those who refuse to die for it are criminals, while those who willingly do so are model citizens. Society can make utilitarian calculations while still believing itself to respect consent absolutely. This belief is not entirely true, of course. The majority of society obviously maintain their rights to preserve themselves; no principle of justice, morality, or common sense says they must suffer rather than harm an individual who will not suffer to prevent harm to them. This right, however, can hardly impose a duty on the individual; for the same reason that they may prefer their own preservation to his, he may prefer his to theirs. The inability to take on obligations to neglect one's own preservation means that rights may conflict. Society must, however, feel that it has the greater right: a representational doctrine of obligation, even if ultimately flawed, permits it to consider those who, out of fear or some other motive, refuse to risk themselves in service to the commonwealth to be, in fact, criminals. The basis of every society's being effective is, in the end, either a sense of nobility or compulsion, either an attraction to something high or a fear of something low. Locke, in refusing to legitimate the former, must conceal the latter.

Society usually does not have to make such hard decisions, of course. Which is to say that it is not usually forced to face such hard facts. Most of the time, people obey the law and pay their taxes because it is simply easier to do so than to avoid it. Performing one's civic duties is hardly burdensome when they are trivial. Decency can reliably motivate decent people when it does not literally cost an arm and a leg. The legalistic prejudice is the great political lubricant, so effective in fact that it can smooth over some bits of sand in the gears. Indeed, considering the state of nature, who would not want to pay honest judges and honorable soldiers? But it is precisely in these circumstances that obligation is not needed; nothing requires that private judgment be suspended. In short, society is good! No one is being asked to do what no rational creature would choose. Here, where obligation is not needed, Locke's account of obligation is not contradictory: promise-keeping is enough to support it.

Given the preceding discussion, the importance of this point might be missed: there are still obligations that arise from consent. Individuals just are not obligated to make real sacrifices. Locke does not give license to tax cheats—he does not justify defectors in every collective action problem—but cowards, collaborators, and the like are vindicated by this argument. They have good reason for their perfidy. Where society functions as we wish it would, however, its members can be relied upon to obey its laws.

Before moving on, it seems appropriate to reiterate some of the claims I have made about obligation and consent. Locke sticks to his story that the essence of political society is the suspension of private judgment. This is reasonable since, most of the time, the limitations of Locke's account do not manifest themselves. There are, however, limits on what one can be obligated to. As obligation arises only from consent, it cannot be contrary to one's own welfare. Ultimately, this means that there cannot be obligations to arbitrary authority: there can be no sovereign. What this means—to have a sovereignless government—is the essence of the rule of law.

The Meaning and Limits of the Rule of Law

Legislative power, the supreme power in society, need not be arbitrary. Indeed, it cannot be so. It must, after all, have the consent of the governed, for this is the only way to give its decrees the status of *laws*, i.e., for them to be commonly recognized and obligatory. Because it is based upon consent, it has power only over those who have actually consented to it (TT II 9, II 87–88). The scope of its authority is further limited by what one can rationally consent to. The effect of these limitations makes the legislative power supreme rather than sovereign. Because the people enforce the rules governing legislative power, the legislative body is prevented from claiming sovereign authority over them.

Of course, Locke explicitly states that the legislative power cannot be an arbitrary power (TT II 135, II 171). No society, in fact, may create an arbitrary power (TT II 149). It is arbitrary in neither sense of the word, natural or political. It is consequently bound by the ends for which it was created (TT II 131). It has been suggested that, by arbitrary power, Locke artlessly followed his contemporaries and meant the indefinite prorogation of Parliament by the king.[40] While this would certainly be an arbitrary act as Locke uses the word, it does not cover all the ways in which Locke uses "arbitrary," even only politically. At the very least, for example, it makes no sense to say that the legislative power cannot be arbitrary if arbitrary power is so narrowly defined. Locke provides four "rules" which give greater clarity to what he means by the lack of arbitrary government (TT II 135, II 136, II 138, II 141; cf. TT II 142).

Obviously, legislative power cannot be an authority to violate the law of nature (TT II 135). The law of nature is "antecedent and paramount to all positive Laws of men" (TT II 168), and the municipal law of a commonwealth is valid only insofar as it is founded upon the law of nature (TT II 12). This by no means suggests that the two must be identical, however: society does not simply inscribe the law of nature on stone tablets and then enforce them. Rather, legislative power is a trust to interpret the law of nature, i.e., to decide what is necessary for "*the preservation of the Society*, and (as far as will consist with the publick good) of every person in it" (TT II 134; cf. TT II 159). Indeed, in Locke's summary of the legislative power, the law of nature drops out and is replaced by the public good (cf. TT II 142). The scope of legislation cannot extend beyond what is required for the public's good, which is to secure "every ones Property" by remedying the defects of the state of nature (TT II 131). It is authoritative because we accept its interpretation of what the public good requires: it is law because it comes from the legislative power.

Nor may the legislative power be politically arbitrary, i.e., it may not rule by extemporaneous decrees (TT II 131, II 136, II 142). Government must be according to standing laws, not commands to perform specific acts, and these laws must be general enough "to have one Rule for Rich and Poor, for the Favourite at Court, and the Country Man at Plough" (TT II 142). To do otherwise would be incompatible with political society (TT II 87, II 136–137). These laws should also include specific penalties for their violation, removing this discretion from whoever judges the particular case (TT II 87–88, II 171). This is because, Locke initially reasons, men do not know the law of nature, or do not agree on its content, and so the legislature's duty is to remove this ambiguity (TT II 136; cf. TT II 124). The purpose of law is to settle disputes, in principle before they even arise.

Yet Locke now interrupts his enumeration of the rules which govern legislative power, in §137, in order to rejustify the first two rules; this restatement is of crucial importance. To understand why, we need only be attentive to what he has not yet said. Prior to this interruptive recapitulation, there was nothing to suggest that law serves as a fence around the people's liberties: the second rule was independent of the first. There is to be a government of laws, not of men, but the reason for this is not that this inhibits the government from offending the public good. Indeed, to say that what the second stricture requires is a government of laws, not of men, may be misleading: the rule of law is contrasted with a condition of (violent) confusion, not one of personal rule.

Section 137 begins, "Absolute Arbitrary Power, or Governing without *settled standing Laws*, can neither of them consist with the ends of Society and Government" (arbitrary power here denoting a supposed liberty to ignore the law of nature). These ends are revealed by reflecting upon what would cause men to "tie themselves up under" society's rulers' will and "quit the freedom of the state of nature." Men would do so only, Locke says, to preserve their lives, liberties, and fortunes and to have their peace and quiet preserved "by *stated Rules* of Right and Property." That men would not give up their natural liberty only to strengthen their enemies is a clear enough reason for why those whom they've strengthened cannot claim a right to harm them under Locke's system: what this section adds is why the rule of law is crucial for the public good.

In other words, this section says why the first and second rules are linked; it brings together what was separate. Returning to the political use of arbitrary, Locke states with confidence that one

> who is exposed to the Arbitrary Power of one Man, who has the Command of 100000. [is in a much worse condition] than he that is expos'd to the Arbitrary Power of 100000. single Men: no Body being secure, that his Will, who has such a Command, is better, than that of other Men, though his Force be 100000. times stronger.[41]

What this statement turns on is the *unknown* character of the ruler. It is this mysteriousness that now becomes the reason that "whatever Form the Common-wealth is under, the Ruling Power ought to govern by *declared* and *received Laws*, and not by extemporary Dictates and undetermined Resolutions." Standing laws do not only inform the people of their duties: they reveal the quality of their rulers' wills.

I wish to dwell on this point a bit, as it is here that prerogative most undermines the ends sought from the rule of law. The requirement that there be a government of laws, Locke concludes in this section, is not merely for the sake of regularity and predictability but so that the rulers "not be tempted by the Power they have in their hands, to imploy it to such purposes, and by such measures, *as they would not have known, and own not willingly*[42]" (TT II 137). He is not saying with this that the laws constrain or somehow limit the prince. Locke was not so naïve as to seriously think that laws could restrain the government—or anyone, for that matter. He vividly notes that law is nothing without enforcement; in every society, there must be someone to act as a "*Terror to Evil Doers*, and by that Terror to inforce Men to the positive Laws of the Society" (TT I 92; cf. TT II 7, II 219). That enforcement as regards the constitutional law and the law of nature comes from the people in the form of a revolution, should their rulers neglect the public good. What law does do is to inform the people of the magistrates' designs, and thus of whether they must "punish" them. Rule without law, either by its absence or by disregarding it, conceals these designs. Here, rule by law is preferable to trust in the prince's moral virtue. Any claim that the prince should simply be loved and trusted by his people, that he should be able to rule arbitrarily, is therefore immediately suspect.

In order that the people may know whether they ought to trust their rulers, these must employ the force of the community placed at their disposal only as the application of a general rule to particular cases. They are not to judge the particular according to its perceived goodness, but according to its legality. This makes *ad hoc* justifications of corruption or subversion more difficult. Questions of justice are to arise only in framing the general rule. They assure the people that they have eschewed naturally arbitrary power by swearing off political arbitrariness.

This also tells us a good deal about Locke's conception of law. The short of it is that Locke must have been what we would call a legal positivist. This is not because such positivism is what we mean by law, or that any other definition of law is necessarily incoherent.[43] That is, Locke does not fall prey to what Ronald Dworkin calls the semantic sting.[44]

At the same time, however, Locke does not follow Dworkin's method of attempting to give the best interpretation of his community's legal practices. Locke was too well acquainted with the dependence of the British courts on some party or another to look to them for any guiding principle. Locke composed a legal brief concerning the sheriff's discretion in composing a list of jurors to aid in the 1st Earl of Shaftesbury's defense at his treason trial. The point of that brief was not to defend a fair system against a corrupt one. Rather, the outcome of the question was to decide *who* would get to rig the jury.[45] What Locke does is to begin from what is politically necessary. What is politically necessary is a law of the sort that judges and executive magistrates could apply in the way that Justice Antonin Scalia says statutes and the Constitution are to be interpreted.[46]

Now there may be the further question of whether rules or maxims called law which fail to satisfy this criterion are nonetheless "law." This question is of immeasurable interest to legal scholars. I suspect, however, that at the onset of such a discussion Locke's eyes would begin to glaze over, but this may just be me projecting a bit here. In any case, laws *should* be tailored such that there is little-to-no reasonable ambiguity about what they command, permit, empower, or prohibit, according to Locke.

The two remaining rules follow logically from the first two. The third rule specifically forbids the legislative from arbitrarily taking the people's property: any taxes must be justified by public necessity and require the consent of the majority (TT II 138–40, II 142). Finally, as legislative power is the permission only to make laws, it cannot justify the delegation of legislative functions: that would be to create legislators, not laws (TT II 141, II 142).

The supremacy of this legislative power, the actual subordination of society to it, is the rule of law in Locke.[47] One consequence of this is that the rule of law is not an aspect of the constitution: it may indeed be preserved to varying degrees by institutional arrangements, but it is not identical with them. Rather, it is a theory of legitimate politics; it is the aim of particular constitutions. The rule of law is an ideal, not a law. It is that for the sake of which the fundamental law (i.e., the constitution) is made.

This seems a good place to address the question of what is this "constitution"? Mansfield remarks that Locke's usages suggest someone who has stumbled upon a word he likes.[48] Yet there is nevertheless a kind of progression in how he uses it and related words. Locke occasionally treats "constitute" as an exact synonym for "create" (cf. TT I 3, I 16, I 23, I 51, I 67, II 99). More narrowly, it sometimes refers to the particular character imparted by *how* a thing was created (cf. TT I 54–56, I 95, I 137, I 168, II 86). With greater and greater regularity, however, Locke narrows his use solely to the *form of government* which the people have created (cf. TT II 76, II 98, II 116, II 132, II 152, II 168, II 205, II 230), and, since this is identical with the form of the legislative power (TT II 132, II 141), to how they have decided to enact positive laws (cf. TT II 131, II 141, II 149, II 153–57, II 212–15, II 218, II 223, II 226–27). It is this final definition that I take to be the essence of Lockean constitutionalism. All other aspects of what we might call a "constitution"—who has the federative power, how the executive is chosen, etc.—are subject to legislative revision (cf. TT II 152). Most of the American Constitution, including the Bill of Rights, would consequently be mere legislation in Locke's sense. (The sections addressing the election of Congress and the president [because of the legislative power to veto], together with the procedures for amending it, would be the exception to this; the parallel passages in the fifty state constitutions would also be a part of the Constitution of the United States; cf. TT II 157.)

Obviously, every individual within society is subordinate to the law, and each has consented to this. The aggregate of persons, however, i.e., the people, is also subject to the legislative authority. The "moral authority of the people," what is usually appealed to in arguments for popular sovereignty, is nothing but legislative power. The people have no power within society. They do not somehow "share" any supremacy with the legislative power: there may be "but *one Supream Power*, which is *the Legislative*" (TT II 149). The result is that the people cannot be supreme "till the Government be dissolved" (TT II 149). In that case, no one may pass laws, no one may make a claim on another's will. The people can entrust and divest individuals, but they cannot command. This is, we learn, what government by consent entails.

The rule of law also implies the total subjection of the executive power. Indeed, both the executive and legislative powers are defined such that this is necessarily the case. The former is nothing but that which employs the force of the community to enforce the laws made by the latter (TT II 144). It has no authority or function beyond this. Anyone who claims more, for whatever reason, simply does not exercise executive power as Locke defines it, and thus can claim no right to obedience (TT II 151); a fuller discussion of this will have to wait until the next chapter. In any event, a power to execute the law is meaningful only if there are in fact laws, and such laws can come only from a law-making power (TT II 150).

This does not, however, mean that the executive body must be independent of the legislative body. An American-style president is a possibility, but not a necessity. An executive is no less the executive, and he does not any the less exercise executive power, if he is appointed by the legislature (TT II 152). Indeed, the executive may be composed of a number of people, Locke speaking of it in both the singular and the plural in the same breath (TT II 156); he does not even say that there must be a chief executive, though this would raise the problem of multiple commands (cf. TT II 148). Executive power may be entrusted to one or to many, and by the legislature, by the people, or by some other means, but none of these options alters its fundamental character. Its authority is inseparable from the law.

Incidentally, and interestingly, this means that the executive power operates only over members of the society (TT II 147). Nonmembers are governed by some other power, presumably the federative (cf. TT II 145–46), though Locke does not really specify: indeed, the fact that aliens are *not* ruled by (political) executive power was used to prove the existence of a natural executive power (TT II 9).

This, then, is Locke's definition of the rule of law. The force of the community is to be directed by the will of the community (TT II 143), and the will of the community is to be declared in standing laws (TT II 151). The legislative power is the keeper of the public will, and there is no room for a will to be exercised outside of it, politically speaking.

It should be noted that under this system the rule of law is most emphatically not the supremacy of the legislature: it is in no way parliamentary supremacy. Legislative power is not limited by the rules by which Locke says it is to be governed; rather, it is more appropriate to say that it is defined by those rules. The consequence of this should be clear: any body of men that violates them simply does not exercise legislative power. It is not the title of "Parliament" that grants authority, but rather a certain, limited trust. A Senate may betray the public good just as surely as a Caesar: tyranny may be exercised by tyrants just as well as by a tyrant (TT II 201). Majority rule, as Locke describes it, applies only to the investment of the authority to make laws; it does not justify the arbitrary rule of the majority or its deputies. The legislature is not the proper judge of whether it has violated the legislative power entrusted to it by the majority: "the positive Laws of Men, cannot determine that which is it self the Foundation of all Law and Government, and is to receive its rule only from the Law of God and Nature" (TT I 126). Should the legislature overstep the bounds of legislative power, it would have no more political authority than any other group of men, i.e., none.

As a result, a system of checks and balances does not vitiate legislative supremacy, even though these allow other branches of government to frustrate the will of the legislature. Indeed, it was precisely in order to preserve legislative supremacy thus defined that Hamilton and Madison advocated checks and balances. Neither, of course, speaks in this way, instead appealing to the stability of law, good government, the interests of the community, etc. The term *legislative supremacy* usually refers to the legislature, not the power it is entrusted to wield. The Anti-Federalists assailed the Constitution for violating legislative supremacy in this sense, while the Federalists paradoxically supported a strong executive in order to protect it in the Lockean sense. This is to say that while the rule of law does not forbid a powerful chief executive, it does rule out prerogative: the president's ability to stand up to Congress would have to come from his veto authority—a legislative power—not from his executive authority or some extralegal right.

Men owe their obedience to the legislative power. Yet this does not tell them to whom their obedience is due. It is, after all, legislators who command, not the legislative power: they might abuse their trust, at which point no further obedience is owed. If Locke is actually to bind men with the legalistic rhetoric of obligation, he must do more than say that such obligation is to the legislative power.

True, Locke does provide rules to govern the legislative power, but these are mere rules: they are meant to control those who have the effectual power to violate them. They are, then, analogous to the law of nature. That law, remember, did not serve to render the state of nature a state of peace. All of what has been discussed in this chapter, political society itself, is necessitated by that failure. The rule of law is, as it were, a moral duty whose content is determined by the inability of moralizing to bring about peace, i.e., by the inconveniences of the state of nature. One might of course respond that Locke intends his doctrine of revolution to counter this inadequacy, a small bit of power politics to ensure that consensual politics triumphs.

Yet Locke does not now discuss popular resistance. Instead, he introduces prerogative. That is, rather than address this concern about the rule of law with a doctrine of popular resistance, or immediately note that James II forfeited his throne for violating the rule of law—the approach taken by Robert Ferguson and in the *Political Aphorisms*, for example[49]—Locke introduces something that only exacerbates the need for that resistance. Faced with this objection, namely, that Locke has not adequately guarded against tyranny, he begins a discussion that heightens, rather than alleviates, the threat of that tyranny.

And he has a very good reason for doing this. Were he to try simply to ensure that actual political systems functioned as described in this chapter by rousing the people to a jealous defense of that system, we would have to assume that he found this system to be adequate. He would be yet another among so many who make observance of legal formalism into a quasi-sacred obligation. Clearly, in order for this to be the case political action would have to be reducible to the application of rules: in order for law to command or prohibit all that it should, it must be possible to codify all such acts into laws. This possibility is a matter of faith, a faith which Locke denies. Now, as if on cue, Locke reveals that things of this world are in a state of constant flux. Law cannot be crafted to accommodate this fact without ceasing to be law. Instead, there must be another power, an extralegal power, in order to address the failure of legislative supremacy: prerogative.

Chapter 3

Prerogative and the Limits of Legislative Supremacy

One cannot acknowledge the legitimacy of extralegal action without weakening the conviction that legitimate action must accord with the law. Yet Locke does precisely this. He argues that the prince possesses, by the "common Law of Nature" (TT II 159), a right to act for the good of society without the sanction of law, even against the law. Why is such a power needed? What would it look like in a liberal commonwealth? How could it be justified without abandoning Locke's account of legitimacy? In the previous chapter I discussed Locke's conception of the rule of law. It is now appropriate, then, to focus on how prerogative stands against it. Once this task is completed, we can move on to situating prerogative within the Lockean commonwealth.

Before beginning, it seems good to outline some of the general features of prerogative which will be addressed more fully in this chapter. This is to provide the context in which the later discussions will occur. Prerogative, I will argue, is not the same as executive power. The executive power sees that the laws are followed—and nothing more. Locke is not being coy here: he is not surreptitiously expanding the scope of executive power by introducing prerogative. He does blur the distinction between the two, more often than not assigning the responsibility of prerogative to the executive, but his presentation maintains that they do in fact have different origins and extents. Similarly, prerogative is not an aspect of the federative power, that power possessed by the society as a whole to protect itself from those outside of it and which also cannot be governed by law. These (namely, the executive and federative) are political powers, whereas prerogative is a natural power.

Prerogative is necessary in every society, Locke argues. Indeed, it does not even necessarily have to be an extraordinary power. True, it does come to light as such, to be used when the ordinary means of executive power are inappropriate, and this is certainly how Locke incorporates prerogative into his political system. Yet it is nonetheless not essential that prerogative be extraordinary: it is capable of being the usual mode of governance, even though this would not be a species of civil government (cf. TT II 162). Not all forms of government, after all, need be what Locke calls "civil." For example, he responds that "*Civil Government* is the proper Remedy for the Inconveniences of the State of Nature," countering the claim that absolute monarchy is the remedy because "Government" is needed (TT II 13): he emphasizes "*Civil Government*," suggesting that it is the alternative to "Government," simply. Additionally, he says that fathers exercise a sort of government (TT II 75), though we would certainly not think to call this civil government unless we were taken in by Sir Robert Filmer's wiles. Prerogative may not be a political power by Locke's definition, but it is certainly capable of being the ordinary and usual form of government. Political power, recall, arises from consent and consists only of the executive, legislative, and federative powers (cf. TT II 3, II 171). (I say "consent" as opposed to "acquiescence." The difference will become important in describing how prerogative can be said to be legitimate in Locke's system.) Locke clearly does not prefer the "non-political" government that prerogative represents (taking political in its Lockean sense), but it is a possibility, and some prerogative must be allowed in every society. Government cannot be wholly lawful.[1]

Prerogative clearly sits uncomfortably with constitutionalism. Indeed, Justice David Davis, writing for the U.S. Supreme Court in *Ex parte Milligan*, went so far as to declare, "No doctrine, involving more pernicious consequences, was ever invented by the wit of man than that any of [the Constitution's] provisions can be suspended during any of the great exigencies of government. Such a doctrine leads directly to anarchy or despotism."[2] Attempts to fit prerogative within a "constitutional" framework have had to stretch constitutionalism past its breaking point, rendering it more a rhetorical trope than a useful analytic concept.[3]

In order to salvage constitutionalism, then, we might want the extent of prerogative to be fixed in the constitution, leaving it as only a power to act without the law "in some things" (TT II 210). So, for example, Locke's prince has the prerogative to convoke and dissolve Parliament, a power that is his by the constitution (cf. TT II 156, II 167).

Yet the logic of Locke's account informs us that such limitation, if intended to be inviolable and absolute, is impossible: just as the magnitude of an unforeseen accident cannot be foreseen, so the power necessary to deal with it cannot be fixed beforehand. Certain prerogatives may be recognized legislatively, even in that part of a written constitution that Locke would consider legislative, not constitutive. What is thus recognized would not, however, be the full extent of prerogative, nor would these powers be prerogatives only because of legislative/constitutional acknowledgment. The power of prerogative, as Locke describes it, is limited only by the public good, and no law can similarly restrain a right of acting without or against the law for that good. The individual's power to do what the preservation of mankind requires is surrendered in political society only insofar as it is consonant with the preservation of that society (cf. TT II 129)—meaning that even if the fundamental law were to deny the prince any right to benefit the people arbitrarily, this would not imply that he is normatively forbidden from doing so.[4] The permission to act for the good of the country by whatever means necessary will still exist.

This is clearly a startling conclusion, especially given what other opponents of Stuart absolutism were writing at the time.[5] Samuel Johnson, for example, wrote in 1689 that

> No Man has any more Civil Authority than what the Law of the Land has vested in him; Nor is he one of St. *Paul*'s Higher Powers any farther, or to any other purposes than the Law has impowr'd him. . . . To judge and determine Causes against Law, without Law, or where the Law is obscure and uncertain, is to assume Legislative power.[6]

The implication of this was clearly that the king possessed no such authority. An earlier, anonymous pamphlet entitled *Vox Populi: or, the Peoples Claim to their Parliament's Sitting* expressed much the same thought: "the King has no Prerogative, but what the Law gives him."[7] This thought is most forcefully put by Robert Ferguson:

> To extend the Governour's Right to Command, and Subjects Duty to Obey, beyond the Laws of ones Country, is Treason against the Constitution, Treachery to the Society whereof we are Members, and through dissolving the Ties by which Princes stand confined, and overthrowing the Hedges by which the reserved Rights, Priviledges, and Properties of the Subjects are fenced about, every Prince is made a Tyrant, and all Subjects are rendered Slaves.[8]

Not all of those opposed to the Stuarts were so stringent, of course. The author of *A Letter from a Person of Quality, to His Friend in the Country*, for example, wrote that, in the opinion of the 1st Earl of Shaftesbury, "a Government could not be supposed whether *Monarchical,* or other of any sort, without a standing Supream Executive power, fully enabled to mitigate, or wholly to suspend the Execution of any penal Law, in the Intervals of the *Legislative* power."[9] Now, this is certainly more than what the authors just now considered would allow and goes even further than what William of Orange claimed was appropriate,[10] but it does not yet go so far as Locke's doctrine of prerogative. The *Letter*, after all, speaks only of a dispensing power, i.e., of a *particular* prerogative of the Crown under the constitution: it does not outline a supraconstitutional doctrine of extralegal action. It is only with the *Two Treatises of Government* that we get a decidedly liberal argument for the prince's right to step outside of the law without that right arising from some other, antecedent positive law.[11]

The Need for Prerogative

Locke gives two reasons why law is insufficient for political ends and so must be supplemented with prerogative. The first involves deficiencies with a well-ordered legislative, namely, one that is not always in being, is separate from the executive, and comprises an assembly of men rather than a lone legislator. Because of the character of legislative power, he says, it is unnecessary for the legislature to forever be in session: it can pass whatever laws are needed and then dissolve, each legislator returning to live under the laws he has made (TT II 143, II 153). Moreover, it would undoubtedly become burdensome to the people for it to sit throughout the year, year after year (TT II 153, II 156). The people's property would be as secure under such a legislative as it is under an absolute monarch (TT II 138). It is for this reason that it must dissolve and reform as needed and that, in all well-constituted commonwealths, it is separate from the executive power (TT II 143, II 159). It is also for this reason that the legislature must be an assembly, for a legislature comprising a single legislator by definition dissolves only with his death (TT II 153; cf. TT II 143, II 153–57).

These aspects of the well-constituted legislative power are the very ones that introduce inadequacies into the rule of law. In such governments, there must be "a latitude left to the Executive power, to do many things of choice, which the Laws do not prescribe": the legislature is not always in being and is usually too numerous for it to act with "the dispatch requisite to Execution" (TT II 160).

There is, however, a more fundamental problem with the rule of law. The above criticisms, after all, apply only to "some Governments" (TT II 160). This is to say that, so far, the problem is merely structural. It is produced by how Locke (and the Whigs in general) sought to obviate the dangers of absolute power: Parliament would pass laws that the king would enforce; there could be no power beyond what the laws demanded. This deficiency with the rule of law could therefore conceivably be remedied by finding some other institutional check on absolute power, one that did not occasion the above difficulties. That is, it is a problem with *how* the law is made. Yet there is a more intractable flaw, one which involves the nature of law itself.

There are, Locke says, many things "which the Law can by no means provide for" (TT II 159). This is a fundamental inadequacy in the rule of law. Its cause lies in part in the very genesis of the rule of law, a genesis which strikes at the logic underlying legislative supremacy. Locke now informs us that, in fact, most laws were created only in order to limit magisterial discretion (TT II 162). According to the view he had been limning thus far, the power of the prince flowed from the law (TT II 151–52). It is an interesting feature of Locke's argument, at least as he had been expressing it up to this point, that the executive and legislative powers were not placed in different hands in order to limit the executive. The executive would, after all, already be limited by his being the executive. Rather, they were placed in separate hands in order to keep those who are authorized to wield legislative power honest. That the prince's power had its source in the legislative was a necessary consequence of legislative supremacy and was essential to it. Were this not the case, the prince would have had a source of power beyond that of the law, and so his power would not have been by definition subordinate to that of the legislative. In one view, the legislative power is supreme for the simple reason that all other powers flow from it; in the other, there is a power that does not flow from the legislative, and so the latter's supremacy is called into doubt. Since the law functions as a limit on the prince's discretion, we now learn, his power would actually flow from some other source: it comes directly from the people, who therefore do him no wrong in clarifying the true nature of his prerogatives (TT II 163). That is, here, the prince is *not* the legislative's creature. Rather, the legislative was created in order to contain his *preexisting* power. Levies do not turn watermills, though they may channel rivers toward them.

It is according to this view that the executive and legislative powers were placed in separate hands in order to limit the executive, or rather to reduce the prince to the level of a chief executive. It may be that this trick requires a sort of creation myth regarding the prince's power. In the beginning, there was no prince, Locke's account of the origins of all political societies goes, but the law spoke and with that *Fiat!* the power was created. And that might even be true if we are talking about legitimate power, or power to which men are obligated. That force or energy which can now be described as legitimate preceded the law's creating, however, like primordial waters and darkness on the face of the deep. This was the original form of government, Locke eventually concedes. There is always the question of whether this potency is ever fully subdued, whether the prince is ever completely tamed, or whether instead waits to overwhelm its bounds. The whole reason for revolution or checks and balances is of course precisely that the torrent of executive energy does not always obey the course set for it by the laws. What Locke is concerned about when it comes to prerogative, however, is whether the laws can direct this energy such that it does every good thing that the primordial, prerogatival government did. Can even the best laws govern well? It is this foundational critique of the rule of law which is of enduring interest to us and to which I now turn.

The making of law, Locke tells us, requires foresight. Yet legislators are not able "to foresee, and provide, by Laws, for all, that may be useful to the Community" (TT II 159). Locke repeats this in the next section, saying "it is impossible to foresee, and so by laws to provide for, all Accidents and Necessities, that may concern the publick" (TT II 160; cf. TT II 167). The ability to be "so much Masters of future Events" as to legislate well for every occasion is beyond human capacity (TT II 156). We can of course predict, and hence regulate, a good number of things—a point not to be forgotten—yet the reduction of *all* action to the mere application of rules would necessitate a near-total capacity to foresee the future. Even limiting ourselves only to those things which are "politically important," this is just an unreasonable demand to make.

This lack of foresight is key: it allows Locke to broaden the scope of prerogative. In mentioning it, he also provides his readers with its cause. This cause marks a turning point in the *Second Treatise*.[12] We do not possess the requisite foresight, he says, because of the constant flux of things.

> Things of this World are in so constant a Flux, that nothing remains long in the same State. Thus People, Riches, Trade, Power, change their Stations; flourishing mighty Cities come to ruine, and prove in time neglected desolate Corners, whilst other unfrequented places grow into populous Countries, fill'd with Wealth and Inhabitants. (TT II 157)

This is true, he states, of all things, not simply of the mundane examples he gives; these examples, moreover, result in politically significant shifts.

The emphasis on prescience in these statements might suggest that the problem is largely epistemological. And indeed, a reading of the *Essay Concerning Human Understanding* supports this impression. We cannot have certain knowledge concerning causes and effects in the natural world, and so it is always possible that something surprising will arise (cf. especially ECHU IV.3). Of course, the probability that our understanding of the basic laws of physics is wrong in any catastrophic way is relatively low, and an extralegal power that finds its justification in our inability to predict earthquakes or asteroid impacts is of only a marginal interest to politics.

What is more undetermined, and thus most in need of an extemporaneous response, is the result of human interactions. We might say that it is not so much the dearth of physics as of economics and political science that is problematic.[13] This dearth takes on what might seem to be comically absurd proportions. Locke's weighty judgment, stated in such a way as to signal that a profound thinker is revealing an important truth, namely, that the fundamental character of worldly things is a constant flux, that there is no *cosmos*, only *chaos*, no being save what our minds fix in ideas and that these minds too are becoming—this pronouncement on the ancient quarrel between Parmenides and Heracleitus, Socrates and Protagoras, is made manifest in the fact that Old Sarum sends two members to Parliament, even though nobody lives there anymore (cf. TT II 157)! An analogous situation surrounds the prince's exercise of the federative power: it cannot be regulated by antecedent laws because, being "done in reference to Foreigners," it depends "much upon their actions, and the variation of designs and interests" (TT II 147).

John Dunn, in his interpretation of Locke, devotes much of his chapter on prerogative to how revealing it is of the depth of Locke's piety. The stable world of Locke's archrival, Sir Robert Filmer, by Dunn's contrast, rested on Filmer's "naïvely providentialist assumptions."[14] Against this optimism, Locke argued that men make their social world and so are responsible for it—they cannot blame God or expect Him to resolve their difficulties. As Dunn phrases Locke's position, "God made Human Nature, the potentialities inherent in the species, the framework within which human life takes place. But men make human history."[15] This means accepting that there are real difficulties to which there may be no complete resolution. Prerogative, the inability to legislate difficulties away, is the acceptance of this truth. Pasquale Pasquino gives the same account, except with History taking the place of Providential neglect.[16] And Harvey Mansfield sees in this flux the resonances of Machiavelli's *fortuna*, *necessità*, and *accidenti*.[17] Tellingly, Kirstie McClure, who attributes to Locke the very theology that Dunn denies, has no place for, let alone account of, prerogative.[18] The same story can be told with or without God, as the moral is that God will not resolve our political problems and that the fundamental fact about politics is disorder. That is, what appears to be a cosmological statement about the flux of all things in fact reveals an anthropological or political truth.

There is a problem, however, with Dunn's procedure of reading a theological position into this anthropological or political truth, or at least with his making them the focus of what Locke is talking about. Dunn's interpretation recasts the debate between Locke and Filmer. One might have thought that the latter opposed to the natural equality of mankind a hierarchy set by God himself and that Locke confronted this supposed hierarchy in order to reestablish the plausibility of equality. Instead, Dunn informs us, Locke struck at Filmer's fair-weather piety with one which could command the submission of a deeply thoughtful and noble-minded believer. Unfortunately for this interpretation, however, the *Two Treatises* gives every indication of its author's having believed that the issue revolved around the existence of a divine mandate to rule, not the unmanly cravenness a desire for such a mandate would reveal.

What Dunn sees is that prerogative results from man's being alone in his struggle to live together with other men. This is neither a reference to God's punishment of Adam and Eve, nor incompatible with it. What is certain, however, is that Locke does not tie the flux of all things to religious principles. Dunn is one of the few scholars operating within the Cambridge school who gives Locke's doctrine of prerogative its due, but his handling of it has more the mien of forcing an octagonal peg into a round hole: if Locke's theory is so steeped in Puritan worldviews as Dunn suggests, then it should be possible to see everything as an expression of those prejudices. Yet doing this with prerogative requires that we take Locke's concerns to be radically different from those which he states them to be or conclude that Locke was just a poor expositor of his own ideas. For Locke does not direct our attention toward the facets of his doctrine which Dunn discerns there.[19] I think what we have in Dunn's case is an interpretation which explains how someone might have written something like the *Two Treatises*, but one which does not explain the *Two Treatises* that Locke actually wrote.

As Harvey Mansfield notes, the flux of all worldly things is a Machiavellian rather than an Aristotelean objection to law: the problem lies in the mutability of things, not in that the generality of law cannot account for what is exceptionally good.[20] The end of law is not the promotion of individual and civic virtue, according to Locke, even if the commonwealth must sometimes rely upon these things. Rather, political society ought to be concerned only with the preservation of property—life, liberty, and estate. That is, the problem is not that the law cannot provide both for the common good and for the highest individual human flourishing in virtue: the law does not look to the latter, and so its inability to provide for both is not problematic. Instead, even the rather modest goal of preserving property is uncertain because of constantly shifting conditions. These latter, moreover, can differ so radically that no general rule could be applicable in every situation.

There is the question, of course, of whether Locke recognizes the Aristotelean critique of law, i.e., of whether this difference is merely one of emphasis. Aristotle, after all, was not oblivious to the problem Locke notes: he simply does not dwell on it. So, for example, he states that Socrates erred in the *Republic* by attributing the fall of the best regime alone to fortune: rather, Aristotle states, fortune causes *all* types of regimes to fall (*Politics*

1315b39–1316a18). Moreover, fortune rules over the very things to which Locke's commonwealth is dedicated (cf. *Politics* 1323b26–29, 1332a29–33, 1333b15–16).

In favor of the idea that Locke in turn recognized without dwelling on the Aristotelean objections, there are remarks that he makes in passing that suggest that he, too, did not consider it possible to codify justice perfectly as a set of rules. I will speak of these in more detail later, but he does speak of a man who must be pardoned for a crime on account of which he actually deserves reward (TT II 159); he lets slip that he does not believe that God would govern the universe according to the law of nature, or by some more sublime, eternal law, but rather as a species of prerogative (TT II 166).

These passages are not conclusive, however. They are, after all, isolated remarks, and perhaps we cannot read too much into them. If Locke recognized the Aristotelean objections, it would mean that there could be no law of nature, Thomistic, Hobbesian, or otherwise. And Locke's use of the word *arbitrary* as a synonym for *irrational* at least gives the impression that there is a useful analogy between reasoning and the application of law.[21] A. John Simmons finds it more plausible that Locke be a rule-consequentialist than an act-consequentialist, as though moral action were the following of rules and moral reasoning an examination of those rules.[22]

Resolving the question of how well Locke understood Aristotle's critique of law would require delving deeper into the foundations of Locke's more obviously metaphysical thought, something I attempt to avoid for the most part in this book. It suffices for now to say that the primary need for prerogative stems from the flux of all things. While we can imagine reasons for our lack of foresight that are not related to flux, and while the generality of law might be criticized on grounds other than our lack of foresight, Locke's rhetorical focus is on the instability of circumstances to which law must be addressed.

To continue to obey laws whose reasons have left them, Locke continues, can lead only to "gross absurdities" like England's famously rotten boroughs. Moreover, under the system that Locke had been describing prior to this flux, "this [particular] inconvenience is thought incapable of a remedy" (TT II 157). Locke does not adduce this particular example in order to recommend redrawing legislative districts. Rather, he assumes that his persuadable readers already agree that this is necessary and so may accept a broader doctrine of extralegal action as following from that necessity. We might comfortably counter this argument with the observation that redistricting need not be extralegal. Yet Locke does not take for a law just any standard but rather only one whose violation ought to be clear to just about everyone, i.e., one that can be applied mechanistically. The battles fought over redistricting in the United States suggest that we have not solved this problem, as do the solutions proposed for those battles: entrusting the process to the discretion of an impartial judge relies more on that judge's honesty and prudence than on having found a rule by which to limit that discretion.[23]

Providence may not be friendly toward mankind, but this is not simply the result of the appeal to Heaven's being nothing but an appeal to force. Rather, this violent world is not even stable in matters mostly unrelated to force, e.g., demographics, fires, and justified crimes, among other things. These things are of paramount political importance, however. Flux and violence conspire to undermine temporal felicity. Law itself cannot rule, and so Locke introduces and justifies an *extralegal* power as the proper remedy to its deficiencies.

Redefining Prerogative

Prerogative was traditionally taken to be the right of the king, and what was debatable in seventeenth-century English politics was its extent, a question usually resolved by determining whether it was the foundation of the laws or their creation. Which is to say that either an extralegal authority was recognized as absolute[24] or there could be no such thing.[25] Locke retains the word of his monarchist opponents, yet he gives it an entirely new definition, wrenching it from the constellation of legal rights for which the king could demand respect and unquestionable obedience. Locke himself points to the peculiar character of his definition, stating that it "*is* that which is called *Prerogative*" (TT II 160). Not all that is called prerogative is actually so. Yet, what *is* prerogative *is* essential and legitimate and unmistakably extralegal. He defines it five times, i.e., five times he employs some form of "prerogative is such and such." It is important that we pause here and examine his redefinition carefully.

Locke's first definition immediately follows his statement on the constant flux in which all things are.

> *Prerogative* being nothing, but a Power in the hands of the Prince to provide for the publick good, in such Cases, which depending upon unforeseen and uncertain Occurrences, certain and unalterable Laws could not safely direct, whatsoever shall be done manifestly for the good of the People, and the establishing the Government upon its true Foundations, is, and always will be just *Prerogative*. (TT II 158)

The second definition (the first that occurs in the chapter "Of Prerogative") runs as follows: "This Power to act according to discretion, for the publick good, without the prescription of Law, and sometimes even against it, *is* that which is called *Prerogative*" (TT II 160). Four sections later, he defines it again: "*Prerogative* can be nothing, but the Peoples permitting their Rulers, to do several things of their own free choice, where the Law was silent, and sometimes too against the direct Letter of the Law, for the publick good, and their acquiescing in it when so done" (TT II 164). In the last definition that Locke provides within the chapter on prerogative, he states that "*Prerogative is nothing but the Power of doing publick good without a Rule*" (TT II 166). Finally, in the last section of the chapter on tyranny, he notes that prerogative is "an Arbitrary Power in some things left in the Prince's hand to do good, not harm to the people" (TT II 210).

We can immediately see that two things remain constant through all five definitions. We might provisionally say that these form the essence of prerogative. First, it is a power to act for the public good and is limited by that good. Ostensible abuses of prerogative were therefore never *actually* prerogative in the first place (TT II 166). Second, prerogative is not bound by (positive) law. Prerogative is discretion above and beyond the law: it permits the prince to act in the absence of law and furthermore to act against the law.

These two aspects, on their own, can obviously leave us desiring more of an explanation. For greater clarity regarding what Locke means, then, let us turn to the particular examples of prerogative that he provides. There are in total five such examples (TT II 156, II 158, II 159 twice, II 167), though the first and the fifth are almost identical and can be treated as one.

Locke begins rather innocuously: he tells us that it is an exercise of prerogative to assemble the legislature when needed rather than as dictated by law. As Clement Fatovic put the point, "When Locke actually turns to prerogative as the focal point of his discussion in Chapter XIV, it becomes apparent that the executive's power to convoke and dissolve the legislature is an exception to the paradigmatic use of prerogative in cases of emergency where the fundamental natural law of preservation is at stake."[26] This example is preceded by a discussion of the *executive* functions in assembling the legislature, making such seem like the normal exercise of executive authority (TT II 154–155). I wish to examine what he says there before moving on to the actual example of prerogative, as this informs that discussion.

At first, the executive is merely charged with convoking the legislative body. If the people had set certain times for its assembly, he merely calls elections, issuing whatever orders are necessary to that end. Otherwise, the calling of elections is left to his prudence, depending on when occasion requires laws to be created or amended, or requires redressing or preventing certain inconveniences (TT II 154). Importantly, an executive who misuses this power enters into a state of war with the people (TT II 155).

Now, something curious happens: it is at this point that Locke adds the power of dismissing the legislative to the executive's normal functions (TT II 156). That is, having just raised the possibility that the executive might misuse his authority, Locke states its scope more expansively, rather than less. Yet we must remember that, in reminding his readers of the Stuarts' questionable prorogations of Parliament, he makes explicit the fact that this authority is restrained, in the final analysis, by the threat of popular resistance. It is precisely this extraconstitutional threat that renders such broad constitutional authority acceptable.

Locke continues to expand the power which the prince should possess over the legislative body. He had initially suggested an alternative to trusting the prince to convoke and dismiss it when appropriate, namely, setting the times at which it is to be assembled in the constitution (cf. TT II 154). Yet he now states that this would be unwise.[27]

> [It is not] possible, that the first Framers of the Government should, by any foresight, be so much Masters of future Events, as to be able to prefix so just periods of return and duration of the *Assemblies of the Legislative*, in all times to come, that might exactly answer all the Exigencies of the Commonwealth. . . . What then could be done, in this Case, to prevent the Community, from being exposed sometime or other to eminent hazard . . . but to intrust it to the prudence of some, who being present, and acquainted with the state of publick affairs, might make use of this Prerogative for the publick good? And where else could this be so well placed as in his hands, who was intrusted with the Execution of the Laws, for the same end? (TT II 156)

Setting the times of the legislative session in the constitution might seem preferable to trusting in the prince's goodness. It is, after all, the alternative to trusting in the people's ability to punish a faithless executive, or rather in their prudently knowing when to do so. Locke advises against this alternative. At most, there might be a mixture of the two, with constitutional provisions susceptible to the prince's discretionary override.[28] The latter power, however, cannot sensibly be avoided; in saying this, Locke renders the situation such that there can be no check but popular resistance.

In making this argument, Locke for the first time calls this power of convoking and dissolving the legislative "Prerogative." He does not refer to it as such until he notes the frailty of human foresight and the fact that only the people can judge its use. This example eases one into the vast extent of prerogative that is to come. It is also essentially the same example which Locke uses to ease one out of the discussions of prerogative (cf. TT II 167).

Whereas the first example involves convoking and then dissolving the legislature, the second example actually alters it. Or rather, Locke says correcting himself, it reforms it, restoring it to what it should have been all along (TT II 158). It is introduced by his solemn pronouncement regarding the constant flux, which flux results, among other things, in the problem of England's rotten boroughs (TT II 157). The problem at hand is such that the previous extent of prerogative is inadequate. The scope of that prerogative must be expanded. This expansion, furthermore, must be justified somehow. Indeed, Locke does not simply add yet another "prerogative." He ceases to speak as if there were simply a set of powers called "prerogatives."

Instead, he now introduces a broad doctrine of prerogative, in the singular—a general definition that encompasses and therefore justifies each particular instance of it. Regarding the rotten boroughs, Locke states, "This Strangers stand amazed at, and every one must confess needs a remedy," and yet Locke's own principles seem to render one impossible (TT II 157). Because the creation of the legislative is the original and supreme act of society, because no inferior power can with right alter it, and because the people cannot alter it while the government stands—that is, because we are to accept Locke's account of the beginning of all lawful governments—we cannot see a way to remedy those inconveniences occasioned by a simple shift in demographics (TT II 157; cf. TT II 134, II 149, II 150).

Locke's solution to the problem is also introduced by a solemn pronouncement, ultimately taken from Cicero.[29] "*Salus Populi Suprema Lex*, is certainly so just and fundamental a Rule, that he, who sincerely follows it, cannot dangerously err" (TT II 158). The good of the people is the supreme law. While a perfectly reasonable rule, assuming that Locke is correct about there being no danger in following it, it does seem to require that one contest, if only temporarily, the authority of the legislature which claims the unique right to interpret this natural law (cf. TT II 87, II 89, II 129–30).

Were it not for this example, one might get the impression from the rest of Locke's discussion that prerogative allowed for arbitrary, i.e., lawless, acts, but could not be a power to make law. Here, however, a new electoral law seems to have been made, the old one being abandoned. This is no mere reform of some aspect of private law, but the imposition of a new constitutional law.[30]

Since this would certainly be an odd conclusion, given Locke's arguments thus far, we might try to interpret his statements here so as to avoid having him say this. Ruth Grant does precisely this, asserting that "there is no legitimate alteration of the legislative even if the alteration brings good government."[31] We could say, provisionally, that a new electoral law is *not* made, but that the ruler instead exercises prerogative in this case as a one-off affair: the practice which he commands and which leads to "a fair and *equal Representative*" (TT II 158) would instead be made into a more permanent law by some other means. And yet, if we are to prefer this alternative, what might these other means be? Two candidates seem plausible, namely, ratification by the legislative and acquiescence by the people. They do not, however, make this example less problematic.

As regards the first, it hardly seems reasonable for this one-off affair to be made permanent by the acclamation of those who gained their position though the affair, namely, the "restored" legislature—the "corrupt" legislature certainly wouldn't go for it![32] Consequently, this example also prevents us from saying that the legislative is always the proper judge of a use of prerogative. We might have been tempted to think otherwise: the legislative is, after all, the supreme power within society. Several scholars have taken this to have been Locke's argument.[33] And this interpretation does have a textual foundation: in one place, Locke remarks that the executive may act in the absence of law "till the Legislative can conveniently be Assembled to provide for it" (TT II 159). It might perhaps be quibbling to note that Locke mentions this only in the context of cases "where the municipal Law has given no direction," i.e., not in cases where the executive acts contrary to the stated laws. Looking at how Locke phrases this, however, any such legislative ratification would have to take the form of legislation providing for the deficient municipal law. If it were simply to acquiesce in or confirm the particular use of prerogative, the legislative would be guilty of issuing an extemporaneous decree rather than a general law (cf. TT II 136, II 142). This is an unacceptable result, as it is not clear how the ruler's extralegal act could be made conformable with lawful government though a misuse of the legislative power. Moreover, immediately after saying this, Locke reveals that "Many things there are, which the Law can by no means provide for" (TT II 159). These are necessarily within the realm of prerogative yet cannot be "ratified" by subsequent legislation. These things are simply incapable of legislative treatment. Tellingly, and I think conclusively, whenever Locke mentions any sort of ratification for prerogative when defining it, he identifies the people, not the people's representatives, as the proper judge (cf. TT II 164, II 165). And, as noted, we cannot have the legislature be the judge of its own reformation by prerogative.

So, let us say that it is the people at large who are to ratify this action. If that is the case, then a law is made by acquiescence rather than consent (cf. TT II 158, II 164, II 165, II 176, II 227).[34] To avoid this possibility, however, we are forced to say that the prince did make a new law and so that prerogative somehow or other is not restricted in this manner. Yet this would be "legislation" of the highest sort, the creation of the constitution, by fiat—the people would not be involved at all!

Locke does not provide us with an easy way to resolve this difficulty, and I do not pretend that this brief exploration settles this issue. I am not sure it can be resolved, unless we take Locke's entire message about rights, consent, the rule of law, etc., to be an exoteric approximation of the teaching he reveals most startlingly regarding prerogative: *salus populi suprema lex*. This possibility, however, is irrelevant for my purposes in this book: as I said at the beginning, the substance of popular counsel cannot be presented esoterically.

Regardless of how one reads these passages, the extent of prerogative is broad indeed, capable of legitimate action against even the constitutional law. It is with this example that we get the first definition of prerogative.

The third and fourth examples are drawn from the same section—indeed, from the same sentence (TT II 159). The former involves tearing down an innocent man's house in order to prevent the spread of a fire to the entire neighborhood.[35] The innocent man's house is not yet on fire, but it is torn down in order to save other homes, also not yet on fire. This is presented as an example "wherein a strict and rigid observation of the Laws may do harm" (TT II 159). A great many would suffer just because the law does not allow the prince to demolish homes whenever he thinks it necessary. Law must protect property from being taken without consent, i.e., unlawfully (TT II 138–140), but necessity compels the unlawful taking of property. The unfortunate owner is expressly called innocent.

This example appears as an aside, set off from the rest of the sentence by parentheses; it consists of a mere twenty words. Moreover, it does not obviously contribute to the conclusion of the sentence, which is the power of pardon based on the preservation of all, even the guilty, whenever feasible. (I will suggest in a bit that it does contribute to the conclusion of the sentence, but this contribution is by no means obvious.) More interesting, however, is that this is the only example which sacrifices the rights of the individual to the public good.[36] There is no law in this case which allows for this; it therefore raises the possibility of essential laws remaining unpassed. Why might this be so?

Locke says that the enclosure of land does not harm anyone *after* having proven its necessity (cf. TT II 26–32 with II 33); following this, he even says that enclosure improves men's lives, as if its not harming others did not yet reconcile men to its necessity (TT II 37, II 40–43). Locke follows the same rhetorical pattern in discussing civil society, saying that its formation does not harm anyone after having already established that it is needed (TT II 95). Might the legislative refuse to countenance certain actions, regardless of their necessity, should that necessity require harming others? Might the legislative, or even the people, refuse to countenance the possibility of certain necessities, as if truly hard choices were necessarily false choices? Might this not, that is, be an additional deficiency in the rule of law, an additional reason why some extralegal authority is needed? Tearing down the innocent man's house is but one example of where a departure from the law is necessary to avoiding a greater harm. It is an easy example because the government may, if it wishes, pay restitution. Not all cases where the rights of the individual must be sacrificed *pro salute populi* are similarly recompensable. Rather than trust the legislative to formulate a general rule for such hard cases—a rule which almost certainly would be applied to the disadvantage of a considerable number due to problems with its formulation—Locke leaves it to the prince's prudence to judge each case on its own merits.[37]

The fourth example of prerogative is similarly baffling in its details. It is the example of pardon. Locke provides two reasons why the ruler should have a power "to mitigate the severity of the Law, and pardon some Offenders" (TT II 159), one much more unusual than the other. The second reason Locke gives is simple mercy, such mercy being demanded by the end of government "where it can prove no prejudice to the innocent." It is the first reason that continues Locke's attack on the adequacy of law to rule. Of the two, it is by far the more interesting.

After stating the above example of the fire, Locke continues, "a Man may come sometimes within the reach of the Law, which makes no distinction of Persons, by an action, that may deserve reward and pardon." Law makes no distinction of persons, but now this is presented as though it were a mark against it. Impartiality means to have "one Rule for Rich and Poor, for the Favourite at Court, and the Country Man at Plough" (TT II 142), but it also means that law does not respect illegal actions that benefit society: Locke says that this man's actions deserve *reward*. That is, he is not to be pardoned out of mercy, but rather out of gratitude for what he has done. Moreover, it is the action that brought him within the reach of the law that deserves reward and pardon. It was illegal to benefit society as this criminal did. Locke does not suggest that he actually be rewarded for his illegal act, only that he not be punished for it.

What Locke says here is so bizarre, or at least it took me so much by surprise, that I went searching through the Oxford English Dictionary for some archaic, obsolete definition of "reward" that would render it less peculiar. I even made an allowance for the possibility that Locke, learned as he was, did not use the word in any attested English sense, but instead according to its etymology, or some French or Latin cognate. After all, Locke is asserting, with nothing more than a single word, that pardon is necessary in order to avoid punishing citizens to whom we owe a public debt of gratitude. I have failed, however, to uncover any cause why I should not be compelled to interpret this lone word. Locke made much greater corrections to subsequent editions of the *Two Treatises* than this single word, were it misleading.

Law cannot dictate when illegal actions are allowed and when they are not: what is illegal must necessarily be forbidden by the law. Some extralegal discretion is therefore required, and the prince is not always at hand. Someone else can, then, stand up and do what must be done. Locke does not call this act prerogative, however, for reasons that I will address below. At the same time, a good ruler should step up, exercise prerogative, and pardon him; as this is an example of prerogative, the public-spirited criminal ought to be pardoned even if the law does not allow it, even if the law forbids it. Pardon of the public-spirited does not depend upon constitutional or legislative sanction. One need only imagine that law-breaker who took matters into his own hands and tore down his neighbor's house to save the city from the fire; after all, the example of the fire is included as a parenthetical insertion into the reasons for why there must be a power of pardon.

Beyond Political Society

We are now in a position to identify several broad characteristics of prerogative. Aside from its most obvious features (namely, that it is extralegal and works for the public good), its scope is unlimited by anything other than the law of nature, it is distinct from the executive and federative powers, it is a natural power, and its use cannot be judged on earth. It is beyond political society. I will explain more about what I mean by each of these in turn.

Let us begin by asking whether these facets of prerogative make it arbitrary. Locke suggests both that they do and that they do not. He says in the first example he gives that prerogative is not arbitrary (TT II 156), then that it is not an arbitrary power to hurt the people (TT II 163), then that it *is* an arbitrary power to do good (TT II 165), and finally, in the final definition of prerogative, that it is an arbitrary power to do good, and not harm, to the people (TT II 210).

These equivocations become coherent in light of Locke's statement that prerogative is bound by the fundamental law of nature and government: "as much as may be, *all* the Members of the Society are to be *preserved*" (TT II 159). The public good is constant through each of Locke's definitions (one of only two things that are). Prerogative is, it turns out, exercised according to a law, i.e., according to a law of nature, and so is not arbitrary in the natural sense.[38] It is, however, exercised without regard for any positive law of civil society and so is arbitrary in the political sense. Prerogative is absolute and arbitrary in the political sense. Tyranny is also absolute and arbitrary in the political sense, but it is arbitrary in the natural sense, as well. It is only in this that prerogative differs from tyranny. Tyranny is naturally arbitrary, while prerogative is not: prerogative is a politically arbitrary power that avoids being naturally arbitrary by working for the public good. We here see the importance of Locke's redefinition of arbitrary power: whereas his contemporaries said that arbitrary power was simply illegitimate (if they opposed the power of the Stuarts, that is), Locke's implicit distinction between naturally and politically arbitrary power allows him to distinguish prerogative from tyranny. It allows him to save a place for prerogative.

If a constitution—either Lockean or American—is not the source of prerogative, it would seem that prerogative was possessed before society was constituted, i.e., that it is a *natural* power.[39] Yet there are scholars who say that this power, which stands beyond every positive aspect of the constitution, was nevertheless granted by the people.[40] And there is some warrant for this in the text (cf. TT II 163–64).

I begin by noting that Locke explicitly makes prerogative into a right of nature. The executive, "having the power in his hands, has by the common Law of Nature, a right to make use of it, for the good of Society" (TT II 159). Consequently, he would not have gained this right as a result of the social compact and so could not have gotten it as a result of the constitution created by that compact. Presumably, this natural power is not surrendered to political society, else it would have to be under positive law and so could not act against it, i.e., could not be prerogative. This of course contradicts Locke's statements that all natural power is surrendered to society (TT II 136); I think this can be resolved as easily as the problem regarding the rotten boroughs, discussed above.

Moreover, in order for prerogative not to be a natural power, some aspects of the constitution would have to be tacit, or the people would have to be capable of granting authority without such grants being a constitution, or the fundamental law would have to state that some provisions are more fundamental than others. The first possibility would allow tacit consent to form a commonwealth (cf. TT II 122); the second cannot be reconciled to what Locke says about the source of legitimacy and the constitution of legislative authority; and the third would render *salus populi suprema lex* the only provision of the fundamental law (all others would be subordinate to it), which, if a constitutional matter, would mean that the fundamental content of no constitution results from convention but rather from the law of nature.

Locke states that the prince has the power of society in his hands and that the law of nature justifies his use of it for the public good. This deserves careful attention. He has the power in his hands because he is the executive, i.e., as a result of the constitution (in our, more expansive sense) or some form of legislation and thus, ultimately, as a result of consent. Normally, he has a right to use that power only as directed by law: if he acts on his own will, he violates the conditions upon which he was granted that power in the first place (cf. TT II 151). He may of course still retain that power—his subordinates may continue to listen to him—but he loses his *authority* to exercise it. It becomes, as it were, stolen property. His subjects, moreover, could not possibly have consented to other conditions: that would be consent to arbitrary power (cf. TT II 137). This is crucial: if he may act beyond the law, it cannot be as a result of any compact and so must be a natural power. Locke explicitly states that this is the case. The executive's ability to exercise prerogative seems, then, to rely on his ability to do so, i.e., upon the power he has in his hands. That is, his ability to act may rest on convention and thus on the trust of the people, but his right to do so does not.

The power granted by the people in those passages which might suggest that prerogative is constitutional (cf. TT II 163–66) is the trust to have sufficient force at one's disposal to break the law; this centralization not only enables him to enforce the law with greater alacrity, but also to pursue more effectively his natural right to help the people without legal sanction. But, should he abuse this trust, these passages continue, the people do him no wrong in defining more clearly the extent of his *legal* authority. These new laws do not, however, define his prerogative per se, for immediately after suggesting that the people may limit his power (TT II 164), Locke states that they let their "wisest and best Princes . . . inlarge their *Prerogative* as they pleased" (TT II 165) and that their struggles were to "get that to be declared not to be *Prerogative*, which truly was never so" (TT II 166). We are able to read these passages as discussing a grant of ability to exercise effectively a pre-existing right, but a right that is not dependent upon a previous authorization. And we ought to read these passages this way in order to avoid attributing to Locke contradictory statements.

A lesser consideration points in the same direction. Throughout the *Second Treatise*, Locke's thematic discussions focus on what the law of nature demands: specific constitutional possibilities are scattered throughout but are not treated thematically. Were prerogative a grant of authority by the people rather than a right by the law of nature it would be the one exception to this.

This naturalness and this extraconstitutionality force upon us the (perhaps counterintuitive) conclusion that prerogative is not a form of executive power as Locke defines it. It is certainly incompatible with the latter power under the rule of law (where the executive gains its will only from the law and is but a private individual in quitting the law; cf. TT II 151), but is it possible that Locke has now coyly expanded what he was so careful in limiting? While I do not believe that he has, this interpretation does have its supporters, prime among them Richard Cox.[41]

And yet it is interesting that Locke refrains from calling prerogative executive power. According to what he argues, *someone* must be trusted with prerogative, and the executive is a good candidate (TT II 156). This does not, however, make prerogative an aspect of executive power any more than possession of the federative power makes *it* executive power, or vice versa (cf. TT II 147–48). Just because an executive possesses prerogative does not mean that it is executive power; Locke is discussing powers, not the bodies that wield them. Prerogative "fell into the hands" of the executive (TT II 156); it is "left to the discretion of him, that has the Executive Power in his hands" (TT II 159); it is "left to the Executive Power" (TT II 160; cf. TT II 167). Locke almost fails once, saying that "'tis fit that the Laws themselves should in some Cases give way to the Executive Power," but he immediately corrects himself to "or rather to this Fundamental Law of Nature and Government" (TT II 159). The "or rather" shows this to be a correction, strongly suggesting that Locke understood prerogative to be a distinct power: there is no need to correct errors that do not exist. Prerogative is separate from executive power.

We are, however, now faced with an interesting dilemma. On the one hand, the *source* of the executive's right suggests that everyone ought to possess it: anyone at all with the power in their hands could exercise prerogative.[42] The law of nature does not, after all, grant superior rights to the merely conventionally superior. When noting that the right of prerogative is possessed by the law of nature, he reminds us that the latter is "common," i.e., applies to all equally (cf. TT II 159). Yet, on the other hand, Locke never says that anyone but the executive (the prince, the rulers, etc.) has a right to this power: he almost always restricts who may use it. One might say that the chief executive simply has more power at his disposal and so is in a better position to exercise this right held by all,[43] but Locke does not say this. We can take this even further: prerogative has the same juridical character as individual resistance, both being nothing but an individual's execution of the law of nature. They are exercises of private judgment regarding what that law requires.[44] Yet Locke, again, does not say this. Why *can't* anyone who has the power in their hands use it for the public good, despite the fact that the law says otherwise? Locke does not say.

Or does he, at least implicitly? Remember the example of pardon. There, prerogative is needed to indemnify a man whose illegal behavior paradoxically makes him deserving of reward. By what right, we might well ask, did this criminal violate an express prohibition of the law? Positive law cannot grant rights to violate positive law, for then there would be no violation. There seems no alternative to the conclusion that it was a natural right, i.e., the same law of nature which justifies prerogative.

What, then, is the difference between the two cases? Again, the example of pardon is probative. A criminal may be pardoned, which presumes that he may be effectually judged in a court of law: pardon is only for those who have been or may be found guilty. Who, however, is to pardon the executive?—which is to ask Locke's favorite question, Who shall be judge? If prerogative is extraconstitutional, there can be no judge on earth. In political society, on the other hand, everyone else's exercise of natural power does have an earthly judge, namely, the government. Now we can conjecture as to why it is only rulers who may exercise prerogative: it is not only a natural power but also a natural power for which there is no judge on earth.

Locke also says that the federative power is somehow natural (TT II 145). Additionally, one might say that, in practice, most emergencies wherein prerogative would be vital to the survival of the commonwealth will be occasioned by foreign dangers. Charles II's Declaration of Indulgence, for example, suspended the operation of penal laws that punished religious dissenters for the sake of domestic tranquility during the Third Anglo-Dutch War. Richard Cox argues for a profound link between prerogative and the federative power.[45] Yet, if this is the case, why does Locke provide no foreign examples in his analysis of prerogative? Whatever the answer to this question may prove to be—and I think the various answers are more or less credible depending on the resolution to the question upon which those answers are expectantly intended to shed light—prerogative is not an aspect of the federative power, nor do they share a common source (as do prerogative and resistance). The federative power is a natural right of society to protect itself and its members, not of any individual within it. Its exercise may certainly be entrusted to officials, but they lack any claim to it apart from their office: their claim is entirely conventional. It is not the remnants of man's natural authority to execute the law of nature but rather "answers to" it (cf. TT II 145): it requires the social compact in order to create a society possessed of this right. Prerogative, on the other hand, is a natural power of the individual: it is the direct application of the law of nature in civil society. It is exercised by parts on behalf of the whole, not by the whole on its own behalf or that of its parts.

There are also jurisdictional differences between the two. The federative power is exercised with regard to persons over whom political society has no conventional authority, namely, foreigners of various stripes. Prerogative, however, while it does not itself call upon prior obligations, does directly touch those who are obligated to obey the law. Furthermore, the federative power possesses a judge on earth: it is subordinate and ministerial to legislative authority and must be surrendered at the pleasure of that body (TT II 153). This common judge is precisely what prerogative lacks.

Locke has not finished describing his political system until he has introduced prerogative. This is suggested by the placement of chapter 15, "Of Paternal, Political, and Despotical Power, considered together." Early in the *Second Treatise*, Locke had stated that he would distinguish these three powers (TT II 2); he dealt with despotical power in chapter 4 and paternal power in chapter 6. Once he begins to discuss political power in chapter 7, however, the flow of the argument does not allow him to cease until he has finished discussing prerogative, in chapter 14; I suggest this is because political power is incomplete and must be supplemented by prerogative. Prerogative is not a part of political power (it being natural), but it is required for political power to function. Chapter 15 also indicates, therefore, to a discerning reader precisely how far Locke has moved from his initial presentation of legitimate government. Political power demands legislative supremacy and the rule of law, while prerogative is unbounded by law. Political power comes from men's relinquishing their natural power, while prerogative is the exercise of natural power. Natural power is needed for politics to function: political power by itself is insufficient. This goes a long way toward explaining why Locke's strict separation of political society and the state of nature seems to blur upon close scrutiny.[46] The rest of the *Two Treatises* builds up to the right of resistance as a necessary consequence of Locke's appending prerogative to political power.

Prerogative is necessary to Locke's political theory because it highlights the problems with the rule of law; it highlights the difficulty with saying that consensual government requires strict adherence to the rule of law. Political society must be adequate to its purposes; if it is not adequate, then no rational creature can be presumed to have given his consent to it (cf. TT II 98). The argument that government requires legislative supremacy is based on the adequacy of legislative supremacy to the ends of government; this not being the case, government requires prerogative, as well.

Beyond Obligation, Consent, and the Social Compact

Legislative supremacy is legitimate because it arises from the consent of each individual. Prerogative is also legitimate, but from where does its legitimacy spring? The problem I am getting at is this: can one consent to prerogative? That is, can one obligate oneself to do what its wielder commands? The answer to this question is not obvious, for one cannot consent to arbitrary power, either as an individual or as a society (TT II 49). Locke's discussion prior to the introduction of prerogative implies that we must answer this question negatively: in order for society to be consensual, men's wills must be directed by general, antecedent laws issuing from those with legislative power (TT II 134). The power to act illegally seems incapable of gaining political legitimacy through consent.

Upon reflection, however, Locke did intimate that the opposite was true in his political anthropology, describing the "probable" history of men leaving the state of nature for political society (TT II 112; cf. TT II 105–12). As an aside, the fact that Locke calls his political anthropology "probable" should ring alarm bells: he viciously attacked Filmer for using the word "probable" in describing an improbable past in a rather memorable passage from the *First Treatise* (cf. TT I 35–36). The serious purpose of Locke's anthropology cannot be to show that all governments have indeed had their origins in consent (cf. TT II 112): it fails rather spectacularly at this. The criticisms of Locke's political anthropology are too many to mention. Locke himself intimates that his account is fictional, noting that it applies only to those governments "that were begun in Peace" (TT II 104); we will later learn that it is "the noise of War" that is heard in history (TT II 175). Attentiveness to the examples of founding he provides suggests that commonwealths are more often founded in blood.[47] Examination of the details of Locke's anthropology undermines the general impression that it leaves, namely, that government did actually begin by the consent of the governed, that free government is not novel.

To return, Locke retells his foundation myths in the chapter on prerogative, a significant repetition because these myths are in fact tied to prerogative's legitimacy. They appear to stretch our conception of what one may consent *to*. This, I think, is their serious purpose. As it turns out, men are permitted to submit to rule by extraordinary virtue, though this theme has thus far been absent from the second of Locke's two treatises (cf. TT I 142, I 158). This submission, moreover, signifies not so much "consent" to prerogative as "acquiescence" in its use. That is, Locke's fanciful history not only casts into doubt its own historical veracity, but furthermore sits uncomfortably with Locke's arguments regarding legitimate government. Consider the debates among scholars regarding early monarchy and whether Locke considers it a form of political society[48]—debates, I think, which reveal that Locke intended that monarchy to be ambiguous.

Locke, conceding that most governments are monarchies, asserts that monarchy originally arose from the consent of the governed. He gives two ways in which this happened, both of which are essentially the same (TT II 110): by submission to the father and by submission to a man of great virtue. It is easy to imagine, Locke says, how men first came to accept their father as their king (TT II 162). After all, he had been a ruler of sorts during their childhood, and they were accustomed to obeying him (TT II 74–75). When most families did not mix, there being much land, government likely began under the father, Locke says. He was possessed of paternal affection for the governed, and custom made it easy to submit to him (TT II 105). This shift from fathers to kings largely went unnoticed (TT II 76). Locke is quick to point out, however, that this shift was not occasioned by respect for paternal authority (TT II 106, II 112): all petty monarchies, i.e., almost all monarchies at their founding, have been elective at some points in their history (TT II 106).

Treating those times when the monarch was not the father, Locke establishes goodness and virtue as a sort of natural authority (TT II 94; cf. TT II 54). When the heir of the father was unfit to succeed him as king, or when several families came together, the people chose the ablest man and the one most likely to rule well to be king; even fathers could be disqualified for negligence, cruelty, or any other defect of body or mind (TT II 105).

However the king was chosen, there were in general very few laws to constrain how he governed: this is key to Locke's anthropology. The king merely executed the law of nature on behalf of society, not needing any other law to limit his power to the nature and ends of government (TT II 74, II 110). There were, of course, or would have been, few occasions in that time for controversies over what little property his subjects possessed (TT II 75): their meager possessions left little room for covetousness or ambition, and so little need to fear or guard against either (TT II 107), and the commonwealth was little larger than a single extended family (TT II 162). The rule of the father was sufficient to procure and preserve all the happiness that men sought in society, at least so long as that rule was exercised with care and skill (TT II 107). They felt, and rightly so, that under such conditions his power was "safe enough in his Honesty and Prudence" (TT II 112). At that time, Locke states, government was almost all prerogative (TT II 162). Even now, a good prince cannot have too much prerogative, and the wisest and best princes have always possessed the most (TT II 164–65).

Locke does not, however, simply praise this time. The grant of such power to one man was negligent, the product of unforeseeing innocence (TT II 94). Monarchy has the advantage of being the *simplest* answer to the problem of the state of nature, and men must be taught to reason about forms of government by harsh experience (TT II 107, II 111): men soon found that their property was not safe under the rule of one man (TT II 94). They began to rein in the monarch by laws; they limited his discretion as soon as they could once it became the discretion to pursue his own, separate interests (TT II 94, II 162). They placed several parts of the government in different hands (TT II 107).

Monarchy was not, however, simply a mistake; while it might have been unforeseeing innocence to grant their monarch total and unrestrained power, a monarch was nonetheless needed. All governments would have fallen had early kings not made war well (TT II 110). The ablest ruler was the "stoutest and bravest," or the "wisest and bravest" (TT II 105, II 107). It is war that makes monarchy necessary. Foreigners cannot be directed by laws or predicted in their actions (TT II 147), and men are naturally mistrustful of those outside of their society, regardless of how much property they possess (cf. TT II 107, II 110). Thus, they choose kings primarily to lead them in battle, even in lands "out of the reach of the Conquering Swords" of imperial neighbors (TT II 102, II 105, II 108–09): societies may have to engage in hostilities even if their neighbors do not care for aggrandizement beyond what is necessary. This ruler, moreover, had to be a monarch, for the conduct of war "admits not of Plurality of Governours" (TT II 108). A single ruler was needed, but for external affairs; the mistake of this age was to grant the king *internal* sovereignty. In a way, their mistake was to confound the federative, executive, and prerogative powers.

One may, however, *acquiesce* in the lawlessness that characterized such rule if it is necessary to the ends of political society. Once Locke has introduced prerogative, he makes this explicit: where a "Rational Creature . . . finds a good and wise Ruler, he may not perhaps think it necessary, or useful to set precise Bounds to his Power in all things" (TT II 164). This can and must include quite a bit of internal discretion.

But is this acquiescence really "consent"? That is, does it bring with it all the obligations that consent does? As discussed in the previous chapter, obligation arises only from consent, and consent obliges. This early monarchy seems like a form of political society—the subjects do have a judge on earth in their dealings with each other—yet at the same time seems incongruous with what Locke has said about legitimate government. The subjects may in effect have a judge on earth, but what the problem regarding the relationship between acquiescence and consent points to is the question of whether they are obligated to listen to that judge or instead do so out of habit or private judgment.

There are textual reasons to doubt at least that Locke means consent and acquiescence to be interchangeable. He refers to the people's "allowing" prerogative to persist, and even that is done only tacitly (TT II 164). The people "permit" their rulers to exercise prerogative and "acquiesce" in it once done (TT II 164; cf. TT II 165). Were it not for an isolated instance where the people "Consent" to prerogative (TT II 158), one might suspect that Locke studiously avoided that word in discussing extralegal power. Even there, however, he is speaking of a post hoc legitimization, not a forward-looking submission to another's judgment. That is, he never discusses a contractual obligation to obey a prerogative exercised at some future date as he does with legislative power.[49]

Prerogative cannot obligate, according to Locke's genesis of obligation. Recall that obligation comes only as the result of consent, and even then, only when such obligation is required for the thing consented to. One cannot, however, consent to arbitrary power in the political sense, i.e., in the sense that prerogative is arbitrary (TT II 136–37). Men may be obligated to the will of society, but only as it is articulated in the laws of that society.

Indeed, it is questionable whether Locke grants the existence of such a societal will apart from these laws: no one who acts without the sanction of law can truthfully claim to act in the name of society's will, as opposed to its good (TT II 151, II 212). The members of the society may acclaim such illegal acts to have been the will of society all along, but only after they have occurred (TT II 158).

It is the law that obligates, and such obligation cannot be directed toward anything that does not issue from the legislative power.

> Nor can any Edict of any Body else, *in what Form soever conceived*,[50] or by what Power soever backed, have the force and obligation of a *Law*, which has not its *Sanction from* that *Legislative*, which the publick has chosen and appointed. For without this the Law could not have that, which is absolutely necessary to its being a *Law*, *the consent of Society*, over whom no Body can have a power to make Laws, but by their own consent, and by Authority received from them; . . . nor can any Oaths to any Foreign Power whatsoever, or any Domestick Subordinate Power, discharge any Member of the Society from this *Obedience to the Legislative*, acting pursuant to their trust, nor oblige him to any Obedience contrary to the Laws so enacted, or farther than they do allow. (TT II 134)

The last sentence is key: men may not be released from obedience to the law, nor can they be obligated to act against or beyond it. "The Members [owe] no *Obedience* but to the publick Will of the Society" (TT II 151). The introduction of prerogative does not change this, for even after it he states, "a*gainst the Laws there can be no Authority*" (TT II 206). In sum, early monarchy is not a form of political society, although it would go too far to say that men are therefore forbidden to acquiesce in it. The members of society may opt to follow their ruler in exercising his prerogative but are not *obligated* to do so.[51]

Such acquiescence is likely to occur, however. The people are not particular about the details of law, Locke tells us, so long as they are benefited (TT II 161). Moreover, they judge rightly when they acquiesce in unlawful action, believing it to support the ends of the law (TT II 165, II 166). The law is but a tool, and is not even the best tool for the ends of government. One does not act to the detriment of the laws when one breaks them, for one fulfills their purpose, namely, the public good. This is done according to one's own interpretation of the law of nature and government, provided that the people acquiesce.

What Locke states here is in sharp contrast to what came before he began to discuss prerogative. Legitimate government was consensual government, which meant that every legitimate government action was obligatory.

Stated another way, subjects, police, and judges could be legal positivists, needing only some rule of recognition à la H. L. A. Hart:[52] appeals to the natural law from within political society, instead of to the pronouncements of the legislature, were illegitimate, forbidden by the law of nature. One of course appeals to the law of nature in determining whether the government as a whole is legitimate, but this decision occurs outside of political society. What one is obligated to do when one is not engaged in a revolution is determined solely by the positive law. With prerogative, however, the legitimacy of a particular government action is indeed a matter for natural law. Yet this reversal also splits legitimacy from consent: the prior consent of the governed is not the sole basis of legitimacy. Authority, understood as concomitant with a duty to obey, is no longer the sole political problem worthy of normative treatment.[53]

Prerogative and Absolute Monarchy

Locke was not, of course, the only liberal or protoliberal in seventeenth-century England to recognize the shortcomings of the rule of law, or to justify their resolution on a liberal or protoliberal basis. The passages in *A Letter from a Person of Quality, to His Friend in the Country* which defend the Declaration of Indulgence are, according to the narrative conceit of the letter, a response to those Whigs who would deny Charles II such a dispensing power. There was a recognition that exigent circumstances might require an extralegal response (in this case, reduced religious strife at home during war against the Dutch). What needs further explication, however, is why it is the king who is to address these circumstances.

For example, the tract entitled *Of the Fundamental Laws, or Politick Constitution of this Kingdom* speaks about the ends and limitations of the law in terms very reminiscent of those that Locke would later employ, except for the conclusion it draws. It observed that Parliament is not

> guilty of an arbitrary Government, [nor] is it destructive to the Petition of Right, when as in providing for Publick-weal, it observes not the letter of the Law; . . . because the end of making that Law, to wit, the publick Preservation, is fulfilled in the breaking of it, which is lawful in a Parliament that is chosen by the whole for the whole, and are themselves also of the Body, though not in a King, for therein the Law saith, *Better a mischief than an inconvenience.*[54]

The author of *Vox Populi* seems to see Parliament playing a similar role, for he says that it is Parliament that "ought to sit to Redress Grievances, and provide for Common Safety, especially in times of Common Danger" and lists among "*the great ends of Parliaments*" the curing of "*Exigencies and Necessities*."[55]

In light of these pamphlets, we see that Locke's doctrine of prerogative could have been an explosive expansion of parliamentary power: whereas before he had limited its authority to law-making (cf. TT II 135, II 142), now it could do whatever it judged to be useful to the public. Those who opposed Stuart absolutism, when confronted with the frailty of legislative foresight, sought to confer the power to face emergencies upon Parliament. Locke's decision to suggest that prerogative is a power best wielded by him who has the executive power in his hands is, consequently, a conscientious break with radical proponents of parliamentary supremacy.

Why, we might ask, cannot the Parliament be entrusted with this power? Why leave it in the hands of the prince? Locke does not address this directly, in a single quotable sentence. He does, however, say that "in some Governments the Law-making Power is not always in being" (TT II 160), and that "Constant *frequent meetings of the Legislative*, and long Continuations of their Assemblies, without necessary occasion, could not but be burthensome to the People, and must necessarily in time produce more dangerous inconveniences" (TT II 156). Taken together, these point to the reason given against a parliamentary dispensing power in the *Letter from a Person of Quality*: "a *Legislative* power always in being, is, when considered, no other than a perfect Tyranny."[56] Locke continues, however, noting that Parliaments are "too numerous, and so too slow, for the dispatch requisite to Execution" (TT II 160). Emergencies cannot be handled by committee. There is a need for a monarchic element in government, for someone whose power is not simply that of a satrap of the legislature's pleasure.

Prerogative is further linked to monarchy of the absolute variety. Prerogative ought to be an extraordinary power, but it need not be so: it was once, in the beginning, the norm (TT II 162). In discussing the foundations of political societies, Locke treats the "Encroachments of Prerogative" as synonymous with the "Inconveniences of Absolute Power": they both threaten to give rise to tyranny (TT II 107).

Both the need for prerogative and the early need for monarchy show the primacy of prudence in politics. "*Law*, in its true Notion, is not so much the Limitation as the *direction of a free and intelligent Agent* to his proper Interest . . . [and could] they be happier without it, the *Law*, as a useless thing would of it self vanish" (TT II 57). In short, law is but formalized prudence. Yet as no law (with the possible exception of the law of nature) can meet this standard for the reasons already discussed, actual prudence must reemerge if men are to be happy. Politics requires prudence; law is valuable only insofar as it serves political ends; law is subordinate to prudence in this regard.

Has, then, absolute monarchy been made into a sort of civil government? Locke never says this and, indeed, denies it on several occasions (e.g., TT II 90, II 174).[57] Monarchs, when they are justifiable, are justifiable as not being absolute and arbitrary: they are useful when numerous laws are not needed. When numerous laws are on the contrary needed, such lawless governance must become extraordinary: Locke's civil government must be established as the ordinary mode of rule. One could at most have a limited monarchy. The ability to exercise prerogative must be limited so that only true prerogative is exercised. And, as I will argue in chapter 5, it is limited by the spirit of the people, not by law. Why it cannot be limited by the latter has already been discussed.

And yet Locke says that a government of true prerogative alone would be best. A good absolute monarch appears as a superior *alternative* to Locke's civil government. It is the government of the Golden Age (TT II 111). It is also how God rules the universe, and virtue indeed provides a "Title to Arbitrary Power": "Such God-like Princes indeed had some Title to Arbitrary Power, by that Argument, that would prove Absolute Monarchy the best Government, as that which God himself governs the Universe by: because such Kings partake of his Wisdom and Goodness" (TT II 166).

Incidentally, I should note this statement here is yet another insurmountable problem if consent, or even bare acquiescence, is the only legitimate basis of power. Just what, we might ask, does Locke mean by "Title" here? If he intends it to be a right of its possessor, as would be true presumably of God's title, then the prince should be able to claim it regardless of the actual acquiescence of the people: God after all asserts his right to rule over rebels and atheists, and so too ought the "God-like" prince rule over even ignorant and disaffected masses. If, on the other hand, this "Title" is the delegated power from the people, and so not a right inherent to the person of the prince at all, then God's title to rule is based solely on the tendency of His actions toward the benefit of the people, as judged by the people themselves, or even the individual (cf. II 168). It does no good to say that God is exempt from Locke's political theory, for that would merely force us to accept the first of these two possibilities, i.e., to assimilate the prince to God rather than God to what we wish were true of princes.[58]

Locke presents prerogative as a superior alternative, but in practice government by prerogative alone is an unavailable alternative: princes must share in God's wisdom and goodness for absolute monarchy to be best, yet princes are but men, made as all others (TT II 165–66).[59] While a God on earth would be ideal, no such earthly God exists or can be created. That government is needed does not mean that the governor exists (TT I 81), and it is foolish to think that all the people require is a judge among themselves, as if no protection from that judge could be necessary (TT II 93). Good rulers are rare enough that Locke does not rely on their existence.

Locke has, however, revealed that prerogative would be the best form of government, were it not for the fact that, looking to the restraints of positive law, it is indistinguishable from tyranny. Civil government is only second best, and recourse to the best is still necessary on occasion. Locke will seek to balance the dangers of prerogative with revolution, but he also appeals to the prince, to the prince's vanity, in the hope that it need not come to that. The prince who exercises prerogative rather than make himself a tyrant is "God-like," partaking of God's "Wisdom and Goodness" (TT II 166). Looking deeper into what Locke says, this does not vanish as false flattery; indeed, such princes are actually superior to God in doing what He is only said to do but does not, thereby creating the political problem in the first place. The only other time that Locke called a prince "wise and godlike" was for promoting private property, thus overcoming the penury to which God banished mankind after the Fall (TT II 42).[60] Princes who fail to do this, i.e., princes who are arbitrary in the natural rather than merely in the political sense, are contemptible. It is their susceptibility to servile flatterers and gross error that leads them to claim that the powers exercised by their beloved ancestors are theirs to become hated and despised (TT II 162, II 164). This desire to oppress others must stem from some sort of weakness or ill nature, Locke says (TT II 205).

Locke does not leave flattery as the only restraint on the monarch, encouraging him to exercise prerogative rather than seek tyranny, just as he does not rely on self-interest to accomplish this. After all, Locke's arguments from self-interest abstract from a fundamental fact about politics: a tyrant generally has more to fear from his subjects than from foreign powers, and so would be foolish to increase the power of his subjects so as to become "too hard for his neighbors" (cf. TT II 42). Locke really does not have anything other than flattery or stern chastisements regarding the natural rights of man to convince a ruler that tyranny is not what he really wants in life—other than, that is, the threat of revolution. The *Two Treatises* would not be needed if the *Two Treatises* was addressed primarily to rulers.

Locke limits the monarch by subordinating him to the laws, leaving revolution to enforce this limitation. But prerogative once again leaves him unlimited: the people must know when to resist, and prerogative makes this difficult. The people cannot simply look to the law for guidance if some illegal acts are legitimate. In bringing prerogative so close to absolute monarchy, Locke increases the dangers of absolute monarchy. In discrediting legalism's intuitions about the shape of legitimate government, he risks losing the support legalism lends to anti-tyrannical fervor. Prerogative must be judged, and judged effectively, if it is not to undermine legislative supremacy altogether, in ordinary as well as in extraordinary modes of government.

Judging the Exercise of Prerogative

Locke does not work to give the impression that prerogative is incapable of restraint or judgment by anything other than the appeal to Heaven, i.e., by force of arms. He provides a number of suggestions as to how it might be restrained, but in examining the logic of prerogative and the fact that Locke does not consistently suggest the viability of any of these suggestions, one must conclude that they are offered only to make prerogative seem less radical rather than actually to function as restraints. He initially suggests that the legislative ought to ratify the executive's use of prerogative, but he immediately abandons this possibility for the reasons indicated above. Locke sets up the people as judge in the legislative's place, but his further discussion of revolution, particularly that it is the appeal to Heaven, calls into question the viability of their judgment, as well.

"*Tyranny*," Locke says, "is *the exercise of Power beyond Right* . . . , [which] is making use of the Power any one has in his hands; not for the good of those, who are under it, but for his own private separate Advantage" (TT II 199; cf. TT II 159 for verbal parallel). "*Where-ever Law ends, Tyranny begins*," he declares, "if the Law be transgressed to another's harm" (TT II 202). The unitalicized portion of this last sentence is key: it is Locke's comment or addition to the strongly worded phrase for which he is often quoted. His point is that it is not the outward character of the acts (namely, that they are illegal), but rather their beneficiary, that distinguishes prerogative from tyranny.

Because men may make mistakes, both prerogative and tyranny are usually judged according to the tendency of the prince's rule rather than by any single act (TT II 161, II 165, II 199, II 210), unless that act is so egregious that it must stem from malice (TT II 222). The example Locke provides for so diabolically unforgivable an act is the formation of a political party, which no doubt strikes us as a bit curious. We might suspect, therefore, that Locke is ironically understating what he objects to here, and indeed the way that James II went about creating a party in Parliament is subversive of representative government in a way that we normally do not consider either Democrats or Republicans to be. It is nonetheless interesting to note that what Locke criticizes here is not the violations of ancient charters to ensure a favorable electoral result—he himself desires that the same thing be done, though to a different end (cf. TT II 157–58)—but rather the creation of a bloc of representatives who do not listen to arguments given but only to what would become known as party whips.

The unforgivable lapse in judgment, the act which incurs instant and irrevocable guilt, is the corruption of the legislature. We might say that it is an attack on the constitution, except that we know Locke supported some such reformations (cf. TT II 157). The character of this crime might also resummon the suggestion that acts of prerogative are to be judged by the legislature: acquiring a party in the legislature would therefore eviscerate this check upon abuses of extralegal power. I have already addressed the legislature's incapacity to judge, especially given the fact that prerogative may be used against it.

One might think that Locke considered the power of the purse to be a great check upon prerogative, and indeed many of his contemporaries viewed it as the greatest power possessed by Parliament in its dealings with the king. For this reason, it is odd that Locke never mentions the power of the purse—except to say that the legislative power must exercise it responsibly and with the consent of the people (cf. TT II 138–40, II 142). He never mentions it as a weapon in the legislative's hands to preserve its supremacy. Locke does note that the separation of powers might better preserve the people's property by ensuring that the legislative is not always in being, but he neglects to suggest that its ability to levy taxes helps it to maintain its supremacy vis-à-vis the prince (cf. TT II 138). That is, the separation of powers protects the people from Parliament, not the latter from the king.

Locke's silence on this matter is telling. On the one occasion that Locke mentions money as tipping the scales toward one power or another, he says that it favors the power of the *prince*: the "Treasure . . . of the State" is his to employ (TT II 218). Locke does not even bother to disparage Parliament's power over the purse; he simply omits it entirely. After all, power is most useful to those who have it, not to those who have only a claim on it. If the prince is acting for the public good, the people can be expected to acquiesce in his emergency requisitions in the absence of legislative approval. They will oppose him in the name of Parliament's right of taxation—and this is key—only if they judge that his actions are not truly prerogatival, i.e., if they should resist anyway. And in that case, it is the people, not the power of the purse, which reins in the wayward prince. At least, in the best of all cases.

Prerogative cannot be restrained by civil government. By definition, it is not restrained by the law, nor can it be restrained by the legislature. Prerogative is wielded by him who has the united force of the commonwealth in his hands (TT II 159), the very problem with any form of absolute monarchy. This is a problem regardless of whether the absolute monarch is led "by Reason, Mistake or Passion" (TT II 13).

Locke does name the proper judge of prerogative, and it is the people. If the legislative is outmatched by prerogative, the latter being free from the former's instructions, then only the people can remove the prince (cf. TT II 168). In attempting to do so, they remove any judge on earth, or judge it to have been removed by the prince's unlawful actions (cf. TT II 13, II 137). Government, both as legislative supremacy and as extralegal prerogative, was instituted for their benefit, and so they are the best judges of whether it works to their benefit or not (TT II 240). It is the community which retains supreme power, but it cannot exercise this power while the government stands (TT II 149, II 243). Its judgment must take place outside of political society, i.e., as revolution. By making the people judge of prerogative, Locke says in effect that only a countervailing natural force can restrain the natural power of prerogative; the people acquiesce in prerogative by not resisting it.[61]

The people judge prerogative. This might seem unproblematic, especially in Locke's discussion of prerogative, but what this means is confused by Locke's discussion of revolution. The people judge by judging whether to appeal to Heaven (TT II 168), immediately raising the problem I discussed in chapter 1: has Heaven now become a competent judge of right, or is it still simply one that is common to all parties? Heaven judges adherence to the law of nature, but its standard of judgment, in the absence of munificent Providence, is not the law of nature but might. Heaven's jurisdiction arises from the fact that it is common, i.e., that all must accept it or face even further judgment and penalties. Locke does not take this back; he does not suggest that Heaven's judgment possesses serious moral significance. Unlawful acts masquerading as prerogative are proven, by the highest Court imaginable and the only Court then in existence, to be tyrannical because the people overthrow their ruler, just as they overthrow a corrupt legislative (cf. TT II 149).

Locke cannot mean, however, that the martial superiority of the tyrant makes him into a wise and godlike prince![62] But neither can the mere presence of resistance, even if crushed, prove a prince to be a tyrant. It is normal for right to be determined by might, but the law of nature is an attempt to escape this. Political society is an attempt to escape this. But political society requires both prerogative and resistance, and Locke's doctrine of resistance casts doubt upon how prerogative is to be judged. The consideration of prerogative compels us to assay what Locke says about revolution.

Chapter 4

Resistance, Revolution, and the Limits of Politics

Locke does not speak of revolutions so much as of a right of resistance (cf. TT II 223, II 225). With regard to the latter, however, he does seem to differentiate between actions taken by an individual and those of a more popular sort. I will, therefore, speak of *resistance,* on the one hand, and *revolution,* on the other, introducing a terminological distinction absent from the *Two Treatises* that mirrors the conceptual one. This is done for the sake of clarity. Both resistance and revolution are related to that natural executive power possessed in the state of nature, governed by the law of nature, and surrendered only by consent (cf. TT II 6–8, II 13, II 87, II 89, II 95). It is the relation between these two conceptions, however, that resists any easy, satisfactory articulation. The popular right of revolution must be built upon the individual's right of resistance: it is individuals who must choose to fight if there is to be a revolution. It is in this transition that the problem lies. If revolution—in the name of Lockean principles—is to be an effective check upon government abuses, we should expect that it be possible to participate in a revolution without abandoning Lockean principles.

Resistance, as I shall use it, is one form of man's natural executive power. Like the latter, it is possessed by the individual and is employed for self-preservation (TT II 6–8, II 129, II 168, II 205–8). Revolution, on the other hand, appears as one form of resistance, but is possessed by the people rather than the individual and cannot be reclaimed until the government is dissolved (TT II 155, II 243).

That Locke favored the Glorious Revolution is no secret, nor can anyone miss that he provides a general doctrine of revolution. His participation in politically radical conspiracies has been well-documented.[1] Locke is far more forthcoming in the *Two Treatises* than he is in the *Letter Concerning Toleration* about there being a right of revolution for the obvious reason that circumstances rendered its inclusion in the former both more necessary and less repugnant. Yet the *Treatises* is no mere apologia for some odious action which becomes necessary perhaps only infrequently, or which can be ignored as irrelevant most of the time: revolution is not so divorced from politics as the question of what is permissible or obligatory if two men are adrift at sea aboard a plank than can support only one of them is from how much to tip your waiter. The doctrine of the right of revolution, the threat of revolution, and therefore the real possibility of a revolutionary reaction to policy are a part of the normal operation of the Lockean commonwealth. Only revolution, Locke implies, can ensure that the rulers do not needlessly violate the constitution and the rule of law, or transgress them in order to subvert the public good under the guise of serving it.[2] As James Tully states, "the conventional means to check the abuse of institutionalized forms of political power are all found by Locke to be insufficient."[3] For Locke, as for us, the price of liberty is eternal vigilance.

Yet this carries with it problems of its own, problems which Locke recognizes. Such vigilance, after all, makes it easier for "ill affected and factious men" to stir the people to an unwarranted revolution "when the Prince only makes use of his due Prerogative;" to this, Locke responds only that the people will have to judge (TT II 240). Everything relies on their knowing when to revolt and, just as importantly, when not to. Revolution, even when successful, can destroy a commonwealth. It produces "Effects very little different from Foreign Conquest" (TT II 218). A needless civil war is no more to be hoped for than an unduly submissive populace. The people must therefore be carefully instructed by Locke in the proper use of revolution. They must be vigilant without becoming paranoid.

Even were the people willing to revolt when necessary, however, we could not say that this alone was sufficient to the establishment of a good political order. Locke's theory also requires that the *individual* have an independent right of resistance, and not simply because this is necessary for there to be popular revolutions. Rather, it is also necessitated by the callousness of the people to individual suffering. It is individuals who enter into society, and they do so for their own felicity. For the commonwealth to be good according to his own standards, it cannot deny individuals a right to their own property—i.e., life, liberty, and estate. Even when the majority cannot respect this right without harm to itself, it cannot reasonably expect to bind the individual's conscience to self-destruction. This is especially true as the majority often fails to revolt when justice demands that it ought to. The majority of men are blind to the injustices suffered by others.

This is the same problem that was faced in the state of nature. In that discussion, Locke had granted the objection that "Self-love, . . . Ill Nature, Passion and Revenge" would lead to partisan enforcement of the law of nature, i.e., that the problem would be *over*-enforcement (TT II 13). Yet in discussing why men actually leave that state, he also cites "the irregular and uncertain exercise" of executive power to protect others as the major inconvenience (TT II 127). Men refuse to stand against the rapacious, which allows the latter to do as they will. This refusal, moreover, is only too reasonable (TT II 126). The "*Legislative and Executive Power*," as well as society and government itself, have their "original *right and rise*" in the relinquishing of the right to punish, but the point is to create that power. The point of the social compact is to bring into being a reliable power of enforcement.

Nor does the average person's indifference to the suffering of others change in political society. Even there, "The examples of particular Injustice, or Oppression of here and there an unfortunate Man, moves them not" (TT II 230; cf. TT II 208, II 223). The individual, however, is not obligated to suffer and die due to public servility or apathy: he is obligated only insofar as his own preservation requires (TT II 129). Locke must, then, say when and how such resistance is to be exercised. For these reasons, I will begin with the individual's right of resistance before moving to the people's right of revolution.

Resistance and the Right of Self-Preservation

Resistance is man's natural executive power, i.e., the right possessed by each in the state of nature to enforce the law of nature (TT II 7). It is, then, inextricably bound up with the appeal to Heaven. In this way, Lockean resistance differs from what we might call "resistance." We might speak of passive resistance, whereas for Locke resistance can never be passive: it is always an act of war. Or at the very least, passive resistance would always be a belligerent *tactic*, and thus one ill-suited against an enemy who recognized it as such.

What holds in the state of nature with regard to threats to one's life holds also in political society, Locke says. "*In all States and Conditions*[4] the true remedy of *Force* without Authority, is to oppose *Force* to it" (TT II 155). "Whosoever uses *force without Right*, as every one does in Society, who does it without Law, puts himself into a *state of War* with those, against whom he so uses it, and in that state . . . every one has a *Right* to defend himself, and *to resist the Aggressor*" (TT II 232). True, if the use of such force is hopeless, Locke on occasion recommends patience (TT II 176). This patience, however, is not demanded by justice. In fact, it actually allows the injustice to continue: it is a concession to the power of the unjust. The ideal situation is for the aggrieved to be capable of forcible resistance and to make use of that capacity.

Yet how is one to know when one's resistance is justified? Locke says, "Of that I my self can only be Judge in my own Conscience" (TT II 21).

Conscience is called upon to judge "whether another hath put himself in a State of War" with the applicant (TT II 21), i.e., whether the act he is contemplating is aggressive or defensive. This difference is not so much in the action—both aggressive and defensive acts are offensive in nature (cf. TT II 235)—but in the justification for that act. Conscience is called upon to judge whether one is contemplating murder or self-defense.

While the individual is judge of this in his own conscience, he is not the final judge: he may be mistaken. Should he err in this judgment, i.e., should he mislead himself in his own conscience due to self-love, ill nature, passion, or revenge, he is answerable as a murderer "to the Supream Judge of all Men" (TT II 21). It is Heaven, then, that is the judge of the right (TT II 21, II 241). Furthermore, as Heaven's judgment of a law that concerns men in this world must have consequences in this world if that law is not to be in vain (cf. TT II 7), such judgment must involve his punishment as a murderer, i.e., his susceptibility to punishment by those charged with executing the law of nature. Heaven's court by definition issues no verdict which cannot be enforced in this world. A favorable verdict necessarily puts the power to enforce it into the victor's hands.

The most important thing, then, is that *Heaven* judge one to have been right in resisting. Locke does not, however, tell men that they may commit what violence they can and be free from criminality. He does not say that might makes right. The appeal to Heaven may judge adherence to the law of nature, but it is an incompetent judge: the law of nature is reason, and the appeal to Heaven is decided by force. Locke therefore tells us when a reasonable man possessed of the power to resist will do so. Reason is the standard by which he, if not Heaven, judges resistance.

Contrary to more collectivist readings, Locke is clear that the individual retains a right of resistance within political society.[5] He appeals to our common understanding that self-defense is permissible. This is, he says, a natural right. Society, moreover, cannot demand that its members surrender or abridge this right. The reasoning behind this is straightforward. The state of war is possible in political society.[6] Such a state of war exists wherever the appeal to law is frustrated, either because of corruption (presumably slight enough as not to dissolve the government) or because of the immediacy of the threat, law being unable to compensate for the loss of life (TT II 19–20, II 87, II 207). There must, therefore, be a right of personal self-defense within society, and it would be curious indeed if the "Fundamental, Sacred, and unalterable Law of *Self-Preservation*, for which they enter'd into Society" (TT II 149) were in fact granted, and consequently to be regulated, by society.

The right to make war, moreover, is not a sign of political power (TT I 131) and so ought not need the consent of others in order to be a right. One might respond that the individual gives up this right in joining political society (TT II 129), but Locke is clear that the individual reserves such judgment regarding his own survival (TT II 129, II 131). This is a judgment that he cannot surrender (TT II 135, II 168). The entrance into political society might at most restrict the right of resistance on behalf of "the rest of Mankind" (TT II 129); this last right cannot be reclaimed without challenging society's authority.

Added to these reasons for why the individual must have a right of resistance are several explicit statements on Locke's part to that same effect. The right of the body of the people, namely, revolution, is shared by "any single Man" as a power common to all mankind (TT II 168). It is not, then, a matter of compact and so not reserved to the creations of a compact, namely, the people. It is shared by everyone in the state of nature (TT II 205). Oppressed individuals have a right to resist and recover what was taken from them by force, even though such is hopeless without the majority (TT II 208). That it is hopeless without the majority means that it is a right that is rarely exercised, but it does not make it any less of a right (cf. TT II 180).

Locke is at pains to emphasize repeatedly in a clear manner when the individual is justified in his resistance in part to highlight the sorts of acts that are impermissible. Men who stir the people to revolution without cause are condemned, and while such men will always be present, they go to their own just ruin and perdition (TT II 230). There can be no resistance where there is an appeal to the law. One may kill a thief in political society, but not rob him, as there is recourse to the law, and no force is to be used when the appeal to law lies open (TT II 182, II 207).

Almost as important is a case that Locke fails to say is illegitimate: one may resist even the just exercise of prerogative, for reasons that will be more fully discussed in the next chapter. Whether one is truly obligated to follow one exercising prerogative is doubtful as it is, but it is all the more so when such exercise requires that one be sacrificed *pro salute populi*. Whoever uses force within political society without the sanction of law and to another's harm puts himself into a state of war with whomever he uses it against. They have a right to oppose the aggressor (TT II 232). In such a case, the prince puts himself into a state of war only with those against whom he uses such force: he does not declare war on society by aiding it extralegally. Because rights may conflict, one man's wise and godlike prince is another's tyrant, and this without resorting to moral relativism.

Locke's Doctrine of Revolution

To distinguish popular resistance from individual resistance, I have resorted to calling the former *revolution*. Such a distinction is necessary, for while the latter is natural, not resting on any compact among men, the former is in a way artificial: it is possessed by, and so its existence is tied to that of, an artificial creation, namely, a people. Revolution is, however, quite similar to individual resistance, though exercised by the body of the people (TT II 149, II 155). It is in this way akin to the federative power, which "one may call" a natural power held by the community, i.e., not by any person (TT II 145). Revolution occurs when the people reclaim their "natural" power, i.e., the power possessed by the people upon its creation but prior to the institution of a common judge among them; such requires that they still exist as a people. It is the appeal to Heaven, exercised to prevent tyranny and to give the people an opportunity to reestablish their legislative (TT II 155, II 168).

As a practical matter, the majority must in some way participate in or support the revolution, else it could not be counted an act of the people (TT II 95). A few individuals cannot hope to prevail, even if they are genuinely oppressed: they are as likely to be followed by the majority, if it does not itself feel threatened, as are madmen or demagogues, and failure carries with it the promise of servitude or extirpation. That such men must suffer is not necessarily just under the law of nature, but should they fail in their resistance, the only common judge would have declared it just. Revolution, then, is limited not only by the law of nature but also by the spiritedness of the people. When a revolution is right is judged by the majority. The individual's judgment as to whether to take part in an attempted revolution must therefore look not only to what reason says is just but also to what the majority will decide.

Locke's main focus, however, is on when a revolution would be reasonable. He emphasizes what the law of nature would say about revolutions. He attempts to bring what the people are willing to do closer to what they ought to do. This is the essence of Locke's rhetorical project, visible most clearly in what he says about revolution.

His discussion centers on the dissolution of government, the necessary condition for justifiable revolution. He names three modes in which government may dissolve, namely, by conquest, by alteration of the legislative, and by a betrayal of trust.

In many ways, the case of conquest can be assimilated to that of an altered legislative. Conquest may, after all, be nothing more than foreign usurpation or tyranny, a sort of conquest that always destroys the frame of government but which cannot erect a new one (TT II 175, II 192, II 197). Another sort of conquest, however, stands as a separate mode of dissolution. As will be discussed later, society may survive the dissolution of government should the legislative be altered or either it or the executive betray their trust. An especially severe conquest may, however, destroy society itself and in this way dissolve the government.[7]

> Thus Conquerours Swords often cut up Governments by the Roots, and mangle Societies to pieces, separating the subdued or scattered Multitude from the Protection of, and Dependence on that Society which ought to have preserved them from violence. (TT II 211)

Locke states that he need not say more about this mode of dissolution, it being obvious and giving frequent enough example to instruct the world. That is, Locke states Hobbes's thesis regarding conquest as being obvious: since the society can no longer protect its members, their obligations of loyalty to that society cease; without such obligations, society cannot persist.[8]

Locke devotes much more space to the other modes of dissolution. Society must have one will, and that will is declared, perhaps even kept, by the legislative (TT II 96, II 151). Government cannot, then, survive should that legislative be altered (TT II 212). Since it is impossible to provide guidelines for when this has occurred without knowing the particular form of government (an important point to keep in mind), Locke describes a thinly veiled English constitution, as understood by the Whigs, to illustrate his point (TT II 213). Under such a form, the legislative is altered when any single person or prince sets up his own arbitrary will in the place of the laws (TT II 214). Additionally, should one endeavor to restrict the legislative's freedom of debate and action, or refuse to assemble them as directed or needed, the legislative is altered (TT II 215; cf. TT II 155). Similarly, it is altered if anyone uses arbitrary power to refashion how or by whom legislators are elected, without the consent and contrary to the common interest of the people (TT II 216). This last qualification is of vital importance: it distinguishes the criminal usurpation discussed here from the praiseworthy reform of the rotten boroughs which introduced the topic of legitimate arbitrary action (cf. TT II 157–58). That Locke qualified himself in this way is highly suggestive of his having kept prerogative in view while deciding how to formulate his thoughts on the dissolution of government.[9] Giving the people over to the dominion of a foreign power likewise alters the legislative, possibly a reference to establishing the Roman Catholic Church (TT II 217; cf. TT II 192, II 209–10). In these cases, it is the prince who is to be blamed: he had the force to stop these acts and so must have acquiesced in their progress (TT II 218).

Locke states another way that such a legislative may be altered, namely, if it is rendered irrelevant. The laws must be executed in order for government to persist. Law is not made simply for the sake of having a law, but that by its execution it might hold society together. An unenforced law, then, is inconsistent with the concept of law itself, and so is no law at all. When execution of the laws ceases, "the *Government* visibly *ceases*, and the People become a confused Multitude, without Order or Connexion" (TT II 219).

Just as in the case of conquest, society's inability to fulfill its mandate results in its dissolution.

The third mode by which government may dissolve is its betrayal of the people's trust (TT II 221). This differs from the mode mentioned above, for the legislative need not yet be altered for this betrayal to occur: if the people retain a power to remove or alter their legislative after they feel their trust has been betrayed, such betrayals cannot be in themselves sufficient to remove or alter it (TT II 149, but cf. TT II 157). Revolution is justified, the government is dissolved, in this case according to a far less demanding standard than that discussed above.

Revolution must of necessity be justifiable by this lesser standard, however.

> To tell *People* they *may provide for themselves*, by erecting a new Legislative, when by Oppression, Artifice, or being delivered over to a Foreign Power, their old one is gone, is only to tell them they may expect Relief, when it is too late, and the evil is past Cure. This is in effect no more than to bid them first be Slaves, and then to take care of their Liberty; and when their Chains are on, tell them, they may act like Freemen. This, if barely so, is rather Mockery than Relief; and Men can never be secure from Tyranny, if there be no means to escape it, till they are perfectly under it: And therefore it is, that they have not only a Right to get out of it but to prevent it. (TT II 220)

To deny a right of revolution in such cases, i.e., to deny that the government may be dissolved without the legislative first being altered or shattered by conquest, is like asking the passengers to sit quietly until their captain actually succeeds in delivering them to the slavers of Algiers (cf. TT II 210).

Locke provides examples of what such a betrayal might entail; these obviously are not meant to be exhaustive. The legislative possesses no commission to invade the property of the subject (TT II 221). The whole purpose of erecting a government in the first place was to protect property, and society's creature cannot be supposed to have a power to destroy its charge; such invasion puts the legislative into a state of war with the people (TT II 222). The executive, on the other hand, betrays its trust if it seeks to form a political party in Parliament:

> For the People having reserved to themselves the Choice of the *Representatives*, as the Fence to their Properties, could do it for no other end, but that they might always be freely chosen, and so chosen, freely act and advise, as the necessity of the Commonwealth, and the publick Good should, upon examination, and mature debate,

> be judged to require. This, those who give their Votes before they hear the Debate, and have weighed the Reasons on all sides, are not capable of doing. (TT II 222)

I discussed the significance of this example in the previous chapter.

A determination that the government is proceeding in bad faith must usually be preceded by an established history of abuses. When asking whether the executive has betrayed his trust, Locke notes that it is the tendency of prerogative that will decide the question (TT II 161). The people forgive occasional lapses due to human frailty and judge their governors by taking their deeds as a whole (TT II 165). Indeed, they, as with any single man, cannot help but be persuaded by a long train of actions, for good or for ill (TT II 210, II 225).

This is, of course, the way that the people actually behave. Consequently, revolutions will not occur upon every slight provocation, but they also may be lacking in the face of manifest tyranny (cf. TT II 207–8). A track-record of misgovernment must precede a revolution as a matter of practice, not of right. By right, a single outrage is enough, should its severity be such that its perpetrator can never again be trusted. As the individual is less able to sustain repeated injuries than is the body of the people, taken as a whole, Locke notes only that the people as a whole do not stir over each manifest injustice.

Taken together, these three methods by which government may dissolve point to a single core principle: all attempts at a power so overwhelming that its use or misuse is dependent solely on its possessor's whims, be these attempts internal or external, advanced or nascent, dissolve the government, i.e., are causes for revolution. Just as any individual may resist whoever attempts to get him under his power on the presumption that threats to liberty endanger life as well (TT II 17), the people may reasonably revolt should anyone make an attempt upon their freedom. While "there cannot be a wiser Constitution" than one whereby the person of the prince is sacred, such sanctity contributing greatly to "the peace of the Publick, and security of the Government," this holds true only "whilst the Government stands" (TT II 205). Attempts at absolute power, however, dissolve the government, at which point stability no longer serves "the peace of the Publick." As Locke remarks, "ancient Names, and specious Forms, are so far from being better, that they are much worse, than the state of Nature, or pure Anarchy" (TT II 225).

Taking the above into view, however, we can see an interesting problem arise. While Locke states that society may survive the dissolution of government (TT II 211), he does not say how, and he frequently seems to equate the latter with perfect anarchy. If the right of revolution is to be meaningful, as distinct from the individual's right of self-defense, the people must survive, as a people, after government has dissolved. How it does so—even *that* it does so—is not immediately clear.

There are powerful arguments against society's survival. Locke states that the legislative and society are one, and treats "*Community*" and "Government" as synonymous (TT II 89, II 95). Moreover, society's will is declared in its laws, and it is of its essence that it possesses a single will (TT II 96, II 151, II 214, II 221): it is in the legislative that this will is lodged, and the constitution of the legislative is the first and fundamental act of society, required for the latter's continuation (TT II 221). The legislative is the soul that gives form, life, and unity to the commonwealth, the knot that binds the people together into one community (TT II 212, II 227). How can society persist if it lacks a soul, form, life, and unity, if its binding knot is cut? Locke states that the nonexecution of law destroys all order and connection among the people and is incompatible with human society (TT II 219). The dissolution of government, moreover, begins the state of nature (TT II 205).

And yet Locke explicitly states that the dissolution of society is *not* the same as that of the government, noting that this distinction is necessary for clarity in speaking of the latter (TT II 211). As he says this, he now notes that society is the compact to create one distinct community. This echoes something he had said earlier, remarking that society is the *consent* to make one community or government (TT II 95, II 99): that is, society requires the intention to create a common government, not the actual existence of that government. It is, then, but the decision to break from the rest of mankind (TT II 128). The essence of a commonwealth is its being an independent community (TT II 133). And it is this decision that is usually dissolved only by conquest, i.e., by something that prevents the creation of a single government and so makes the ends of the compact impossible (TT II 211).

Government is, then, entirely society's creature; it cannot survive its creator's death. The existence of a common judge cannot survive the absence of meaningful consent to create that judge. The intention to create that judge, however, can survive in that judge's absence, at least for a time. Men, habituated into reasonable action by political society, may continue these habits once government is dissolved. They may approximate that condition wherein truly rational human beings live together in peace, without a common judge, and without widespread injustice.[10] As it is only an approximation of that state, however, and as the support for these habits is no more, such a relationship cannot long last. The habits will fade as men realize that they are no longer rewarded in this world. The inconveniences of lacking the judge provided for by the government, namely, the inconveniences of the state of nature, will soon tear the community apart. Those who desired to continue a common life required political society, Locke says; "Government is hardly to be avoided amongst Men that live together" (TT II 105; cf. TT II 101, II 127). The intention to create a judge is no substitute for having a judge.

It is this community, however, which survives the dissolution of government. This requires that a community be able to survive in the state of nature. Locke notes that men who lack "a decisive power to appeal to" are in a state of nature, "however associated" (TT II 89). This suggests that more than one sort of association is possible in the state of nature. Men in that state are not necessarily isolated individuals and may have ties of loyalty to each other (cf. TT I 131).[11] The rights of the community remain while it persists, just as they do under conquest, namely, to consent to its own legislative (TT II 211–12, II 220, II 222). The community, however, lacks its potency, for it does not possess a judge to prevent the state of war among its members (TT II 212). Every member of the community is in a state of nature, just not the "loose State of Nature" when all mankind was one community (TT II 211). This is important for which law of nature is enforced: the community that one must protect is the society to which one belongs, not all of mankind (cf. TT II 211, where individuals are free to seek their safety in some other society only if their own has dissolved). Individual resistance and prerogative, all of man's natural powers, are to be exercised on behalf of that community. Revolution can support but not alter the people.

Difficulties Regarding Revolution

Resistance and revolution, taken separately, make perfect sense; the problem lies in the transition from the former to the latter. In order for a revolution to occur, in order for the people as a whole to be defended, the individuals who constitute that people must each choose to exercise resistance. This raises numerous concerns, including the individual's rights' being trumped by the majority, the seat of judgment regarding revolution, and the stability of the commonwealth. I shall go through each of these in turn.

A reasonable individual may choose to engage in resistance. A regard for one's own life may clearly cause one to risk it, a fact that even that philosopher of cowards, Thomas Hobbes, recognizes: the man led to the gallows and the soldier in battle may court danger in order to escape it.[12] All that is required in these cases is that opposition be the less risky option. A regard for liberty, on the other hand, may or may not justify life-threatening assertiveness. If slavery is likely to be worse than death, one may of course die in opposing it. Such is the case if one is condemned to slavery rather than drudgery and if the master is likely to slay the slave at some point (TT II 23). If this is not the case, however, patiently waiting for the appropriate opportunity may be in order, a course which Locke also counsels (TT II 176, II 196). Valuing one's estate would not normally be cause enough to recommend that one risk one's life to defend it, but resisting robbers is justified as defending one's liberty (TT II 17–18).

A popular revolution may also be reasonable, if we may attribute reason to a group. The people created the government to protect certain things, namely, life, liberty, and estate, and there is no need for a government that fails to protect them (TT II 123–24, II 134, II 149). More importantly, the life of a people is more secure than that of an individual, and so a people can do more with less risk to itself: the mere threat of absolutism is sufficient to justify revolution. The analogue to the law of nature's regard for self-preservation in the law of nature and government is the preservation of the society; preserving the rest of mankind becomes preserving, so far as possible, all the individual members of the society (cf. TT II 6 with TT II 88, II 134, II 159). Revolution is required, from time to time, in order to secure the end of government.

The difficulty lies, however, in the relation of resistance to revolution. It is not the people that decides to revolt: the decision-making body of the people, namely, the legislative, cannot pass judgment precisely at the moment when revolution would be justifiable. Rather, the revolution is contemplated and made, or not made, by all the individual members of the people, and it is here that the argument breaks down. It makes sense for a man to fight in order to protect himself, but it may not be reasonable for him to do so for others. This same problem was faced in the state of nature, where there is much danger in enforcing the law of nature and men have a duty to preserve others only when their own preservation comes not into competition (TT II 6, II 126).

The opposite of this problem, though related to it, involves the majority's support for the individual. Above, the problem was that the individual might choose not to take part in an attempted revolution unless he is directly threatened. The aggregate result of this, however, is that the majority of individuals may not take part in a revolution for the sake of an oppressed minority. This can result from two things. The majority might be benefited by such oppression, as it is when prerogative is used to sacrifice a part for the whole. Alternatively, it may itself be in danger from the government. Still, if the government's designs currently oppress only the few, the greater part of the community might not act to save either itself or the currently oppressed individuals. The end result in either case is that the rights of the minority are trampled due to the actions of the majority.

Locke is quite clear that the individual has rights apart from the majority's will (TT II 208), but rights are like laws: they must be defended if they are to be rights at all (cf. TT II 7). Since it would be suicide to act without the majority (TT II 208), however, what rights does the individual in practice have? How could any individual justify pressing unpopular rights? Such would certainly violate the duty each has to preserve himself (cf. TT II 23, II 135, II 168, II 172). The right to resist is based upon the rationality of resistance, both as to the purposes of resistance and as to the ability to do so successfully. Thus, it is unlikely for individuals to resist without the majority. In a sense, they have no right to do so, for they lack the ability to do so. And in a sense, they do have such a right, for their incapacity is based only on the unrighteous behavior of others. Again, the problem lies with the judge of right. The appeal to Heaven signifies that force judges the claims of reason, and reason must therefore consider this in determining what is just or reasonable.

Locke's final note is to have conflicts between the individual and the majority be resolved by the majority, even though the general principle of justice requires that no one be judge in their own case (TT II 13, II 90–91, II 242). After noting that the individual must decide whether he has been wronged sufficiently for resistance to be reasonable, Locke establishes the body of the people as judge (cf. TT II 241 with II 242). We should not forget that prerogative may legitimately and unlawfully harm an individual, as was shown by the example of the fire discussed in the previous chapter. As Locke states, "*Where-ever Law ends, Tyranny begins*, if the Law be transgressed to another's harm" (TT II 202)—this is the only instance in the discussion of conquest, tyranny, and the dissolution of government of prerogative's not being exempted from what is being blamed (e.g., prerogative may alter "the Electors, or ways of Election," but may not do so "contrary to the common Interest of the People" [II 216; cf. II 158]).[13] In having the body of the people judge the individual's complaint, however, Locke creates (or sanctions) a situation wherein the judge looks to how it has been benefited (i.e., whether it really was an act of prerogative), in addition to the effect on the individual.

The individual both has and does not have rights, while the majority—in effect, if not by its self-deceiving words—judges the individual to have rights only so far as it benefits the majority, i.e., not on any principle of justice.[14]

This is the case where the majority actually is benefited by the individual's misfortune. As an internally binding moral matter, neither the individual nor the majority has a claim on the other. Locke does not privilege one over the other, except to say that the majority usually wins out. The individual cannot demand respect for his rights, insisting that the majority significantly harm itself by its own decision, for he lacks the authority to press his claims. The majority, however, cannot demand obedience from the individual in such cases, for should he have it within his power to avoid the majority's decision, he is under no obligation not to do so.[15]

The conflict between the two goes even further. The above mostly assumes that the majority is benefited, but even when they are being brought under absolute dominion, a perceptive and interested minority will often find that its cause lacks majority support (a fact that Locke and his political allies knew only too well).[16] The people can be counted upon to treat aggrieved individuals as raving madmen or heady malcontents, which in no way, of course, actually makes them mad or impetuous (TT II 208).

> For till the mischief be grown general, and the ill designs of the Rulers become visible, or their attempts sensible to the greater part, the People, who are more disposed to suffer, than right themselves by Resistance, are not apt to stir. The examples of particular Injustice, or Oppression of here and there an unfortunate Man, moves them not. (TT II 230)

The real problem with the tension between the individual and the majority, politically speaking, is that the majority may be too slow to act for their own good. They may let the disease fester until it happens that they actually are oppressed or, at best, wait until they have much innocent blood to answer for.

This tension is played out again in Locke's favorite question, Who shall be judge? Locke has noted when revolution would be reasonable, but who is to judge when it is reasonable, applying those general rules to particular cases? The problem arises not so much in judging whether the legislative is altered but of whether it or the prince have betrayed the trust placed in them.

Given what we have discussed to this point, the obvious response would be the majority. The reasonableness of engaging in revolution, i.e., of individual resistance for the public good, is after all dependent in part on the majority's view of the situation. Moreover, they appear as the proper judges, since they are the ones who deputized the government in the first place (TT II 240; cf. TT II 149).

This is all well and good, but if the individual is legitimized in his partaking in revolutionary action because of the decision of the majority, the majority must be a practical, not just theoretical, judge. The one body that represented the people, however, and gave voice to the majority's desires, namely, the legislature, is precisely the one body that cannot be trusted to judge whether it has betrayed its trust or not. It would in that case be the only effectual judge in its own case. Nor can the majority's judgment be known apart from that of its "deputies." One cannot really expect a public, or accurate, referendum on the matter.

Perhaps, one might surmise (Locke does not suggest this as a possibility), their participation in the revolution or lack thereof, or acquiescence in it after the fact, is their form of "voting." Yet this does not solve any problems, for then one could not know their vote before one would have to act. The community may, after all, and indeed probably will, disagree, and visible behavior before the battle will most likely give credence to the claims of both sides. Chief Justice Taney expressed this problem nicely with regard to the Dorr Rebellion in Rhode Island: "Could the court, while the parties were actually contending in arms for the possession of the government, call witnesses before it and inquire which party represented a majority of the people?"[17] As an additional difficulty, those who support a revolution are always less visibly active than those who oppose it. That one acts with the support of the majority is almost a matter of faith. This faith is clearly not enough. If the judgment of the majority is to be at all binding, if it is to direct the actions of the individual, it must be knowable. As it is not, arguments as to the justness of the majority's being judge are to no practical, and hence political, avail.

Gaining no reliable guidance from the majority, we might next turn to the individual. After all, the dissolution of government begins a state of war (TT II 155, II 227), and only the individual can judge whether a state of war has begun (TT II 21, II 241). Yet it is clear that he cannot be the seat of judgment regarding revolution: one heady malcontent cannot decide that the government is dissolved and demand by right that the rest of society recognize it. Locke does, after all, hold out the possibility of illegitimate resistance and revolution. None of this, of course, argues against the individual's right of resistance, but that resistance is reasonable for one does not make revolution reasonable for all.

Locke therefore sets up the appeal to Heaven as the only judge of revolution. He does not grant the people a right to judge each case, only the right to judge whether to appeal to Heaven for judgment (cf. TT II 168). As such, the individual must begin the appeal to Heaven, convinced of his justice and believing that the majority will join, or at least acquiesce, in his decision. He cannot know whether they will actually do so before he begins his appeal. The correctness of the individual's judgment is knowable only after he has judged. Only then can the majority join him.

Furthermore, as a practical matter, the majority almost never takes the field; even the combined number of all the armies on both sides is usually far less than a majority of the subjects. A man may, therefore, be convinced that the has the support of the majority with an army numbering significantly less than that, and even than that of his opponent. How is he to know his true support? In the state of war, whether it judges rightly or wrongly, the only judge is in Heaven. The outcome of the battle is, at least at first, the judge of the revolution. True, victory gives the revolutionaries no right to constitute a new government, even if the government had been dissolved according to the judgment of reason; in this case, they are akin to a just conqueror liberating an oppressed people (cf. TT II 175). The outcome of the battle is judge, however, since those executed for treason cannot usually regroup to form a government.

The people, i.e., the majority, then, appear only as a secondary judge; they are a secondary judge because Heaven must weigh the revolution first. Should the revolutionaries succeed, the people may further resist them, attempting to reinstate the old government as the new government, just as they may with conquerors, or they may create a new government that does not punish the revolutionaries. So long as they are given an opportunity to choose freely, i.e., so long as the state of war actually ends, the outcome can be taken to be that of the majority. The people judge only after the revolution, and as they are then in a state of nature, they do not necessarily have to be heard at that point, either. Those who do not fight have a say only if the victor gives it to them.

Heaven and a Stable Commonwealth

The people, then, are the final judge of revolutionary acts: in this way, it is their consent that forms the basis of the commonwealth. In practice, however, not all appeals can actually reach this final court: the people do not get the opportunity to adjudge the defeated unless a further appeal to Heaven grants it to them. That is, compulsion forms the commonwealth's foundations. The primary arbiter of a revolution, the one in Heaven, undermines the commonwealth's basis in consent. Consent is necessary for its creation, but it is insufficient to make such a commonwealth possible in the first place. It cannot guarantee that it will be consulted or respected. It is force that lies at the root of the commonwealth, consent having the opportunity to count only if the reasonable, i.e., those who would rule by consent, succeed in their violent acts against their adversaries.[18]

That the commonwealth is based on force would not be such a problem, however, were that coercion just. Even within the commonwealth, after all, violence must be directed against criminal elements. The justness of such compulsion relies on the justness of the commonwealth. Everyone agrees that legitimate governments may enforce legitimate laws. The judge in Heaven, however, is an incompetent judge of justice.

As an incompetent judge, Heaven need not decide aright the first time: robbers, pirates, and conquerors are often victorious, but they gain no (rational) right of empire by their victory (cf. TT II 176). One may legitimately oppose what Providence brings about (cf. TT I 16, I 47–48, I 118, I 147).[19] For this reason, one is not morally obligated to accept Heaven's decree. That Heaven has spoken does not preclude further private judgment. Appeals to Heaven may be repeated.

Locke thus legitimizes holding on to ancient grievances. The conquered retain a right to their ancestors' possessions, a right shared by all individuals (TT II 176, II 192). Those dispossessed in this way must, however, wait upon God's Providence. Filmer had elicited Locke's disgust for advising men to do this (TT I 121), but Locke now states that one must be patient if the law does not act and God removes all other remedies (TT II 176; cf. TT II 168). What Filmer had praised as just (thereby earning a rebuke), Locke acknowledges as a regrettable necessity. Once that necessity is lifted, therefore, the dispossessed may with right appeal to Heaven, as Jephthah did (TT II 176). They always have a right to shake off usurpation or tyranny, like Greek Christians against their Turkish masters, whenever they have the power to do so (TT II 192). Locke clarifies this a little further on: they may cast off the yoke of oppression when God gives them courage and opportunity (TT II 196). He does not say that God provides anything more.

This aspect of Locke's doctrine is an invitation to the sort of anarchy that society was established to prevent. As a practical matter, no commonwealth can afford to ignore its own basis in some form of compulsion, in its having once been a sort of successful conqueror. In the best case, this violence was and continues to be victoriously directed against the unjust, i.e., the irrational. But the defeated almost always consider themselves both just and rational. Locke therefore lays a foundation for perpetual disorder, should the defeated ever increase in power. This doctrine, namely, that Heaven judges the right, or that "some day" justice simply must prevail, can be destructive of the entire commonwealth, should a significant but doomed minority "discover" an ancient grievance. Their ultimately unsuccessful revolution may cast men into the state of nature without establishing a power around which they can rally to once again escape. This irascible passion may be ubiquitous, but it is Locke who inflames it with talk of Jephthah, oppressed Christians, and a great tribunal which cannot be deceived.

Locke's response is that this doctrine is no more dangerous than any other which grants all men a chance for justice: that is, he does not say it is not dangerous (TT II 176). The fault lies, he in effect says, with the appeal to Heaven, not with his doctrine: he but recognizes Heaven's dominion over earth. Yet the logical conclusion from this fact is to recognize ancient grievances, and in this way to destabilize the commonwealth. It should come as no surprise, then, that much of what I have been discussing is not explicit in the text but is rather the completion of the argument whose foundations he sketches out.

Locke states on more than one occasion that disturbing the commonwealth without erecting a new one is "certainly the greatest Crime Men can be guilty of one towards another" (TT II 218).

> This I am sure, whoever, either Ruler or Subject, . . . lays the foundation for *overturning* the Constitution and Frame of *any Just Government*, is guilty of the greatest Crime, I think, a Man is capable of, being to answer for all those mischiefs of Blood, Rapine, and Desolation, which the breaking to pieces of Government bring on a Countrey. And he who does it, is justly to be esteemed the common Enemy and Pest of Mankind; and is to be treated accordingly. (TT II 230)

This is the crime that carries with it the greatest dangers, though it is the most avoidable (TT II 168, II 209). One issues a declaration of war on the people by removing the bar to war from among them (TT II 227). But it is not just one's own people that one offends: by moving even one community from a condition where war is barred to one where it is not, a real and deadly harm is done, not just to that community, but to all mankind. All mankind can demand justice from the offender (TT II 13, II 176).

Worse still, having a right to defend oneself does not preclude such punishment: one can be held to account also for lacking a right *worth the upheaval* caused in pursuing it (TT II 176). The right of course remains, but the judge of that right is unsatisfied. It should go without saying that its dissatisfaction need not be reasonable (as when the oppressed minority is not joined by a people that ought to revolt). Society deems the pursuit of certain rights to be impermissible, not because a reasonable person would have surrendered them (for it is reasonable to oppose the possibility of death by all means available), but because they are disruptive of society's peace. In this way, what is rational in a state of nature composed of individuals becomes irrational in political society or a state of nature composed of a community, the just becoming unjust because of the greater penalties threatened for pursuing one's right and the greater likelihood that those penalties will be imposed. Again, such penalties are imposed so as to preserve order, not to preserve the individual.

Acting in a manner that disturbs the public peace, even for one's own safety, draws the just condemnation of both God and man (TT II 204). The supreme tribunal of which Locke speaks (cf. TT II 176) is not just divine; it has human sanctions, as well. It is the latter that are important where politics is concerned. God follows the condemnations of men, and so both condemn for political purposes. In this way, though not necessarily with good reason, the public good gains its paramountcy over that of the individual. Again, the consent of the individual is depreciated: the requirement for consent had privileged the individual's good apart from society.

This subtle yet significant shift has some interesting consequences which help to cast some of Locke's statements in a new light. So, for example, his argument forces the conclusion that there must be limits to one's freedom of speech. Certainly, the *Letter Concerning Toleration* does not permit every religious doctrine to be preached. And something similar is hinted at in the *Two Treatises* regarding teachings that are not expressly theological. Those who propagate wrong notions of government, as Filmer and all flatterers do, commit the greatest mischief for prince and people that is possible (TT Pref.). Locke cites James I in calling them vipers and pests to the commonwealth (TT II 200), the implication being that, like all noxious beasts, they must be punished, if only to prevent the harm that they do (cf. TT I 39, II 8, II 11, II 16, II 171–72, II 181). Writing after the Glorious Revolution, Locke suggested that all who do not renounce the doctrine of divine right should be treated as enemies to the king and his government.[20] While they "would have all Men born to, what their mean Souls fitted them for, Slavery" (TT II 239), this is not why they must be silenced. Greatness or meanness of soul is not a consideration in Locke's politics (though his inability to restrain himself from that remark may show some concern).

Rather, they must be silenced because they overturn all governments with their errors. Their theories "can serve for nothing but to unsettle and destroy all the Lawful Governments in the World, and to Establish in their room Disorder, Tyranny, and Usurpation" (TT I 72). "This I am sure, their Civil Policy is so new, so dangerous, and so destructive to both Rulers and People, that . . . former Ages never could bear the broaching of it" (TT II 239; cf. TT I 3, I 10, I 65, I 70–72, I 75, I 77, I 105–6, I 124, I 161). Flattery leads rulers to abandon civil government for absolute monarchy and to think themselves incapable of control (TT II 91, II 218). The emphasis on their impact on rulers suggests, here at least, that a major part of the problem is that flatterers speak to those who are strong.

Part of Locke's argument, then, is to counter that such flatterers actually undermine the strong,[21] and for reasons unrelated to the fact that Locke himself is awakening the people to their potential for greater, future strength. Filmer and his like must make usurpation a legitimate title to rule (TT I 121). This is Filmer at his most senseless (TT Pref.), and requires that he reduce all government to force and, more importantly, nothing more: because the method of gaining monarchic power is so confused in Filmer, it would seem that the only test for legitimacy is whether one actually wields supreme power, "which in plain *English* is to say, that Regal and Supreme Power is properly and truly his, who can by any Means seize upon it" (TT I 79). Filmer, it turns out, is a closet Hobbesian!

Filmer does more than reduce all government to force. The real problem is that this reduction is destructive of the public peace. The surface of such arguments, the supposed legitimizing force that they might have, "cuts up all Government by the Roots" (TT I 126). Only one other class of people does so in the *Two Treatises*: conquerors (cf. TT II 211). This is because, while providing the rules by which we are to know who is the legitimate king, Filmer fails to give the practical knowledge necessary for determining who is actually king by those rules (TT II 113): "For so it be a Power, *i.e.* Right to Govern, it matters not, whether it be termed *Paternal*, or *Regal*; *Natural*, or *acquired*; whether you call it *Supreme Fatherhood*, or *Supreme Brotherhood*, will be all one provided we know who has it" (TT I 122). Locke equates agreeing "that [government] shall be monarchical, but [appointing] no way to know or designe the person that shall have the power and be the monarch," with having "no forme of government at all" and "anarchy" (TT II 198). The standard that Locke applies to every doctrine (except perhaps his own) is whether it will tend toward civil peace; those that do not should be reviled as false and, if necessary, banned.

Locke further seeks to undermine support for such doctrines among those who might be tempted to adhere to them, namely, those who would support a polity founded upon Scripture (cf. TT II 13). Rather than according with the practice of religion, he avers, Filmer scandalizes Christianity and brings in atheism (TT I 154). His impiety is so great as to make kings greater than even God Himself, for even He is bound by His promises (TT I 6, II 195). Filmer seems more like Hobbes with each passing minute! At last, we know why he was the first to speak out against the Monster of Malmesbury. At last, we know why he adopted his "way of writing" (TT I 20). Like "a wary Physician," Filmer diluted the "odd and frightful Figure" he would have us swallow with more pleasing stuff (TT I 7).[22] And because the church supports the view of divine right, a view so opposed to the Divinity and the "Just and Natural Rights" of man, the complaints against the "Drum Ecclesiastick" do not cease to be valid (TT Pref.). Rather, Locke assures his readers, such doctrines are like the Tower of Babel, an impious abomination ready to fall (TT I 143). After Filmer's discussion of Nimrod, all monarchs must be either tyrants or established by consent (TT I 148). Those who would see the divine hand in politics but not have it support tyranny must agree that lawful government arises from consent alone, not from any divine hand.

Locke's method here is one of war. He makes a sustained attempt to convince his reader to abandon the divine right of kings, or that his previous abandonment of it was justified. Still, and importantly, he does not recommend that the commonwealth blindly entrust its security to his or his allies' rhetorical abilities. Should they be unsuccessful in their attempts at persuasion, those who fail to convert are to be treated as public enemies. This is the consistent application of Locke's pragmatism: were his intolerance here unnecessary, there would have been no need for politics in the first place.

The preservation of the commonwealth is primary, justifying his treatment of those whose doctrines would undermine it.

It bears repeating, given the harshness of these statements, that a commonwealth for Locke signifies a certain kind of political order: this is not a justification for similar measures by "the State," or some other term that has been consciously stripped of normative connotations. We should not attempt to understand what Locke says here from within a framework of legalism.

Given the viciousness with which he attacks them, then, Locke is at great pains to show that he is not one of these commonwealth-destroying thinkers. Indeed, he presents the *Second Treatise* as necessitated by a desire to save himself from this charge (TT II 1). Showing the error of Filmer's doctrine and all those who would argue along similar lines in the *First Treatise* is not enough to avoid the imputation of punishable anarchism, even though that thesis, upon deep examination, also overturns all lawful government. After all, Filmer's writings equate might with right only after careful analysis and so may be serviceable so long as men do not examine them too closely. Inviting men to trace out and extend the logic of his doctrines, however, renders them useless for the preservation of peace, and so the one who does so without providing an alternative is guilty of disturbing the peace. Still, Locke's claims that his doctrine will cause no tumult seem curious in light of the problems discussed thus far. Let us then turn to these claims.

Locke exculpates himself from the charge, or tries to, that he lays a foundation for rebellion by clearly asserting, "*Force* is to be *opposed* to nothing, but to unjust and unlawful *Force*" (TT II 204). Of course, Locke's entire doctrine, his entire political system and its *raison d'être*, is premised on men's not following this injunction. If most people actually obeyed this, there would be no reason to leave the state of nature. Locke appears to recognize this: the reason for why no "Danger or Confusion will follow, as is often suggested," follows this statement.

At a minimum, one might suspect the sufficiency of this statement in §204 to prove Locke's point based on the fact that he continues to adduce argument after additional argument for the public safety of his doctrine. Examining the section in question, we find that what he says about force requires the condemnation of God and man in order to prevent "such Danger or Confusion." Even this, however, is not sufficient, for the paragraph ends with an incomplete sentence introducing those paragraphs that follow as the *reason* for why the statements regarding force and the just condemnation of God and man lead to the conclusion that no tumult will result from the doctrine ("For,").

Locke also claims that no tumult will result from his doctrine since it "operates not, till the Inconvenience is so great, that the Majority feel it, and are weary of it, and find a necessity to have it amended" (TT II 168; cf. TT II 209). On the one hand, this slowness to act is good, for it preserves the public peace (TT II 205). Indeed, Martin Seliger goes so far as to say that the "apathy of the masses is regarded as a factor of stability and attains the stature of a civic virtue."[23] Were things otherwise, a right of revolution might actually leave anarchy and confusion (cf. TT II 203). On the other hand, however, Locke blames this tendency of the people, for they are

> hardly to be prevailed with to amend the acknowledg'd Faults, in the Frame they have been accustom'd to. And if there be any Original defects, or adventitious ones introduced by time, or corruption; 'tis not an easie thing to get them changed, even when all the World sees there is an opportunity for it. (TT II 223; cf. TT II 157)

Locke can hardly claim that his teaching is salutary, or at least is not pernicious, because people are ill disposed to govern their actions by it.

Moreover, Locke's reasoning here (TT II 223) states only that the form of government is not lightly abandoned, not that there will not be paroxysmal episodes. Locke refers to "the many Revolutions" which England had seen in his and in former ages. He therefore continues by creating an objection that his hypothesis will foment frequent rebellion (TT II 224).

Locke's response to this is hardly encouraging.

> First, No more than any other *Hypothesis*. For when the *People* are made *miserable*, and find themselves *exposed to the ill usage of Arbitrary Power*, cry up their Governours, as much as you will for Sons of *Jupiter*, let them be Sacred and Divine, descended or authoriz'd from Heaven; give them out for whom or what you please, the same will happen. *The People generally ill treated*, and contrary to right, will be ready upon any occasion to ease themselves of a burden that sits heavy upon them. (TT II 224; cf. TT II 205)

Locke begs that he not be blamed for how the people would act even without his doctrine, even as he tells them that how they would act without it is indeed just. He then again repeats that the people are slow to revolt (TT II 225), even though he considers this a mark of blame, and finally concludes that it is tyrants who are the real rebels (TT II 226–27).

Even overlooking the inadequacy of these claims, it is likely that Locke's doctrine will cause tumults that may not have otherwise occurred. Locke tells the people to guard their liberty as they would their lives and that the regard for this liberty "has often occasioned Contest, and sometimes publick Disorders" (TT II 166). The threat of revolution is necessary to keep the legislative and executive in line and to compel men to exercise arbitrary power as prerogative, not as tyranny; revolution is "*the best fence against Rebellion*" (TT II 226). I have already touched upon the problem of ancient grievances.

In the end, Locke defends his thesis by saying that, for all its faults, it is no worse than any other that he has met with. At least it will wreak no more havoc "than Justice does, where she lies open to all that appeal to her" (TT II 176), i.e., than the state of nature, a state so convulsive that men were compelled to leave it! Locke's doctrine, however, at least does not lead to absolute monarchy, namely, a perpetuation of that state in its worst form.

But now Locke appears to have contradicted himself. He defends his doctrine by saying that the people would revolt anyway whenever his doctrine would grant them a right to (TT II 209–10, II 224). That is, his doctrine ought not to result in any improvement of man's estate, for what improvements might be had through revolution are inevitable. On its own, this fact would be a problem only for my interpretation, for I affirm that Locke was attempting to bring about a revolution in ideas for the sake of good government, i.e., that he was not simply explaining what had occurred. The flip side of Locke's suggestion, however, implies that there can be no danger from Filmer or others who deny the right of revolution, if political theorizing does not affect the willingness to revolt. If this is the case, why inform princes that flatterers endanger them, rather than their people, and why inform the people of their natural rights? The fact that Locke includes such statements only when defending himself against the greatest mischief that can be done to prince or peoples ought to give some pause.

Locke therefore falls back on yet another reason why his doctrine ought not to be banned as destructive to the public peace, a reason much more in accord with his other arguments. He responds that men must be allowed to defend themselves against the unjust and that the resultant violence is to be charged to those that necessitate it, not to those who say that men must defend themselves (TT II 228). Not peace, but the *quality* of the peace, must be considered.

> If the innocent honest Man must quietly quit all he has for Peace sake, to him who will lay violent hands upon it, I desire it may be consider'd, what kind of a Peace there will be in the World, which consists only in Violence and Rapine; and which is to be maintain'd only for the benefit of Robbers and Oppressors. Who would not think it an admirable Peace betwixt the Mighty and the Mean, when the Lamb, without resistance, yielded his Throat to be torn by the imperious Wolf? (TT II 228)

Locke drops, then, the claim that his doctrine will not cause any tumult and asserts in its place that the peace that he brings is a better peace.

> The end of Government is the good of Mankind, and which is *best for Mankind*, that the People should be always expos'd to the boundless will of Tyranny, or that the Rulers should be sometimes liable to be oppos'd, when they grow exorbitant in the use of their Power, and imploy it for the destruction, and not the preservation of the Properties of their People? (TT II 229)

Locke's pursuit of a certain kind of peace, however, namely, that dominated by the rational—which is to say, political government—requires a recourse to war not required by less demanding desires for peace. In reality, most absolute monarchies, bad as they are, do not begin to approach Polyphemus's den.

Locke's concern cannot, therefore, be nothing more than public peace. His project cannot be justified simply upon that basis. One might say that Locke rehabilitates a desire for liberty from Hobbes's debunking,[24] yet given the grounds of Hobbes's position, this would also require something of a rehabilitation of pride—and Locke does not so openly champion what was still to be considered a vice, the sin of sins. Moreover, as will be discussed at greater length in chapter 5, Locke frequently makes liberty seem nothing more than a fence around one's life, and so something that should be in the service of public peace; this does not explain why a desire for it should be permitted to upset that peace, as it plainly may in Locke.

The fact that we must speculate, or make more or less reasonably educated guesses, regarding why and to what extent Locke's concerns extended beyond the maintenance of public peace means that the *Two Treatises* does not contain his reasons for writing it. It is, as Leo Strauss notes, "less Locke the philosopher than Locke the Englishman who addresses not philosophers, but Englishmen."[25] It ought to go without saying that this in no way proves that Locke did not give serious consideration to why he held to the politics that he did, that he was nothing more than the articulate spokesman for a particular faction in a particular time. Nor does it license let alone necessitate a religious reconstruction of his thought, especially given the religious implications of what he did write. It does, however, suggest that the *Treatises* is not self-sufficient, philosophically speaking. It contains many arguments of philosophical interest, but it does not contain all of the relevant arguments. It is doubtful whether Locke ever wrote them all down.[26]

While the ultimate justification for Locke's system may be tantalizingly obscure, the outline of that system is not. We can say what Locke was arguing for, given the text as it has come down to us. The sort of society that he wished to produce can be gleaned from the pages of the *Two Treatises*, as can the sort of government which regulates it. The "traditional" opinions that its people must hold, those things which they must all think (if not think through), are discernible. We can also piece together at least some of the reasons that may have led Locke to adopt his political views. Let us then turn to these matters.

Chapter 5

The Lockean Commonwealth

The commonwealth exists in order to avoid those inconveniences incident to the state of nature. That state is of course largely rhetorical, serving to establish the ends of civil government precisely by begging the question. Locke cannot possibly have known that it existed, nor need it ever have. Or rather, this irrelevance applies to the existence of the state of nature *qua* anthropology, i.e., the anarchic state of nature discussed in the latter portion of chapter 1 of this study, not *qua* juridical relationship. The existence of the latter is, of course, a certainty for Locke: it exists wherever there is no government that can claim authority, namely, almost everywhere.[1] With regard to the anthropological version, Locke says that there would be no records of such a state since writing could not have flourished prior to government (TT II 101). His examples from ancient historians' and travelers' accounts do not depict the state of nature but rather are similar enough that they can give a sense of what it would have been like, especially if one is attentive to their details and original context. His "history" is "probably" what followed from that state, a conjecture founded upon a supposition. This is all he needs it to be so long as the supposition is in some significant way indicative of reality. In a similar vein, anthropological research would be irrelevant in assessing Locke's political system, especially as the state of nature is constructed so as to challenge the authority of those relations which govern in most communities.[2]

To say that the state of nature is the proper starting point in considering justice is already to presume rather than establish what is most important in life and politics.[3] But this limitation is noteworthy only if we wish to step beyond the circle traced round our feet by our Lockean heritage. Nor should the fictitiousness of the state of nature prevent us from seeing Locke's serious point. His theory is based upon the truth of his understanding of the world, an understanding which the state of nature reveals. The latter is, as it were, a *mythos* containing a *logos*, a story crafted around an account; it is his version of a morality play. It is the truth of his account, not that of the story, upon which he will stake his claim to have solved the political problem: it takes the world as it is, not as we would have it. His story threatens what we take for granted in order to show how dearly we cherish it but does not establish the rightness of our concern. Nevertheless, Locke will claim for his system that at least it actually does preserve and foster what common sense acknowledges is to be preserved and fostered.

It is with this in mind that we can see the centrality of prerogative to the argument advanced in the *Two Treatises of Government*. We are left resourceless if we do not recognize in Locke the attempt to grasp the fundamental character of political things and to craft—actually bring about—the regime best able to address them. It is not sufficient to say that he was in favor of the right of revolution, as if we already knew what he meant by such a right from our reading Tyrell, Shaftesbury, Sidney, or Barclay, as if it were simply a matter of being for or against it: Locke's final chapters are after all devoted to clearing up what a right of revolution would mean. Likewise, when the natural law tradition includes both Hooker and Hobbes, we learn very little by placing Locke within that tradition. As Martin Seliger writes, "Established practices are almost invariably a matter of controversy amongst contemporaries . . . ; it bears repeating that historical conditions need as much explanation as they provide one."[4] And while we may be able to say that Locke was in general a supporter of the rule of law, what is the significance of this observation when we cannot even agree ourselves on what that phrase entails?[5] Nor is it particularly enlightening to note that Locke was in favor of prerogative. He outlined a *doctrine* of prerogative, and so the task falls to us to understand what it means, for him, to advocate that power.

This question is inseparable from the commonwealth as a whole: the doctrine cannot be separated from its logical context. (He certainly does not advise, after all, that *primordial* prerogative be exercised; cf. TT II 162.) This means that it serves a practical purpose, a function which cannot be understood or justified apart from the commonwealth's *raison d'être*. Prerogative reveals that the questions of authority and obligation cannot be the sole focus of political theory; its place within the commonwealth reveals that these questions cannot be abandoned for being incoherent, however.

In short, we cannot understand these parts in isolation from the whole. The latter is in turn incomprehensible without the state of nature, or the view of nature it suggests. We could at most remark that "Locke says this" or "Locke asserts that," but we could not provide the "why" which gives all of his statements their meaning and importance. By examining the components, by endeavoring to see how they fit together, we can bit by bit come to appreciate Locke's political doctrine. We can see the view of politics it engenders, we can see what the people must be taught and what they must believe, and we can, perhaps most importantly, see the world in which Locke saw himself, the world against which his politics are a reaction.

An Outlook, Not a Constitution

Locke does not provide us with an ideal constitution in the *Two Treatises*, nor would we necessarily expect him to. The only end that such an undertaking could reasonably serve would be to establish a rapport by "proving" what everyone already agreed upon. This, for example, appears to have been Robert Ferguson's intention in arguing that the monarchic form be retained.[6] The Whigs took great pains to make themselves appear as the defenders of the old regime, and the monarchy was in no real danger of being abolished: neither the Duke of Monmouth nor the Prince of Orange was going to seize the throne simply to relinquish it, and even in the Rye House Plot the objective was merely to call a Parliament and strengthen it against the king.[7] "Common sense" does not sit well with "radical change," and Locke labored to appear as the spokesman of common sense; the persistence of at least the *form* of monarchy set certain limits on what could and could not acceptably be said. To suggest a type of regime different from the English constitution would have rendered his views irrelevant and quite likely have brought disrepute to whatever policies he advanced.

This is not to say, however, that Locke absolutized the regime as it stood. A legitimate government might take another shape, he said (cf. TT II 132). He is not silent about constitutional matters, even though he well could have been (cf. TT II 153 [on separating the legislative and executive bodies], II 205 [on the sacredness of the king's person]). The most suggestive passage concerning his preferences occurs in the shortest chapter of the entire book, where he defends his choice of the word "commonwealth" as being the best word he can think of, translating the Latin *civitas* (TT II 133). He does not consider, let alone reject, the choice commended by his ostensive guide, Hooker, namely, "polity." Despite his stated willingness to exchange "commonwealth" for a better word should he run across one, it seems that he was insistent about using a term rife with dubious political linkages. Neither Hobbes nor Cromwell would make particularly good associates, and his attempt to suggest that he is only following James I in his usage rings hollow. That seemingly loyal suggestion becomes seditious if one momentarily suspends one's disbelief in Locke's submissiveness to the monarch's idiom, however—for then, Locke acknowledges his willingness to immediately abandon the authority of James I if offered a better one.

Locke's reticence, his refusal to be either bold or silent, rouses a temptation to try to tease out a Lockean constitution from his scattered and isolated remarks. He says enough to make scholars see a preference for freehold suffrage, male suffrage, universal suffrage, and even no suffrage; for cabinet government, a constitutional hereditary executive, and even absolute monarchy.[8] Every scholar who has "discovered" the Lockean constitution has found some palpable support in the text. Locke does not, however, seem to have been concerned with providing one, even surreptitiously. That is, we cannot say what he would have proposed had his audience been in the proper mood.

The unreceptivity of the English people to such an innovation is not, however, the only reason why Locke may have omitted that discussion. It is not even the most interesting. His problem with Restoration England was not its institutions, and so reform could not be achieved merely by altering the structure of government. Constitutions are, after all, akin to laws. Even leaving aside the question of their adequacy to political life, they cannot enforce themselves. They require partisan defenders. Locke's objection to the Stuart monarchy was the Stuarts, not the fact that they wore a crown.

Yet this does not identify the real problem in seventeenth-century England. It was the people, after all, who permitted the Stuarts' transgressions. All the best institutional arrangements in the world are in vain if they are not suited to the popular spirit, or if the latter is not suited to them. It was the belief structure of his countrymen that had brought his country to the point of ruin. As a work intended primarily to persuade, the *Two Treatises* speaks more to this problem than to any other. Free government, as Locke describes it, cannot persist if he convinces the people only to acquiesce in William's *fait accompli*: he must end their intellectual and spiritual subjugation to divine right.

I should be clear that I am not asserting that most people at the time actually believed in the divine right of kings, let alone one based on descent from Adam; I do suggest, however, that the problem which Locke saw as fundamental was that they acquiesced in the rule of those who claimed *de jure divino* a title to absolute power.[9] They did not oppose foolish nonsense, even when that nonsense was deployed for no other reason than to harm them.

Locke's purpose, then, was to interpret the Glorious Revolution, to influence the manner in which it was seen. Every historical event is of course the result of a variety of actions, motives, and circumstances, some more admirable or admired than others. Locke emphasizes some of these while neglecting others, thus casting the revolution in a particular light. This was done not just to strengthen William's position but to make history teach a particular lesson. It was not sufficient that William be offered the crown;

men's recollection of *why* was just as important, and probably even more so. The Prince of Orange did not accomplish, according to Locke's narrative, yet another of "the many Revolutions which have been seen in this Kingdom, in this and former Ages," i.e., which did no more than effect a change of names (cf. TT II 223). Rather, he and the English people had brought about a real revolution (or restoration) in the theoretical realm.

> The King, and Body of the Nation, have since so thoroughly confuted [Filmer's] *Hypothesis,* that, I suppose, no Body hereafter will have either the Confidence to appear against our Common Safety, and be again an Advocate for Slavery; or the Weakness to be deceived with Contradictions dressed up in a Popular Stile, and well turned Periods. (TT Pref.)

The Revolution was in fact about refuting the divine right of kings and proving, once and for all, that government does in fact exist only by the consent of the people: God did not rescue him, once James II lost their confidence. William of Orange is not a usurper because they say he is not, and for no other reason; no other arguments are needed, and none other would be valid.

Locke's purpose, then, was to portray the revolution as teaching this lesson, an entirely new account of legitimate government, dressed up as the common sense of which England needed only a reminder. Locke had of course composed the vast bulk of the *Treatises* prior to William of Orange's landing and almost certainly for a different revolution. His purpose, however, would not have changed had it been the Duke of Monmouth who drove James II into exile. Indeed, Locke could have published it after just about any revolution.

What is intriguing is that Locke's account of legitimate government was not concerned with power struggles between English institutions. The people did not need to be instructed that their only friends sat in the House of Lords and controlled the House of Commons. A well-constituted legislative power would still require the king's assent for its summoning (cf. TT II 156 with II 154). Prerogative remains an essential component of good government. In denying (by ignoring) Filmer's claim that Parliament was nothing more than the king's council and thus devoid of any authority,[10] he does not go so far as to transfer to it sovereignty. And Locke does not so much *contract* the prerogatives of the king (a necessary act for parliamentary sovereignty) as give them a new basis. Indeed, a *doctrine* of prerogative proves to be far broader than any list of prerogatives by right of the Crown. Locke, that is, refounds the English constitution without altering its institutions. We may safely say that it is these new principles of government which form the essence of the distinctively Lockean commonwealth. Such a commonwealth may adopt any number of constitutions and remain essentially unchanged. It is defined more by the people's way of life, or by opinions concerning what is a truly good life, than by its structure.

The new principles of government rest upon a mixture of authority and prudence. Given the focus of other political tracts at the time, this involves a denigration of authority.[11] Locke manages to denigrate authority by asserting earthly ends as the touchstone of a society's goodness. According to Locke, the law has no independent normative value: it is a means. Men do not enter into political society merely for the sake of having a law. Rather, they simply use law to achieve their primary goal, namely, to escape the state of nature. The lack of a commonly recognized law is of course a major source of that state's being intolerable, yet it is the effects of this defect for which men seek a remedy. They do not, in his telling, want a law which reflects the divine one because adherence to law is the heart of morality. A realistic appraisal of the world, moreover, shows the establishment of positive law to be inadequate to the task. Legalism as a prejudice may be useful, but it can also be disastrously misleading. Man without government is exposed to a thousand dangers, but a known, enforced, and rational series of regulations cannot guarantee the elimination of those evils.

Law must, then, give way to the public good. Extralegal action is simply a part of political life. The perfect "legal state" or *Rechtsstaat* is not the goal from which occasional deviations are necessary, for it simply is not achievable. And even if extralegal action were only rarely necessary, there would still be the question of how to justify it. Prerogative does not so much indicate a gulf between the ideal and the possible as compel the thoughtful partisan to reevaluate the ideal itself. Locke does not, after all, advise us to judge politics by an impossible standard, especially if we desire a government that actually does what can be done for the improvement of our lives. The prudent man need not acquire authority in order to act, and this is as true of governors as it is of private citizens.

The goal, then, is to see the public good preserved by both legislative supremacy *and* prerogative, the former when it is able, the latter when it is not. It is to see both Parliament *and* the Crown with all their powers, so to speak. Some things are to be done according to law, others, as the result of prudent flexibility. We cannot, however, know beforehand which spheres of life are to be governed according to which paradigm. That is, we cannot fix the "jurisdictions" of legislative supremacy and prerogative as we can with, say, courts of criminal and civil law. Prerogative, properly speaking, has no "jurisdiction." It cannot be codified into a set of "prerogatives." Justified by law's failure, it is a legitimate exercise of power wherever that failure occurs. The main cause of that deficiency, however, namely, "flux," also prevents us from perfectly foreseeing where, when, and how often recourse to arbitrary actions will be justifiable.

These are not just two different powers, but two different sorts of power. Political power, on the one hand, must manifest itself as legislative supremacy: consent is the catalyst of obligation—the suspension of one's private judgment—and this can be given only to the rule of law. Prerogative, on the other hand, is a natural power. It does not, therefore, bring with it an obligation to obey. Prior consent is not a necessary precondition of its use, nor can such consent ever be forthcoming: no man may bind his conscience to arbitrary power. Each individual member in society is free to judge each unlawful act; a long train of mistaken or perfidious decisions does not so much "release" men from their obligations as persuade them that acquiescence is no longer the best course of action. The commonwealth is, then, a mixture of natural and political power, of things to which one is obligated and of which one must be the judge.

Prerogative stands beyond the constitution because the constitutional and the legal are the obligatory. Where political power is exercised, "all private judgement of every particular Member [is] excluded" (TT II 87). The people are not obligated to accept assertions of prerogative; nor must the prince admit that he exercises something other than prerogative until the opposition of the majority is made manifest.

That there is no constitutional check does not mean that institutional responses to prerogative are contemptible; it means simply that the logic of prerogative does not tell us when the prince must stop pressing the issue.[12] It means we are in a realm where the limits on the acceptable use of power are ill-defined, which means they may be the subject of dispute. Absent constitutional mechanisms, we cannot forejudge when such disputes should or should not terminate peacefully. The trust of prerogative is the trust to be in such a position; the necessity of prerogative shows that the need for such trust cannot be lessened though constitutional checks and balances. The Lockean commonwealth fosters and welcomes the legalist prejudice; it can be supported only by means abhorrently incomprehensible to that prejudice. It is no wonder, then, that we should find prerogative deeply unsettling.

The attempt to translate Locke's doctrine into modern constitutional language misses the point of his discussion, however. Prerogative is not a legal doctrine. It instead points us to flaws with legalism, and thus with the attempt to define legitimate government exhaustively by constructing a framework of corresponding rights and duties. What little discretion is allowable to the executive power under the law in Locke's system is unquestionable: one can dispute only whether it has been lawfully granted. When the prince exercises broader discretionary powers, however, he does so less authoritatively: he may with greater right be opposed. The exercise of executive power carries with it an unambiguous duty to obey. The exercise of prerogative, on the other hand, must be judged by the individual, and the individual's duty to support the public good implies a duty to obey and support the prerogatival acts only to the extent that the people acquiesce in their use. As Clement Fatovic observes, "exercises of prerogative are never unassailable acts of the sovereign."[13]

One cannot have a low tolerance for uncertainty if this mixture is to be acceptable. It is, after all, unstable: every marginally competent usurper or tyrant can make a plausible claim to be acting *pro salute populi.* Yet it also carries with it several implications that might seem necessarily "wrong" to us. The commonwealth, in admitting prerogative, does not satisfy the liberal sense of what political justice should be. It might seem dissatisfying on a theoretical as well as a practical political level. The fact that even *just* prerogative is not obligatory means that one may legitimately resist its use. Not that such resistance renders its use illegitimate, however: this is merely the consequence of there being no sacrificial obligations, no duty to pay that which cannot be recompensed, no consent contrary to self-interest. We might wish all rights and duties to be compatible, that adherence to what the law of nature represents would lead to peace and concord among men. Therefore, if the state possessed a right to compel, the subject would have a duty to obey; if the latter could with right resist, the former could not command. One of two belligerents simply must, our prejudices inform us, have done the other some wrong. It would, then, be possible to craft legal norms that respected all of our rights, followed by a moral obligation to do so.

Yet men do not and cannot possess such duties.[14] Locke clearly indicates that the prince must, at times, act without the cover of legality in sacrificing a few for the good of the many. We see this in the example of the man whose house is demolished in order to save those of his neighbors. This is simply the exercise of society's right to preserve itself, now extralegally. We see this same right when it compels cowards to march into battle and in the treatment of criminals. At the same time, we see that those who are forced to endure some great loss, if they judge it to be too great to bear, are not obligated to do so: if their compliance must be compelled, it is not necessarily because they are reprobates. Society does have a right to sacrifice its members, and a prince may benefit it unlawfully if need be. In all such cases, the individual may resist. Resistance is, after all, legitimate even when revolution is not. Locke's commonwealth is premised on a rejection of this view of rights, duties, and obligations, even as it relies upon this view for its unexceptional operation.

This argument would of course apply to his account of legislative supremacy even if he had not appended to it prerogative. It is the latter, however, that makes the problem more acutely felt. We do, after all, recognize the need for some to be sacrificed. But at least, we can tell ourselves, it is done according to the due process of law. As I argued in chapter 2, Locke's account of consent, representation, and obligation can serve only to assuage society's conscience regarding such actions. If we demand an account of legitimacy that would satisfy the conditions of a social contract, we will never find a legitimate government; as government is needed, however, we must be satisfied with chanting the contractarian charm. Yet prerogative does not possess even this soothing back-story, and thus brings these problems to the fore.

Even accepting this view of rights and duties, however, the mixture of natural and political power in the commonwealth is unsettling. Is not the point of political society, after all, precisely to avoid recourse to natural power? Was not it men's exercise of that power, employing it according to their own judgment, that was the cause of so many evils in the state of nature? These are valid objections. Examining the state of nature more closely, however, it seems that it was not so much natural power that was the problem as its misuse. If it can be turned to good account, it is not an evil. After all, misery was the result of men's not knowing or obeying the law of nature, of the latter's poor enforcement. And, moreover, political society simply cannot do without natural power. It cannot be the legal state. As a consequence, our goal must be to harness this power, not to abolish it.

In practice, this implies the rather mundane requirement that prerogative be limited. It must supplement, but never supplant, the rule of law. It must be employed only where legal forms are inadequate (though as often as that may be) and the prince must be compelled to use this power only for the public good. It is right to be uncomfortable with the union of natural and political power, Locke says. Prerogative is extralegal action in a society held together by laws. It is a reminder that we cannot fully escape the state of nature and a reliance on force. Only the inconveniences of these are avoidable, and even that is not certain.

The Lockean commonwealth is a source of unease because it does not support itself. It requires the constant threat of bloodshed. It does not rest on a system of "checks and balances," or some other invention of prudence. That is, it resists all attempts to "legalize" prerogative, to codify and regulate all aspects of political life in a constitution. There is prerogative, not simply a series of defined prerogatives. The commonwealth does not escape from the necessity of revolution: if war is the essence of the political problem, it does not solve it.

While certainly true, Locke would not consider this to be a real criticism. It would be valid only if we were to deny that revolution had a role to play in a healthy society, if we were to refuse to see it as anything more than medicinal. We would like to have it tamed: protests, perhaps even civil disobedience, should replace saber rattling in a just community. We are, however, bidden to judge health and justice by what is possible. Locke would argue that a society where revolution is not a possibility, both moral and actual, cannot remain rational and is not healthy. Put bluntly, members of the Lockean commonwealth must be militarily capable.

The rule of law is not self-sustaining—it requires extrinsic support—and so the Lockean commonwealth needs a populace ready and able to ensure its proper functioning. Locke's discussion of political society before he introduces prerogative (chapters 7–13 of the *Second Treatise*) simply lays out the rules according to which lawful government is to function. As these are only rules, they may be violated. Without a power *on earth* to enforce them, they are in fact no rules at all (cf. TT II 7, II 219). And yet no part of the government can be trusted with this enforcement. The legislative power has no force of its own: it only commands and hopes that those with force not only obey but also compel obedience from others. Parliament's power over the purse, reaffirmed after the Glorious Revolution in the *Bill of Rights of 1689*, is enforced by the people should the king transgress against it; i.e., its power in this regard is ensured by the governed, not by any part of the government.[15] That part of the government with force, however, namely, the executive power, does not embody the public will and so cannot be trusted with preserving that will. It is the laws, rather, which declare this public will, of which the executive is merely a functionary (TT II 151, II 202). The federative power of course has no domestic mandate (TT II 145). There is, as Locke puts it, "no *Judge on Earth* . . . between the Legislative and the People, should either the Executive or the Legislative, when they have got the Power in their hands, design, or go about to enslave, or destroy them" (TT II 168).

Now, a constitution provides a means of knowing who is authorized in any given case to exercise political power (TT II 198). It identifies the judge on earth. It may do more, but it must do at least this much. Consider how the U.S. Constitution begins: "All legislative Power herein granted shall be vested in a Congress of the United States which shall consist of a Senate and House of Representatives."[16] It then proceeds to tell us how we are to recognize which assembly of persons gets to be this Congress. An anti-Congress of malcontents has no claim to the federal legislative power, just as the generally recognized Congress cannot pretend to authority over, say, the established religion of the United States, or of any one of them. Where the Constitution is vague, e.g., as regards the federative power,[17] Locke would say that it has failed as a constitution (cf. TT II 141, II 157, II 198). (Of course, the very indeterminacy which necessitates prerogative might be reason to leave such matters vague, but this would be already to admit that they cannot be addressed in a constitutional fashion; cf. TT II 147. The same ambiguity is manifest in the question of *who* may suspend the privilege of the writ of habeas corpus when the public safety may require it.)

We are thus in possession of clear definitions of what constitutes a violation of the fundamental law. It might fall out, for example, that some persons claim the right to exercise the authority of a certain office while in fact lacking it. More likely, they might claim for the office which they legitimately occupy powers which are within the purview of another or to which no one may rightfully aspire. A clear constitution can aid in the identification of usurpers and tyrants. Indeed, the former can be said to exist, properly speaking, only where the constitution is clear. Yet discovery is not prevention. A constitution cannot prevent its being contemned with nothing more than the indelibility of its ink. In short, there might be "rebellion."

> For Rebellion being an Opposition, not to Persons, but Authority, which is founded only in the Constitutions and Laws of the Government; those, whoever they be, who by force break through, and by force justifie their violations of them, are truly and properly *Rebels*. For when Men by entering into Society and Civil Government, have excluded force, and introduced Laws for the preservation of Property, Peace, and Unity amongst themselves; those who set up force again in opposition to the Laws, do *Rebellare*, that is, bring back again the state of War, and are properly Rebels. (TT II 226)

Locke's doctrine of revolution deters such rebellion with real, worldly consequences (TT II 229). Though Locke says that he only informs princes of what will happen anyway (TT II 226, II 229), his doctrine actually provides these consequences by making the people more jealous of their rights.

The constitution is, as it were, a tripwire: it warns the people of potential threats to their liberties. What, after all, but ambition could motivate the usurpation of power? Why else would a legislature issue an extemporaneous decree, take property without consent, or delegate its legislative authority, if not to undermine the public good? Enumerated rights and assertions of the legislature's control over taxation function in precisely the same manner, i.e., they are intended to make transgressions of the public good unmistakably clear. The unconstitutional is presumed to be illegitimate. The preceding acts would not have the status of law, meaning that no one would be justified in enforcing them (TT II 135–42). Any executive actions not commanded by the law would be illegitimate (TT II 143–44, II 151, II 202). When the constitution is violated, obligations cease; where one is not obligated, the individual (in general) ought to resist and the people ought to revolt against anyone who claims coercive authority (TT II 155). So long as the initial conditions regarding consent have been met (cf. TT II 95–99), legitimacy is by and large reducible to legality.

It is not a constitution, then, that protects a people's properties. Their lives, liberties, and estates may be secure if it is adhered to, but it is the people themselves who ultimately enforce adherence to it. The rulers, in abjuring legal forms, demand that the people trust in their moral goodness: the people should oppose all who needlessly require of them so blind a faith. Faithful rulers display their honesty by relinquishing their ability to be dishonest, i.e., by rendering their moral virtues invisible because irrelevant. Even angels govern themselves as if they were nothing more than clever devils. Or perhaps more accurately, an enlightened people demands that its governors act like clever devils. This is what the rule of law means. Revolution is necessary to the Lockean commonwealth, at a minimum, in order to enforce the constitution.

Yet a constitution cannot be a suicide pact, and it would be improper to oppose him who prevents it from being one. Acquiescence in every action that is accompanied by a sense of having received some benefit is to be expected, whether the act was legal or not (TT II 161).

And here lies the danger of prerogative: it requires that either the rulers be trustworthy or the people enlightened, yet neither is the case. A society without a presumption against the legitimacy of extralegal actions would find the legislative procedures neglected, i.e., it would tend toward its primordial condition of being wholly prerogatival. Such a government would quickly become tyrannical. Yet it should be obvious that law is incapable of holding its own against arbitrary power. Prerogative is without a defined jurisdiction, whereas legislative power is much more tightly bound. Executives saving their people from the grip of fear are just sexier than legislators amending the language of a bill. Of the two, prerogative and legislative power, the former's scope is more likely to expand over time, especially if well used. The people must recognize the danger in this and work to prevent it: they will love prerogative, but must buttress legislative supremacy.

Prerogative is limited only by the spirited enlightenment of the people.[18] Locke goes even further than this, however. When we examine his text closely, it turns out that such a people is in fact the very genesis of freedom under government. This last point requires further explanation.

The people, we are told, naïvely allowed for government without law, and for a time this worked well enough. When they had accumulated some material felicity under the aegis of prerogative, however, they found their estates, their liberties, and their lives insecure. They therefore limited the power of their prince, subjecting his rule to the commands and prohibitions of law. Prerogative was allowed only where the latter could not safely govern.

It is not the law, however, that was actually responsible for limiting prerogative: it was the people. It was "unforeseeing Innocence" to place so much trust in their ruler's justice (TT II 94). It was a choice appropriate "to Men, whom neither experience had instructed in Forms of Government, nor the Ambition or Insolence of Empire had taught to beware of the Encroachments of Prerogative, or the Inconveniencies of Absolute Power" (TT II 107). In time, however, they "found it necessary to examine more carefully *the Original* and Rights of *Government*" (TT II 111).

That is, the people remembered, as it were, that all government exists only for their benefit and by their consent: their refusal to consent could overturn all rulers, and no dictate of justice prevented them from doing so. They learned Locke's doctrine, so to speak.[19] It was their recognition of their own strength, theirs both by right and by fact, that rendered extralegality safe once more.

Locke is making quite a claim for his doctrine. Only it can preserve freedom, for it alone does not cow the people into dumb submission; according to his fanciful retelling of unwritten history, moreover, freedom is coincident with his doctrine. Prerogative withdrew, leaving a space for the rule of law to fill, because the people had learned they had a right to demand it. Whenever they forget this right, the powerful make inroads on their liberty. This focuses everything—the survival of the commonwealth in its freedom precisely when it is most imperiled—upon the temperament and education of the people. The prince is allowed to act without or against the law only because they allow it. If a spirited people, jealous of its liberty, knows when and why extralegality *should* be permissible, its use *will be* restricted to only those times and for those reasons. Or more properly speaking, any prince who contemns both positive and natural law will find himself face to face with an angry populace, and a powerful one.

Most people readily accept the necessity of government of some sort. The need for law is also pretty straightforward, rhetorically speaking. Prerogative, on the other hand, is not the easiest of concepts. All that was needed to teach men the necessity of law was the experience of lawlessness. They were not, however, taught the uses of prerogative per se: it really did just "happen." Even then, what was present could not really be called a doctrine: prerogative "insensibly" swallowed up the whole of government. Its unreflective origins, however, do not render it childish. Locke argues that it is indeed necessary. As the commonwealth turns on popular enlightenment about politics, the people must be taught a *true* doctrine of prerogative. The latter is safe only because the people know how to keep it safe. They understand its place: revolutionaries cannot limit it properly if they do not understand its proper limits.

Let us turn to a facet of prerogative that I have not discussed yet. It highlights one of the more important aspects of prerogative's relation to the commonwealth, and it is this aspect about which the people require the most instruction. Locke argues that the advances made under *good* princes show why prerogative must walk, as it were, under the noontime sun. The fact that a necessary act was illegal should not be concealed in the shadows, at least in the Lockean commonwealth. That is, the law should not be "construed" so as to be capable of handling every contingency that may arise. This is not so much because an unacknowledged prerogative can lead to feckless legalism (though it can certainly do that) as that it can destroy the most necessary foundation of the rule of law itself.[20]

It is one thing when the people must oppose lawless acts that harm them. Locke's vivid reminder—a reminder that seems out of place in a discussion of prerogative's legitimacy, and so a reminder just that much more striking—points to something more than this.

> Upon this is founded that saying, That the Reigns of good Princes have been always most dangerous to the Liberties of their People. For when their Successors, managing the Government with different Thoughts, would draw the Actions of those good Rulers into Precedent, and make them the Standard of their *Prerogative*, as if what had been done only for the good of the People, was a right in them to do, for the harm of the People, if they so pleased; it has often occasioned Contest, and sometimes publick Disorders, before the People could recover their original Right, and get that to be declared not to be *Prerogative*, which truly was never so. (TT II 166)

Even when the act is for the public good, even when it is truly prerogatival, the people must be ready and willing to ensure that it does not set a precedent for future tyrants.[21]

This is not to say that the people must oppose manifestly good acts, but rather that they must take care that such acts are manifestly seen and acknowledged as extraordinary: they cannot be allowed as lawful. The reason for this is both clear and depressing. The minds of men, educated in society, are dependent upon that society: mankind puts great stock in precedent, in general principles drawn from what the past has considered legitimate. Men are, after all, by and large governed by tradition according to Locke. In this way, any precedent that is not disavowed as extraordinary gains "legitimacy." "And when Fashion hath once Established, what Folly or craft began, Custom makes it Sacred, and 'twill be thought impudence or madness, to contradict or question it" (TT I 58). Private interest may often keep up "Customs and Priviledges, when the reasons of them are ceased," leading inevitably to "gross absurdities" (TT II 157). Even when men recognize that a disorder exists and have knowledge of its cause, they are unwilling to remedy it if it is ancient.

> They are hardly to be prevailed with to amend the acknowledg'd Faults, in the Frame they have been accustom'd to. And if there be any Original defects, or adventitious ones introduced by time, or corruption, 'tis not an easie thing to get them changed, even when all the World sees there is an opportunity for it. (TT II 223)

Past precedents inform the present's view of what is legitimate. A respect for precedent, a respect for tradition, a respect even for patriarchy—all these equate the good with the old, with the established, with what one accepts because it was presented as one's own. This is opposed to the rule of reason, i.e., to a life lived within the bounds of the law of nature.

What was thought to be good in particular cases stands as a surrogate for what is good now: a general principle becomes a substitute for thought in general. If the people were truly Lockean, on the other hand, an appeal to what was historically allowed would not persuade them to permit actions that were injurious to their material felicity: there could be no danger from prerogative, and the reigns of good princes would be unequivocal blessings. But prerogative *is* dangerous, precedent *is* dangerous, and this can only be because people judge the goodness of an act by a standard other than whether it benefits their private, prepolitical concerns. Again, the public good is only the aggregate of these concerns. The people are easily confused regarding the public good; they are often mistaken about their own good, perhaps hoping that there is more to life than the protection of life, liberty, and estate. So it is not just prudence that the people need in times of crisis.

Locke's entire political order is based upon the people's holding a particular view of what constitutes legitimate action. For the most part, this view demands the strict subordination of executive power to the legislative; such subordination is founded on its enforcement by the people, either through the credible threat of revolution or through its actuality. Deviation from the rule of law may be required, and Locke is certain that it is, but such deviation cannot change what is held to be normally legitimate if the ordinary functioning of government, i.e., the rule of law backed up by popular arms, is to be sustained. Precedents, however, change precisely this, and so the necessary deviations from the rule of law must be opposed if they threaten to set such a precedent. The beneficial act can stand, but the one who insists upon its legality, the one who insists that nothing extralegal has occurred, cannot. Those who insist upon the legality of such acts must be considered misguided or bent on subversion: both are criminal in a politician.

Acts of prerogative must then always remain extraordinary, questionable, and a source of unease, even when they are manifestly beneficial and necessary. Moreover, it is not enough for them to cause unease only among the political theorists or politicians who loudly fret over them; in fact, their unease is almost irrelevant in this matter. Rather, it is the people who must be wary when they are benefited illegally: it is the people who must rise up for a revolution to be popular. Locke says that they are "very seldom, or never scrupulous, or nice in the point . . . whilst it is in any tolerable degree imploy'd for . . . the good of the People" (TT II 161), but they must become so. Everyone knows to fear the Achaean army: they must be taught to beware of Greeks bearing gifts.

The People and Popular Philosophy

It seems that everything hinges on the people. Their character, their habits, their beliefs—all must be such as to bear the responsibility for their own freedom. I have already described the view of politics they must hold. They must be Lockeans, even if they have never read the *Two Treatises of Government*.[22]

Now seems to be a good place to examine Locke's connection to the Enlightenment and to the Modern project of remaking politics in light of philosophic insights into justice and virtue. Leo Strauss was fond of Winston Churchill's observation that modern society is built upon low but solid ground: it would pursue what all, or almost all, men reliably desired, whether the sum of those desires would truly bring happiness or not. This pursuit was most readily apparent in the early stages of Modernity, with its pointed avoidance of a reliance on virtue. It reached its perfection in the thought that went into the United States Constitution, as explained in the *Federalist Papers*' justly famous formulation:

> Ambition must be made to counteract ambition. . . . It may be a reflection on human nature that such devices should be necessary to control the abuses of government. But what is government itself but the greatest of all reflections on human nature? If men were angels, no government would be necessary. If angels were to govern

> men, neither external nor internal controls on government would be necessary. . . . [This is a] policy of supplying, by opposite and rival interests, the defect of better motives.[23]

Madison's earlier argument, in *Federalist* No. 10, makes plain that such devices were not needed merely to supply a defect among the governors.

Locke avoids a reliance on the virtue of statesmen. It is certainly nice when it is present, as in the case of a good king wielding prerogative, but a facet of that king's goodness is precisely his reticence to wield a power that he would not entrust to some unknown successor. And while the exercise of prerogative may require certain political virtues such as prudence, perspicacity, and the like, Locke refuses to rely upon the prince's *moral* virtues, nor does he put much effort into convincing kings of their duties. Instead, prerogative leads him to a discussion of revolution, one of the cruder "external . . . controls on government" that Madison alluded to. And it is here that Locke relies very much upon a kind of civic virtue.

This civic virtue was lacking in Locke's day. England, as Locke saw it, came to "the very brink of Slavery and Ruine" (TT Pref.). We should not dismiss this as empty rhetoric on his part. It was, after all, James II's political ineptitude that forged the alliance between Whig and Tory responsible for his downfall, not "the uncanny shrewdness which long, slow, increasing peril engenders, an endless vista of oppression and persecution, decked in a tinsel of fair-seeming toleration."[24] Locke began to compose the *Two Treatises* long before the Glorious Revolution, even before the ascension of James II to the throne. Their rhetorical flow, however, suggests throughout that the climax will be a justification of popular resistance. If Locke wrote a political tract that culminated in such a justification long before the Glorious Revolution, it seems reasonable to conclude that he felt that a revolution would have been justified long before it as well. Yet the Rye House Plot was discovered. And support for Monmouth's rebellion never materialized. And it should be remembered that the Glorious Revolution was really more a foreign invasion facilitated by certain aristocrats than a massive popular uprising. Locke's praise of William III as "our Great Restorer" (TT Pref.) does not ring as obsequiousness or false praise. The people of England seem at best an absent guardian of their own liberties.

The *Two Treatises of Government* was his contribution to this problem. He would insert resistance to tyranny in the name of the natural rights of man into his nation's tradition, a part of what it meant to be English, even if this would, from a strictly historical standpoint, be a complete fabrication. I have argued that Locke intended to teach new principles of government, novelty overlain with a veneer of forgotten common sense. His was an essay concerning the *true* original, extent, and end of civil government, coming on the heels of his overthrowing the false principles and foundation of Sir Robert Filmer and his followers. Locke's strategy with the *Two Treatises* suggests that the needed civic virtue was to be inculcated by an Enlightenment.

Locke makes it seem as though the problem were a matter of dark and superstitious political doctrines. Men, who were strong enough to ensure their own properties, were failing to do so because of the charm incanted about rulers, making obedience even to tyrants seem the Christian thing to do. Locke seems so interested in refuting Jonas Proast—and insulting him in the process—precisely because, unlike, say, Thomas Long's, his attack on the *Letter Concerning Toleration* subversively employed relatively liberal principles.

Yet close examination makes clear that it was not just the fashionable doctrines of his own day that were shot through with disadvantageous confusion. Locke has very little (if any) respect for custom as such.[25] In this way, he is no conservative: tradition is not the accumulated wisdom of long experience. Locke's proof in his *Questions Concerning the Law of Nature* that the general consent of men is no guide to morality begins with the observation, "were we willing to hearken to [the voice of the people] as if it were the herald of a divine law, we should finally hardly believe in the existence of any god at all" (NL VII 62). He goes on to ask, "how many are there in the more civilized nations, living under fixed laws, which all recognize, and under which they acknowledge themselves to have been raised and to be ruled, who do not sanction their vices by their own conduct . . . ?" (NL VII 66). If custom were the result of some scientific discipline, then perhaps the conservatives' encomia to tradition might be reasonable; but Locke traces it *precisely* to men's not employing their reason.

One could object that Locke thought the coming of Christianity to have changed all of this, especially as most instances of vicious customs that he cites are those of Greek and Roman pagans, tropical natives, Turks, Persians, Hindus, Assyrians, and the like. Locke praises Christianity for having made morality profitable: recognizing that the philosophers' talk about virtue had left her "unendowed, very few willing to espouse her," "our Saviour" came with "another relish," one with the "efficacy to persuade men, that if they live well here, they shall be happy hereafter;" *this* was "something solid and powerful to move them" (RC 245). Morality requires the support of a God (RC 241–43, 245; NL VII 76), and although "the works of nature . . . sufficiently evidence a deity," the usual workings of custom made it impossible for the mass of society as a whole to discover one:

> and what dread or craft once began, devotion soon made sacred, and religion immutable. In this state of darkness and ignorance of the true God, vice and superstition held the world. Nor could any

> help be had, or hoped for, from reason; which could not be heard, and was judged to have nothing to do in the case; the priests, everywhere, to secure their empire, having excluded reason from having any thing to do in religion. (RC 238)

Man now has "assistance to support and carry him through" when he feels himself "hedged in with prevailing custom" (RC 246).

Attentiveness to Locke's examples shows that contemporary customs are no better, however, and not just among heathens.[26] "It is familiar among the Mingrelians, a people professing Christianity, to bury their children alive without scruple" (ECHU I.3.9). One need not go so far as the Georgian Caucasus to see Christian atrocities, however: James II's reprisals after his army defeated Monmouth's at Sedgemoor give the sting to Locke's invitation to "View but an army at the sacking of a town, and see what observation or sense of moral principles, or what touch of conscience for all the outrages they do. Robberies, murders, rapes, are the sports of men set at liberty from punishment and censure" (ECHU I.3.9).[27] Locke's description of pre-Christian religion in the *Reasonableness of Christianity* copies even the cadence of what he had said about the customs which one could now see in the world in that stark passage from the *First Treatise*:

> And when Fashion hath once Established, what Folly or craft began, Custom makes it Sacred, and 'twill be thought impudence or madness, to contradict or question it. He that will impartially survey the Nations of the World, will find so much of their Governments, Religions, and Manners brought in and continued amongst them by these means, that he will have but little Reverence for the Practices which are in use and credit amongst Men. (TT I 58)

I have already noted the problems with England's political principles.

We might wonder why reason has so little influence on not just the customs of this or that man but on the aggregation of their customs or on the national custom. Locke gives a couple of reasons (cf. RC 238, 245), but when explaining why any remedy of this defect had to be "suited to vulgar capacities," Locke attributes man's contempt for the "airy commendations" of "learned heathens" to material poverty.

> The greatest part of mankind have not leisure for learning and logic, and superfine distinctions of the schools. Where the hand is used to the plough and the spade, the head is seldom elevated to sublime notions, or exercised in mysterious reasoning. It is well if men of that rank (to say nothing of the other sex) can comprehend plain

> propositions, and a short reasoning about things familiar to their minds, and nearly allied to their daily experience. Go beyond this, and you amaze the greatest part of mankind; and may as well talk Arabic to a poor day-labourer, as the notions and language and the books and disputes of religion are filled with. (RC 245, 252)

If something like *this* is the problem, then it seems that the improvement of nature given license in chapter 5 of the *Second Treatise* would have a marvelous impact on man's reasonableness.

Yet it is not so much desperation as the necessity to work at all that prevents men from engaging in the sort of speculative activity necessary. What is needed is not so much superabundant food, climate-controlled shelter, inexpensive garments, unemployment insurance, and universal access to health care, as the leisure which has been surrendered in obtaining these things. Even in an advanced country, there will be servants and day laborers (cf. TT II 28, 41).[28]

There is also the suggestion that increasing men's rationality to the point where they could in fact comprehend the subtleties of the philosophers would not actually result in social improvement. Locke credits the philosophers with showing the "beauty of virtue" and notes their argument that "she is the perfection and excellency of our nature; . . . she is herself a reward, and will recommend our names to future ages" (RC 245). But he says that the rewards of virtue that were doubtful and distant concerned the other life, not happiness or reputation in this one. Seeing that the "portion of the righteous [is] pretty scanty in this world," men "could not but think" that the rules impressed upon them as virtues could be set aside; after all, these rules "appeared so little to consist of their chief end, happiness; whilst they kept them from the enjoyments of this life; and they had little evidence and security of another" (RC 245). What was needed was a "view of heaven and hell." "Upon this foundation, and upon this only, morality stands firm, and may defy all competition." Given its scant rewards in this world, and absent knowledge of rewards in the next, morality is not "more than a name" (RC 245). What the philosophers provided were "airy commendations" (RC 245).[29]

I mention these things because the revolution in politics which Locke attempted with the *Two Treatises* would labor under the same constraints as did the revolution in morals he claimed for Christianity. Even if Locke did not consider himself to be taking a page from Christianity's spread, namely, conquest by means of a book,[30] that is in fact precisely what he was doing. A change of the sort Locke desired to bring about could, according to his own analysis, be brought about only by the propagation of a simple doctrine, one suited to vulgar capacities, appealing to man's desire for happiness, and premised upon reward and punishment.

And this is, more or less, what he provided. Locke's is a simple political gospel. Hard work deserves reward, and government exists to make sure the rational and industrious get it, regardless of whether they are rich or poor. Be wary of the government. Demand that it rule by law, but recognize that it cannot always do so. In all cases, however, judge its actions by asking whether they are done for your good, and do not feel obligated by anything other than your own consent and basic decency. Government is so much your servant that you may fight against it, if it serves you badly. Be tolerant of other people's religions.

More must be said about the sort of enlightenment that Locke sought to bring about. In certain crucial respects, as it turns out, he inspires more than he enlightens. Peter Josephson suggests that "What Locke proposes is the rule of reasonable customs, not reason," yet this overstates the coherence of what Locke in fact inculcates.[31]

This is nowhere more evident than in Locke's teaching regarding liberty.[32] Freedom, it seems, both is and is not more important than life and indeed must be both for the commonwealth to function. At the same time, however, he equivocates about what this *liberty* even is. Occasionally it is simply action in accord with reason: the irrational are not free. More often, however, it is mere willfulness: it is to be free from external impediments. The people, or at least the decisive fraction of them, must believe all these things at the same time.

The problematic passivity of the English people in the face of absolute monarchy could conceivably be remedied by something like the *Two Treatises*. Locke does not simply inform his countrymen of their rights or coolly suggest that one would be justified in defending them. Rather, he makes their defense a matter of life and death: he who would take away your liberty must be presumed to harbor designs on your life (TT II 17). He describes the effects of tyranny in vivid and sanguinary language (TT II 210, 226, 228, 230, 233, 239). He may be accused of overstating the case, but this would be a mark against him only if his intention were accuracy: instead, he seeks to make his readers more jealous of their liberties and thus more willing to revolt in protection of them. He makes a rhetorical appeal for greater vigilance against tyranny. In this case, at least, he attempts to inflame their irascibility and channel it in a politically salutary direction. Were he successful, this would certainly go a long way toward remedying the aforementioned difficulties.

Yet Locke cannot afford to simply stoke the fires of irascible self-regard. The people cannot treat liberty as an end, as something which is to be valued more than even one's own life. Those who risk their lives in fighting against tyrants cannot hold their lives to be of less worth than their liberties. They cannot have that contempt for survival which aristocrats and ancient republicans claimed was the essence or prerequisite of noble action. After all, revolutions occur only outside of political society (all else is rebellion or resistance); they must at some point end. The *Two Treatises* opens by convincing men that they should surrender their liberty and join political society precisely in order to preserve their lives. A concern for liberty is justified by the regard for one's life that is the principle law of nature. This is the doctrine with which Locke would have men explain themselves to themselves. In short, the people must act nobly without thinking noble thoughts.

We may state the problem as follows. Locke at times presents liberty as a means, namely, to the preservation of life (TT II 17, II 93). Life is presented as the single most needful thing (TT II 6, II 23). Indeed, a man may give up a good part of his liberty, provided that his life is in fact made more secure by such a surrender (cf. TT II 123). In order to preserve his life, he exchanges his natural freedom for political freedom, the freedom and obligations of the law of nature for those of positive law (TT II 57, II 87, II 124). Indeed, the only limitation placed on this surrender of liberty is what is necessary for self-preservation (TT II 23, II 129, II 172).

This account is necessary if Locke is to convince men to join political society (or more accurately, not convince them to not permit it to regulate their actions). Liberty must be the sort of thing which a man can reasonably surrender if he is to put on "*the bonds of Civil Society*" and submit to its "Dominion and Controul," a subjection that "in many things [confines] the liberty he had by the law of nature" (TT II 95, II 123, II 129). Men leave the state of nature, and so accept this diminution of their liberty, in order to preserve their lives (TT II 123). Only if men hold this view of liberty can there be an acceptance of law, which acceptance is necessary for the consensual operation of government. (I am of course omitting the alternative against which Locke is arguing. Government can, and often does, justify its operation based on duties which are not of the individual's own choosing: divine will is but one example.) Yet it is precisely men's right "to order their Actions, and dispose of their Possessions, and Persons *as they think fit*,[33] within the bounds of the Law of Nature, without asking leave, or depending upon the Will of any other Man" that Locke defines as "*perfect Freedom*" (TT II 4). One cannot take on an obligation to obey without surrendering much of the liberty one formerly possessed. Men must be willing to accept limits on their liberty for the sake of other benefits, and so become obedient, law-abiding subjects and (with more difficulty) dutiful magistrates.

That is, his readers' conception of liberty cannot be one that finds legalism to be simply repugnant. We should not forget what political society is, or what it demands. To be obligated to the legislative power, to have it be the representative of one's own will, is to be a legalist. It is to accept the equation of the lawful with the just or, at least, with the right thing to do. Life within any functioning society is likely to foster such a prejudice in favor of the laws, even if it is defeasible, but Locke's account of political society does not encourage this equation with the argument that justice really is reducible to legality under a legitimate regime. Locke's account does not take advantage of this prejudice. Rather, he argues that we must accept that equation *even though* it is wrong, for the alternative is the anarchy of individual, private judgment. The possession of this judgment, the liberty to judge for oneself, must be worth less than whatever is inconvenienced by that anarchy.

Yet the whole point of Locke's project, and the very sort of activity he encourages in the final chapters, relies on an inverted relationship between life and liberty. "Chains are but an ill wearing, how much Care soever hath been taken to file and polish them," and slavery "so vile and miserable an Estate of Man," that it is quite possible that one subjected to them might find "the hardship of his Slavery out-weigh the value of his Life" (TT I 1, II 23). Locke does not counsel that one in such a position commit suicide, however. Rather, one may "by resisting the Will of his Master, . . . draw on himself the Death he desires" (TT II 23). He does not say that, should the slave, even a just slave, prevail in such resistance, he must find someone else to be his master; the effect of victorious resistance in such a case appears to be that he regains his freedom.[34] One subject to slavery may risk one's life for liberty; one need not risk one's life only for one's life.

To view liberty as something more than a mere fence to one's life but rather as that which may be of more concern than one's life is necessary if an individual is to take part in a revolution. Moreover, the decision to rise up requires private judgment, and so an unwillingness to wholly surrender it to be represented by someone else. Consequently, we cannot resolve this dilemma by distinguishing between two sorts of liberty, one which is surrendered, the other, retained. The same liberty must be both surrendered and retained, an object of both alienation and the most intimate concern. Such a concern for liberty, however, might militate against the entrance into political society and one's willingness to live within it under its laws, for the reasons noted above. The sweetness inherent to liberty tends to wane when its bounds are felt. Men naturally chafe under the law, even if it forbids only things they would not normally do. Whatever its cause, the desire must be moderated. Thus, this view of liberty is not emphasized until Locke addresses the proper response to usurpation, tyranny, and the dissolution of government. When arguing for political society, he gives it a passing, ambiguous mention (cf. TT II 23).

The above is not, of course, a damning problem politically speaking. It does not render the Lockean commonwealth an impossibility. Most people, after all, are similarly ambivalent regarding what is most important. It is not as though human beings actually first determine their hierarchy of goods and only then make their choices by that standard: we can often surprise ourselves, learning or revising what we actually hold to be important from our actions, and it is not at all necessary that what we learn be reducible to anything so formal as a "hierarchy."

Still, seeing that we value liberty in some way or another, we might well ask what this "liberty" is. That is, we explain certain of our actions to others with recourse to the word, but what do we mean to signify by it?

Locke is acting as an educator in the *Two Treatises*, informing Englishmen about politics. In the process, he attempts to inform their conception of liberty. He says that it is both right and necessary for them to throw off tyranny and claim their sacred birthright as free members of a free commonwealth. What, then, according to his account, *is* this liberty which the good citizen must both surrender and die to protect?

He at times treats it as correlative with reason (TT II 57, II 63). It is the ability to act according to the law of nature (TT II 6), or according to the laws of political society (TT II 22). Since political society is legitimate society—illegitimate societies not being political societies at all (cf. TT II 13, II 90, II 174)—it is also bound by the law of nature, which governs all positive laws (TT II 12). That is, the law-abiding man in society implicitly obeys the law of nature. The latter, moreover, is reason, pure and simple. This is what it means to be free. The free man follows reason, not some untutored passion or superstition. The essence of liberty is reasonable action: the irrational are not free.[35]

Locke asserts this definition of liberty, he does not prove it (though he does criticize Filmer and others for not accepting it; cf. TT II 22, II 57). Law does not (as he elsewhere says it does) abolish or restrain, but rather preserves and enlarges liberty. We should not, he tells us, call something "confinement" which but hedges us in from bogs and precipices (TT II 57). That is, fences should not be called confinement if they are good for us. We should not give a good thing (namely, law) a bad name (e.g., confinement). This, even though Locke states that the laws "confine" (TT II 129). In supporting this definition of law and liberty, Locke argues that not all confinement is bad. One who lacks the understanding to direct his will in accordance with the law of nature, i.e., according to reason, must not be allowed to direct his will at all (TT II 58). This does not do any injustice to the one so directed, i.e., it does not diminish his freedom, for he was never actually free in the first place (TT II 57, II 60, II 62). No one can have a right to what they cannot possibly possess; the irrational have no "right" to liberty.

What support, however, does Locke give for this definition? That is, why should we follow Locke in subsuming liberty under reason? His justification, the reason he actually provides, is that law is needed. "*Where there is no Law, there is no Freedom*" (TT II 57). Rather than showing this syllogistically from the above definition of liberty, however—i.e., rather than reminding his reader that this follows from the nature of law and from the nature of freedom—he proves it to be true because one cannot be free if one is *in practice* subject to the uncontrolled whim of another, backed up by force and violence; law is in practice needed to defend against these things (TT II 57). In this view, a man under the law of nature whenever its enforcement is lacking or imperfect is not free, even though he acts according to the law of nature, i.e., reasonably. Locke's support for the identity of liberty and reason in fact undermines it. We nonetheless accept it, however, because politics requires that children be viewed as born to liberty, if not yet actually free (TT II 57). This principle is not immediately sensible to one who has read the *First Treatise*: there, Locke had mercilessly ridiculed Filmer for suggesting that Adam was created to be king, but had as yet no kingdom at the time of his creation (cf. TT I 18). Rather, we accept this principle because it justifies what is politically necessary. Society cannot function if we do not accept this opinion.

Locke does not, however, bid us to accept this principle generally. Indeed, to accept it generally would be to wholly and openly subordinate what is normally meant by consent to reason. By "my consent," I mean what I actually choose, not what someone else says I should choose; government by the consent of the people loses much of its appeal if their opinions don't really matter.

For the most part, therefore, Locke seems to treat liberty as nothing more than self-direction, ignoring the niceties of how that direction comes into being.[36] Liberty is a matter of the will, not of reason, and is threatened by other human beings, not necessity. Consent is primary, and we presume people to be capable of giving their consent (TT II 59, II 170). No proof of rationality is required, only an absence of evidence of such irrationality that we could not say they had any will to speak of. We accept this so that we might be able to support a form of government less odious than what preceded the birth of liberalism. That is, liberty-as-self-direction is also justified by expediency rather than its intrinsic persuasiveness.

We accept it, moreover, even though the practices of most men are manifestly irrational (TT I 58, II 12); we accept it even though "To turn [a man] loose to an unrestrain'd Liberty, before he has Reason to guide him, is not the allowing him the priviledge of his Nature, to be free; but to thrust him out amongst Brutes, and abandon him to a state as wretched, and as much beneath that of a Man, as theirs" (TT II 63).

This is a problem that Locke's doctrines cannot solve. The unreadiness of the people to revolt can be remedied by something like the *Two Treatises*: men can be made more jealous of their liberties, just as they had become more complacent regarding them. A spirit of freedom can be both fostered and stifled, so its languid state in seventeenth-century England could be reinvigorated. The same success cannot be had in making such an attachment simply reasonable: Locke's project requires that the people become inspired, not enlightened.[37] Knowingly or unknowingly, he reproduces rather than purifies, explains, or reconciles the opinions of common sense. The people in the Lockean commonwealth must exhibit behaviors whose justifications contradict each other. This is of course an entirely reasonable expectation—it is the opposite that is difficult to bring about—but it does require that they remain essentially unconscious of this tension and how it affects the way they live. It may perhaps be for this reason that Locke notes that the people judge whether to revolt more by feeling than by thinking (cf. TT II 94, II 168, II 209, II 224–25, II 230).[38] As I said before, they must engage in noble actions without being led astray by noble thoughts.

Chapter 6

Justifying Secular Politics

There ought to be something questionable about Locke's turning away from authority as the sole focus in a discussion of legitimacy or, to use the language he does, about his mixing natural and political power. For the Bible speaks in terms of authority. "Let every soul be subject unto the higher powers. For there is no power but of God: the powers that be are ordained of God. Whosoever therefore resisteth the power, resisteth the ordinance of God: and they that resist shall receive to themselves damnation" (Rom. 13:1–2). "Submit yourselves to every ordinance of man for the LORD's sake: whether it be to the king, as supreme; or unto governors, as unto them that are sent by him for the punishment of evildoers, and for the praise of them that do well" (1 Pet. 2:13–14).[1]

Robert Filmer's argument relied on the premise that every people has a sovereign and that the only question is to whom their absolute obedience was due. Nor was he outside the mainstream to see this as flowing from patriarchy, even if his was a far more literal interpretation of how political power flows from fathers. As Peter Laslett notes with regard to Locke's argument in §64 of the *First Treatise*, "In denying, as he seems to do here, that the Fifth Commandment has anything to do with political obedience, Locke was repudiating far more than the principles of Filmer. He was attacking a tradition of Christianity, and particularly of Protestant Christianity."[2] Laslett mentions Tyndale's *Obedience of a Christian Man* as an example of what he means, as well as Martin Luther, who said of honoring thy father and thy mother, "In this commandment belongs a further statement regarding all kinds of obedience to persons in authority who have to command and to govern. For all authority flows and is propagated from the authority of parents."[3] Laslett might also have mentioned George Lawson's *Politica Sacra & Civilis*, which attempts to turn the Fifth Commandment toward the ends of government by consent and the rule of law.[4] John Calvin also generalized the Fifth Commandment's prescription to all "those whom the Lord has set over us."[5]

Yet Locke goes beyond saying that there are no interesting facts about politics that in any way derive from the Fifth Commandment (cf. TT I 62–66). He makes a far more radical claim. The whole question of obedience, whatever its model or source, is not nearly as important as his apparent coreligionists thought it was. It is not irrelevant—his speaking of revolution in terms of the dissolution of government and the return of a state of nature betrays its lingering significance on a rhetorical level, at a minimum and perhaps more robustly—but it is not the sole, or even principle, perspective from which politics is to be viewed.

If we were to understate the opposition between prerogative and the rule of law, we might miss how momentous a shift has occurred away from a focus on obedience to authority. Samuel Rutherford, for example, attempted to defuse the vigor that the Bible lends to absolutist arguments by asserting that it is only *lawful* government that makes a man "one of St. *Paul*'s Higher Powers."[6] Locke himself, in his paraphrase on the Epistle to the Romans, asserts that "St. Paul meant here magistrates having and exercising a lawful Power."[7] Yet the commonwealth is *not* constructed so as to be one of these higher powers. At most, we might say that political power is, but even political power is ultimately justified as good for earthly ends, not as a means of knowing to whom obedience to God requires obedience. Jonas Proast discerned how complete was Locke's departure from the accepted ways of speaking about politics and admonished him in these words:

> Now if according to the *Scriptures*, and even to the *judicious Mr.* Hooker, *God* is the Author and *Institutor* of Civil Society in general; then the *Ends* of it, as your self must grant, can be no other than what *He* has appointed: and all that is left to the Choice and Contrivance of Man, is onely the framing and modelling Commonwealths, and the Government of them, as Prudence shall direct, for the better attaining the Ends which He has fix'd and prescribed.[8]

Locke never calls upon Paul's or Peter's letters to support even the obligatory side of the commonwealth's activities: political power is authoritative because of promise-keeping, not respect for authority. When Locke speaks of the "the Magistrates Sword being for a *Terror to Evil Doers*," he poignantly omits that the ruler is "the minister of God to thee" (TT I 92; Rom. 13:3–4).

We can explain the demotion of authority and obedience, and the attendant promotion of the considerations which justify prerogative, by being attentive to the fact that Locke's politics are secular. The arguments that support deviations from the rule of law—e.g., that it cannot reliably protect life, liberty, and estate—would be persuasive no matter the ends for which the commonwealth was established. That the feasibility of lawful government should lie at the center of Locke's political analysis, on the other hand, is supported only by Locke's avowal that the commonwealth exists for no purpose other than the preservation and increase of its members' properties. And this in turn is plausible only if there are no specifically Christian reasons for men to come together into commonwealths, or if Christianity were to supply nothing additional to the causes that impel all men to seek political society, whatever their religion. In order to better comprehend the secularism of Locke's political theory, we turn now to a work that addresses both politics and theology and that was published contemporaneously with the *Two Treatises—Epistola de Tolerantia.*

Locke and Religious Toleration

It is an interesting fact that John Locke, famous advocate of religious toleration and the right of revolution, was not always in favor of either. Both were condemned in what is now known as the *Two Tracts on Government*, written in the years immediately following the restoration of Charles II. His resistance to toleration, if not necessarily to the right of popular resistance itself, was overcome some years later, when he wrote *An Essay on Toleration*. Locke did not publish either of these, even though the *Two Tracts* was polished enough that his friends encouraged him to make it publicly available.[9]

I will not delve into why Locke chose to withhold the *Two Tracts* and the *Essay on Toleration*, or what events or arguments led him to shift his position.[10] Instead, I will focus on the argument that he finally did defend publicly, the one he cleaved to while writing the *Two Treatises of Government*. That argument is contained in his *Epistola de Tolerantia*, translated almost immediately by William Popple as *A Letter Concerning Toleration*.

There are two parallel arguments that Locke makes in the *Letter*. One is political, the other, theological. Why should the magistrate abstain from enforcing his own religious beliefs through the civil law and instead actively punish all those who affirm his right to that forsworn enforcement? Why should churches cease preaching that the magistrate has the right to enforce religious conformity (aside from the persecution by his hands that this claim would entail, were he to accept the political argument)? The sixty-four dollar question is, Does the political argument rely upon the theological one?

This is a different question from whether the political argument is acceptable only given certain theological premises. It may well be that only Christians of a certain type could accept the separation of church and state suggested in the *Letter* (or others influenced by a similar theology). However true or false this may be, however, it does not touch upon whether Locke's account of what a state *is* refers back to religious principles. That is, one may be a Christian and accept a broadly secular account of the purposes of government. It is this possibility that differentiates the two questions.

The separation of church and state requires that the state be able to stand up on its own foundations. It must be able to justify its existence separately from the church's. This is crucial to its freedom from theological superintendence, either at the hands of prelates or of demagogic preachers, and we can see that Locke recognizes this fact. He does not make a Latitudinarian argument in the *Letter Concerning Toleration*; he does not say that we possess an overlapping religious consensus that enables us to live together, and *therefore* there should be something resembling (if only at a distance) a separation of church and state. After all, were this his argument, those who did not lie within this overlapping consensus would have no claim to toleration. Locke does indeed argue that some must be denied religious liberty, but this is not because they fall outside of this overlapping consensus. Rather, they are to be excluded because they represent a threat to political stability. If being beyond the pale from a religious perspective were a sufficient argument against toleration, Locke would have to argue for the persecution of idolatry and animal sacrifice—practices abhorrent to the religious mainstream. Or put another way, whatever overlapping consensus may be said to exist—the definition of who is within and who without—is defined politically, not religiously. The Latitudinarian argument which Locke does *not* make supports instead the sort of toleration advocated by certain fundamentalist groups, i.e., toleration of the inoffensively familiar. It would not support the separation of church and state that the *Letter Concerning Toleration* explicitly advocates.[11]

Jonas Proast, Locke's sometime-perceptive interlocutor regarding the second, third, and fourth letters concerning toleration, argued for the sort of soft governmental support for religion that Locke rejects. As he wrote in *The Argument of the Letter Concerning Toleration Briefly Consider'd and Answer'd*, the penalties that the magistrate may reasonably impose upon heterodoxy

> are not such as may tempt such Persons either to renounce a Religion which they believe to be true, or to profess one which they do not believe to be so; but only such as are apt to put them upon a serious and impartial examination of the Controversy between the Magistrate and them: which is the way for them to come to the knowledge of the Truth. And if, upon such examination of the matter, they chance to find that the Truth does not lie on the Magistrate's side; they have gained thus much however, even by the Magistrate's misapplying his Power, that they know better than they did before, where the Truth does lie.[12]

Locke's subsequent letters explode the suggestion that this is a soft form of nontoleration, but he is unable to decry its justice without reasserting his definition of a commonwealth, a definition which relies upon the perfect separation between politics and religion.

Now, how Locke's refusal of toleration to Catholics and atheists fits into what I have just said is problematic, and I will address this below. One might try to resolve this tension by saying that Locke *does* ultimately rely upon an overlapping religious consensus. My argument here, however, is that such a conclusion would be a criticism of Locke, not an interpretation. However well-founded that criticism may or may not be, it would tell us nothing of his conscious thought, and so would be of no aid in fixing the meaning of ambiguous passages. It certainly would not justify a religious reconstruction of his thought. For Locke, politics has a logic all its own, independent of religious beliefs, and it is that political logic which determines who is, and who is not, to be tolerated.

From the text of the *Letter Concerning Toleration*, it appears that the greatest theoretical hurdle that Locke faces is not the secular account of government. Rather, it is religious principles which argue against accepting that account of government. And, indeed, it is precisely along the theological axis that Locke was compelled to defend his argument in his subsequent letters concerning toleration.[13]

Consider in this regard a certain movement discernable in the *Letter*. It involves Locke's restatements concerning why the magistrate may not become involved in matters of religion for religious motives. Initially, in his definition of a commonwealth, Locke provides three reasons (LCT 67–71 [26–28]). They are all more or less secular, or invoke religion only negatively. First, the care of souls is not committed to the civil magistrate any more than to other men; he has this care neither by God's assignment nor by his subjects'.[14] Second, the power of the magistrate consists solely in compulsion, while one cannot change belief through force. Third, even if this second point were factually incorrect,[15] the magistrate's possessing such a care would make salvation depend upon place of birth, which is so absurd as to be impossible.

Locke returns to why the care of souls is not committed to the civil magistrate when he discusses the latter's duties with regard to toleration. Here the argument proceeds by answering objections. Locke starts off as above, advocating limited government on relatively secular grounds: why should the ruler compel a man to be saved when he does not compel him to be healthy or rich?

From this point on, however, the objections and Locke's responses to them are almost entirely theological in character. If, for example, we reject limited government—if we say that it in fact should care for the complete happiness of the people, health, wealth, salvation, and all—should not the magistrate ensure that everyone walks that one path strait and narrow all the way to Heaven? Locke's response intimates the possibility, and more, that there is more than one such path. But the chief point, and what determines the controversy, Locke argues, is that, since salvation depends upon faith more than practice, I cannot be saved by a religion in which I do not believe; as a result, the whole reason behind persecution is lost—or, at least, the sole publicly embraceable reason (LCT 91–101 [35–38]).

Locke's focus on theological matters builds even more. His response to an objection that his doctrine would require toleration for idolatry is almost entirely an account of the uniqueness of the Israelite political system. Locke boldly affirms that there is no such thing as, no provision in the Gospel for, a Christian commonwealth (LCT 111–21 [42–45]).[16] It is only once this has been established that Locke details the original rise of commonwealths and limits the legislative power to the ends suggested by that origin (LCT 125–29 [47–48]). It is only once he has silenced the progressively louder voice objecting in the name of politics guided by faith that Locke returns to his purely secular account of politics. The flow of the first half of the *Letter* is one of rising opposition to Locke's account, followed by the subduing of that opposition.

In a real sense, then, the theological arguments are something of a sideshow. Upon analysis, after all, all of the arguments that form a part of the argument for why the magistrate should tolerate those religions (and only those) that support toleration are contained in or derive from Locke's first articulation of that principle. Indeed, it is misleading to say that they are contained in the first definitions of a commonwealth and of a church, for they are in fact already complete in the definition of a commonwealth alone. It does not matter what a church is as far as the policy of toleration goes; or, more accurately, what does not matter is whether Locke is correct about the true nature of a church. The policy regarding toleration is to remain the same regardless of any theological arguments that are offered. If the purpose of religion were not simply the salvation of souls, or if a church were actually something more than a corporation for that narrow purpose, the magistrate's duties regarding toleration would not change.

Of course, should the individual find the government abhorrent to his conscience, Locke honestly advises that, well, religion would not be religion if it did not claim to trump other considerations—it may demand that one suffer for one's beliefs. But at the same time, government would not be government if it cared a whit for such conscientious objections or permitted them to stand in the way of its pursuit of worldly, earthly ends (cf. LCT 123–24 [47], 127 [48]; ET 140–41, 143). The truth or falsehood of toleration's being the mark of a true church is irrelevant to the truth of the magistrate's being obligated to tolerate churches that fit within the secular framework of the commonwealth and to persecute those that are incapable of conforming to that framework.

So if Locke's argument begins and ends with secular considerations, one might ask, why does he speak so much about religion? Why was it that he did not simply reproduce the tone of the *Essay on Toleration*, which contains nary a single theological argument and only one allusion to the Bible, and that a throwaway (ET 139)? It is an unmistakable fact that the major shift that occurs between the *Essay on Toleration* and the *Letter Concerning Toleration* (aside from the permissibility of revolution) is the latter's increased regard for religious objections to toleration and an attempt to overcome them.

But note what this shift in fact indicates: Locke summons these religiously motivated reservations in order to overcome them, not because he found toleration to be unsupportable without the theological arguments which he summons in order to overcome these reservations. What Locke in fact attempts to do with his religious discussions is to reform theology to accord with toleration. It remains a fact that not every religion can accept the separation of church and state, but Locke argues that a true understanding of Christian dogma does.

This might seem at first glance to be Christianity's good fortune. There is nothing accidental about this result, however. For, as Locke makes clear, the truth about Christian dogma becomes known when one's understanding of what God demands is guided by the fact that He demands toleration. That is, Locke makes toleration one of those "reality checks" that guide one's interpretation of the Scriptures, like "does my reading of 1 Kings make $\pi = 3$" (cf. LCT 71–73 [27–28], 131 [49], 145–49 [54–56]).[17] This is because reason teaches us toleration, while the words of Scripture do not directly oppose it. This latter result is ensured by the fact that, upon reflection, most passages admit of interpretation. For example, apparently all the suggestions that Israel's idolatry will lead to their dispossession of the land in the same way that the Canaanites were dispossessed do not mean that the latter were punished for their idolatry (cf. LCT 115–21 [44–45]; Lev. 18:3, 24–28). As even Martin Seliger is willing to grant, the "relationship between reason and revelation is not exactly the same as between reason and Scripture."[18]

While Locke does appeal to religious arguments in order to establish that Christianity is silent about politics, he makes no such analogous appeal to Scripture or to the nature of the human soul in establishing the definition of a commonwealth and the nature of the civil goods which it is to protect and foster. This is not the necessary consequence of the religious teaching, as it might otherwise seem. Ignoring for the moment Locke's presentation of it, the Bible can be read to declare not so much the separation of religion and politics as to denigrate politics altogether. It is the farmer, not the shepherd, whose offerings God rejects and who slays his brother. It is Nimrod who founds empires and cities, and his Babel is the seat of impious ambitions. Abraham was born in the city but commanded to leave and lead a nomad's life: his nephew Lot settles in the midst of corruption, i.e., in the city. The desire for a king like all the other nations is a rejection of God. The fact that John Calvin had to defend the dignity of politics against the Anabaptists proves that the Bible does not unequivocally support a secular civil government by failing to establish a religious one.[19]

For Locke, on the other hand, the Bible's necessary neglect of political matters points to an independent dignity of the political sphere. Yet this should not be taken to imply that Locke establishes that dignity by appeal to the Bible, even to its silences. Indeed, almost half of his explicit references to Scripture are concentrated in the first two or three pages (cf. LCT 59–63 [23–24]). Outside of that impressive flurry of pious passage-dropping, he quotes without citing Matthew 18:20 against the necessity of apostolic succession for there to be a church (cf. LCT 73 [29]); he does the same with Isaiah 1:12, denying the possibility that indifferent things might ever be made necessary in divine worship (cf. LCT 105 [40]). The most extended discussion of the Bible involves the uniqueness of Israel's intolerance toward idolatry (cf. LCT 115–21 [44–45]). Crucially, Locke does not support the nonexistence of a Christian commonwealth with any scriptural quotation, reference, or even allusion (cf. LCT 117 [44]). The precariousness of life in this world and the need to sustain it by the acquisition of earthly goods which come only by toil and industry; the widespread dishonesty of men and the need to form society in order to protect the "secure and private possession of the things that are useful for life;" and the limitations that this places upon legislative power—these are all known and arguable without any appeal to Scripture or religious experience (cf. LCT 125–29 [47–48]).[20]

Let us approach the secular character of Locke's arguments from a different perspective. Recall the strange formula that only tolerant churches are to be tolerated. This can easily appear meaninglessly circular, for of whom are tolerant churches tolerant? Other tolerant churches. Intolerant churches, i.e., those outside of this privileged club of mutual toleration, are not to be tolerated; it might seem that every so-called tolerant church is to be intolerant toward so-called intolerant churches. This conclusion is mistaken, however, for no church is ever permitted to be intolerant (LCT 79–91 [30–35]). It is the *magistrate* who is to exhibit the public's hostility toward intolerant churches. The mark of such a church is to claim this prerogative for itself, or to insist that another church's suitability for toleration should depend on something more than political arguments, i.e., that it should depend also upon religious arguments or its own recognition of another church's membership in the closed and internally defined set of "tolerant" churches. So toleration for the tolerant is not circular, nor does it create a club of favored churches in the place of one favored church, for it boils down to toleration for those who accept the separation of church and state.

At this point, it is easy to see why defenders of that separation are oftentimes keen to deny that it is acceptable upon only some religious principles, notably those of Protestant Christianity, or even just those strands which deny that God punishes the community for the sins of its members. If one begins with the premise that religion is the first and most important consideration in a person's life—if one views politics, economics, business, friendships, and the like through the lens of religion and guides them by it—Lockean toleration might appear to be nothing of the sort. Such a policy of toleration might instead appear to be the establishment of a particular theological doctrine. That is, it appears to be the establishment of whatever religious opinions make the separation of church and state acceptable to churches.

Such histrionics, however, miss the point, Locke would argue, or would prefer to concede. It is indeed the establishment of certain opinions, but of *political* opinions, and only an anarchist could object to the enforcement of political decisions. However much it might seem the ossification of the current overlapping consensus of religious opinions, that "consensus" is instead defined politically. In this way, what is doing the work is not really what John Rawls would have called an overlapping consensus at all.[21] I might note that the religious opinions that appear to be publicly favored are *whatever* ones will reconcile the faithful to what the state requires for thoroughly secular reasons. Those who lie beyond the pale by their denying the theological permissibility of secular politics are to be extirpated, not because their religion slanders God, but because it refuses to renounce threats to nonreligious, civil goods. This is no more or less religious than the forbidding of the Communist Party or any successor to it in the United States was partisan.[22]

The judgment that supports the separation of church and state may be energized by a couple of arguments, and in this way Locke does seem to take advantage of an overlapping consensus of sorts. That judgment can be supported by the primacy of civil goods, similar to Machiavelli's "I love my fatherland more than my soul."[23] It can also be supported by a conviction that religion says nothing about politics such that it would contest that primacy.

Rhetorically, there are costs to saying either of these things, the latter making toleration seem less tolerant, the former, impious. Locke defends himself from both charges, not by saying neither but in effect by saying both.

Still, given that the latter religious road to toleration was open, and given the important fact that Locke's contemporaries would not have frowned on the decision to take it—it is our contemporary liberals who scowl and call for more than a bare "mutual toleration among Christians" (cf. LCT 59 [23])—there is less of a rhetorical justification for Locke to present his thoroughly secular reasons for the separation of church and state. This is to say that Locke risks alienating some of his readers by including this argument. We may reasonably conclude from this fact that he was attached to it, in a way that we cannot assert a similar attachment to more conventional arguments.

There are, moreover, crucial passages in which it is clear that the political argument is the more fundamental, the other arguments being deployed for rhetorical effect. This is in addition to the fact that we are left with the same impression from a comparison of the *Letter* with the *Essay on Toleration*.

Consider, for example, the second objection lodged against the magistrate's being unable to forbid certain religious practices on account of their being anathemata. "You will say: What if some church be idolatrous, is that also to be tolerated by the magistrate?" (LCT 111 [42]). Part of Locke's answer is that the power given to the magistrate to suppress an idolatrous church may also be turned against an orthodox one, and thus be used against Christians in the Indies or Calvinists outside of Geneva. One might respond, of course, that this is merely a prudential reason, and not even a very good one: my toleration of the erroneous does not secure me from persecution at their hands (unless their errors be of a certain fortuitous kind). It might further be urged that this self-interested, prudential reason for why those *with* a right to coerce should avoid doing so—namely, to avoid the coercion of those *without* that right—in no way alters who actually possesses that right to coerce (cf. Locke's discussion of what normally happens when the prince and the subject disagree about the former's due limits, LCT 129–31 [49]).

That is, self-interest and the practical and sometimes psychological necessity of giving reasons to alien people may under certain circumstances suggest a policy of toleration: one cannot reasonably expect always to receive what one is unwilling to grant, and the pagans' refusal to tolerate Christian missionaries must somehow be *wrong*. Yet these arguments are not simply sufficient and do not create a right. They are political only insofar as they are matters of policy.

Locke, importantly, supplements these arguments. "Civil power is everywhere the same. . . . The civil power can either change everything in religion according to the prince's pleasure, or it can change nothing" (LCT 113 [42–43]). The definition of civil power in no way depends upon religious beliefs (which may vary across peoples and over time). The all or nothing approach to government interference in religion is justified, as a matter of right, only by this sort of supplement. It is only the rationalist definition of the political that prevents one from saying, "I am orthodox, and for that reason may do things in God's name which the heretical may not." Locke appeals to the interest in avoiding persecution and having an argument by which the condemnable ought either to change their ways or to condemn themselves, however, because it inclines some of his readers to accept this secular account of politics.[24]

Returning to the general impression left by the *Letter Concerning Toleration*, Locke claims that government has no need to establish a religion and no right to do so. Here he directly contradicts what he had written in the *Two Tracts*. The argument that he presents in favor of this conclusion may turn out to be compatible with only some religious views, but it is not based upon them, just like the argument of the *Essay on Toleration*. His argument has Hobbesian overtones. In this he does not depart from his earlier writings on toleration, either the *Two Tracts* or the *Essay on Toleration*. Proast, unable to reconcile a policy of toleration with the promotion of "True Religion," did concede that such a policy "may tend to the Advancement of Trade and Commerce."[25] To the extent that Locke brings in considerations alien to his earlier arguments against toleration or to Hobbes, these are offered to make Christianity safe for the commonwealth. The problem Locke faces is an understanding of Christianity that is at some distance from the secular needs of political life. It is Christianity as understood by his contemporaries, not politics as understood by himself, that must move to bridge this gap.

To see how far Locke must actually move his contemporaries' understanding of Christianity, is useful to turn to Thomas Long's assault on the *Letter*. Locke's assertion that toleration is the mark of a true church, Long discerns, "in truth would unchurch all Christian societies, that have been since the first assembling of them by Christ and his Apostles."[26] Christianity has, from the very beginning, he says, suppressed heretics. We see the gulf that separates Locke's views from Christianity also in Jonas Proast's objections to how Locke responded to his argument: Locke does not see how someone of the true religion is permitted to do things which someone of a false religion may not, just as the righteous may correct the wicked, but not vice versa.[27] Locke makes no legal distinction between true religion and false, which, as Proast sees regarding 1 Peter 2:13, means that he cannot believe that rejecting the true religion could be an instance of doing evil.[28]

This seems like a good place to pause and address the question, For whom was the *Letter Concerning Toleration* written? I mean both its ostensive addressee and its intended audience. As will become clear, the *Letter* was certainly not addressed to Locke's Arminian friend, Philip von Limborch. Locke attributes to his addressee several positions which Limborch did not hold. While he may not have instructed Limborch to publish the *Letter*,[29] it is impossible to account for its structure and content except on the assumption that it was intended to be a public letter, and thus eventually to be published. It was, however, intended as a public *letter*, not as a revised tract or treatise or essay. Locke himself notes that he has not included every argument that might be made but rather those best suited to his addressee (LCT 71 [28], 155 [58]). The epistolary character may also explain the introduction of theological arguments absent from the *Essay on Toleration*.

Much of the *Letter* is a response to objections characteristic of its addressee. Some of the most interesting material is introduced by *dices* ("you will say"), *sed dices* ("but you will say"), or (once) *quaeris* ("you ask"). This facet of the *Letter*'s structure is unfortunately suppressed in William Popple's translation. Frequently, he translated them as "It may indeed be alleged," "But it may be asked," or even (and least forgivably) renders the objection without translating *dices* at all (e.g., LCT 69 [27], 77 [30], 91 [35]). He translates it faithfully, in the second person, only nine times, mostly involving the suppression of dissenting sects (LCT 95 [36], 109 [41], 131 [49], 137 [51] twice, 137 [52] twice, 141 [53], 145 [54]).[30] There are in fact twenty-six places where Locke indicates that he attributes a position to his addressee.

Locke tells us two other things about the person to whom the *Letter* was ostensibly written (including the postscript on heresy and schism). First, the addressee wishes to hear more about Locke's views on mutual toleration among Christians and why this is the mark of a true church.[31] As the positions attributed to him make clear, he is skeptical of this position. Yet he wants to hear arguments about it all the same. The occasion might be one of inquisition or reasonable curiosity; the sequel shows the latter to be the case. We may also deduce from the opening that the *Letter*'s addressee has no idea just how radical Locke's proposal for toleration actually is: he thinks Locke desires only mutual toleration among Christians (LCT 59 [23]), but it turns out that he would have it for idolaters, as well. In fact, this shift is the first thing Proast criticizes about the *Letter*.[32]

The second thing we are told about the addressee apart from the interjections comes at the close of the postscript. Locke notes that a person of his perspicacity can be satisfied with the bare indications[33] of the argument for toleration that Locke has included in the *Letter* (LCT 155 [58]). Reading beyond the printed text is not the same as reading esoterically, but it may include the latter. In any case, Locke assures us that we are justified in reading beyond the text, at the very least by filling in the arguments.

I should note that I do not believe that we can reliably read anything into the fact that the *Letter Concerning Toleration* is, at least in the Latin printing, addressed to T.A.R.P.T.O.L.A. Raymond Klibansky follows Jean Le Clerc's expansion of the initials to *Theologiae Apud Remonstrantes Professorem*

Tyrannidis Osorem Limburgium Amstelodamensem, Professor of Theology at the Remonstrant [Seminary], Hater of Tyranny, Limborch of Amsterdam.[34] It seems that the significance of these initials is too cryptic for it to have been meant for anyone for whom the *Letter* was made public, rather than circulated privately. That is, we cannot identify the addressee with Limborch, even as the *Letter* is technically addressed to him in a way that only he and his friends would understand. (Incidentally, the initials which identify the author of the *Letter*—P.A.P.O.I.L.A.—expand to *Pacis Amico* (or *Amante*) *Persecutionis Osore Ioanne Lockio Anglo*, Friend of Peace, Hater of Persecution, John Locke, an Englishman)

Locke has his addressee explicitly enter the discussion twenty-six times. From these interjections we learn that his reasonable and insightful skeptic believes or can be brought to say the following.

1. The incapacity to produce belief through coercion does not bar the magistrate from attempting to produce it through argument (LCT 69 [27]).
2. A true church requires a bishop or presbytery (LCT 73 [29]).
3. Observance of ecclesiastical laws can be secured only by coercive power (LCT 77 [30]).
4. The commonwealth must have a care for the salvation of souls, even if its judgments in this matter are guided by the church rather than by a fallible magistrate, for there is only one way to Heaven (LCT 91–95 [35–37]).
5. The magistrate may legislate concerning *adiaphora* (which consequently must exist),[35] and among them are the time and place of worship (LCT 103 [39], 107 [41]).
6. Prohibiting the magistrate from outlawing certain religious practices for religious reasons is tantamount to what we would call in First Amendment law "accommodationism," to the point of tolerating child sacrifice and cult orgies (LCT 109 [41–42]).
7. The law of Moses prohibits Christians from tolerating idolaters (LCT 111–15 [42–44]).
8. The practical upshot of Locke's doctrine of toleration is that all disputes between the magistrate's judgment of the public good and the individual's conscience regarding what God demands will be resolved in the former's favor (LCT 127–31 [48–49]).
9. A regard for public peace means that dissenting churches cannot be tolerated (LCT 137–41 [51–53]).
10. Christians are more prone to religiously motivated factions, tumults, and civil wars than Jews and pagans, and so cannot be tolerated as safely (LCT 145 [54]).

It is clear, therefore, that the *Letter Concerning Toleration* was pitched against a relatively conservative position, both religiously and politically, but appeals to the more reasonable or persuadable adherents to that position. It speaks to the respectably traditional more than to the ardently so; to those who sincerely love the established church (or something like it—the addressee does seem anti-Congregationalist), but who also appreciate its good political effects and, when push comes to shove, are more deeply distrustful of schismatics than of other religions; not quite those who would later be satirized as the Vicar of Bray, but not wholly different, either. Locke's interlocutor moves over the course of the *Letter*, the greatest shift occurring with his apparent acceptance that there is no such thing as a Christian commonwealth. No further theological points are raised in the name of the reader once this is established.

The toleration which Locke advances and toward the acceptance of which his addressee is moved has its limits. These limits are highly revealing. In matters of worship, there is no accommodation to be made for religion (LCT 109–11 [40–41]; cf. ET 140–41); what is demanded is only neutrality. Determinations of the secular public good always trump what in the United States is preserved by the Free Exercise clause.[36] In matters of doctrine, on the other hand, any teaching that might threaten the public peace or any individual citizen is likewise not to be tolerated (LCT 127–9 [48]). This leads to Locke's famous withholding of toleration from Catholics and atheists.

Locke's hostility toward Catholics in the *Letter* has been overstated. If Richard Ashcraft is correct that Locke appeals to anti-Catholic prejudices, it is also telling that Locke fails to exclude them by name.[37] Proast does not pick up on the fact that they are debarred.[38] Jeremy Waldron correctly notes that there was, moreover, no need for coyness on Locke's part if he meant Catholicism when he alluded to a church "which is so constituted that all who enter it *ipso facto* pass into the allegiance and service of another prince" (LCT 133 [50]).[39] They are singled out by name for this treatment in the *Essay on Toleration*, for example (ET 146, 151–53). Instead, Locke seems to have explicitly left the door open for precisely the sort of reformation along the *Letter*'s lines which actually did take place within the Roman Catholic Church. (Those who would tie the straitjacket of historical context tightly around men's minds do not, I think, have anything to say to this imaginativeness on Locke's part).

Locke's attack on atheism ought to strike us as incongruous in a slightly different manner. Locke added a paragraph to his *Essay on Toleration* after it was written, noting that atheism is less a purely speculative doctrine than one with practical consequences (ET 137). He did not, however, explicitly draw from this fact the conclusion which he asserts in the *Letter Concerning*

Toleration, namely, that atheists are beyond the pale of toleration. Why does Locke exhibit such hostility toward atheists?

Let us set aside for the moment the explanation that Locke was frothing at the mouth when he described those who deny the existence of a Deity. Being the easiest explanation, it is also the one most likely to obscure alternatives. Nor does it explain everything that is bizarre about Locke's harsh judgment in the *Letter*: this consideration suggests that the easy explanation actually is obscuring a more suitable account.

Beginning with rhetorical considerations, I cannot say that Locke buys himself much sympathy among his readers when he reassures them, Don't worry, religious toleration won't allow atheists to move in next door. After all, religious toleration *does* demand that the government permit idolatry and blood sacrifices to go on next door. Given the hostility toward Santería in the United States, there is some reason to suspect that the latter is at least as offensive to people.[40] It is, at any rate, more public and hence more visible.

This consideration is balanced by the fact, however, that Locke was more vulnerable to an accusation of Hobbesianism or Spinozism than of pagan worship. After all, his political theory in both the *Two Treatises* and the *Letter*, the considerations which move him to such different conclusions in the *Two Tracts* and the *Essay on Toleration*, the mechanistic hedonism that underlies our knowledge if not the existence and content of the law of nature in the *Essay Concerning Human Understanding*—these cannot fail but to remind one of those "justly decried names," as Locke was cornered into calling them. So his support for prohibiting atheism does perhaps serve to reassure his readers in some way.

Nontoleration of atheists reassures his readers—or it might be better to say that it reassured some of his readers—in the same way that modern scholars use it to argue that Locke could not himself have been an atheist. After all, what atheist, one might ask, would suggest a policy under which he would have to justify his absence from any regular church service by his opposition to all forms of *organized* religion, rather than a hostility toward religion simply? J. R. Milton draws an analogous conclusion from Locke's absolutist *Two Tracts*, saying that it shows his religious opinions at that time must still have been "broadly orthodox," for "it is hardly likely that anyone would have advocated a policy requiring the imposition of a religious orthodoxy that he did not himself accept."[41]

The presumption seems to be that the advocacy of every political policy is in one's self-interest, or at least is not disadvantageous to oneself. No one's claims about justice, it is assumed, exclude them from the category of the just. This presumption cannot be sustained when it is remembered that not everyone is free to advocate whatever policy they choose. There is, moreover, very little cost (except to one's pride in one's probity) to supporting an objectionable policy which one could not change by one's opposition. There is not opposition to acknowledging this, and even more than this, when the subject is not religious. Abraham Lincoln declared several times in his first presidential campaign that he had no desire to abolish slavery in the South, a reasonable declaration given that it would have taken a civil war to accomplish what he furtively desired.[42] Even Hobbes declared that an atheist ought to be punished.[43]

This is to say that Locke's statements regarding atheism do not prove anything about his religious commitments, one way or the other. Only if atheism demanded the same sort of public expressions of belief as theism, which it does not, would these statements be the indicators some take them to be. We must approach Locke's meaning here with a sense of agnosticism about his fundamental beliefs.

Let us consider why atheists are not to be tolerated while Canaanites explicitly are. Locke justifies their exclusion on political grounds, i.e., because atheism is a doctrine with practical consequences (LCT 135 [51]). Yet it is not simply widespread atheism that is problematic; that is, the problem is not just that it would be politically irresponsible to proclaim atheism, or that no society can exist where *everyone* denies any sort of God. While government may be justified solely on secular grounds and for secular ends, it turns out—and very problematically for everything Locke has said thus far—that its functioning requires something that it seems secular reason cannot provide, namely, a reason to keep promises.[44]

Jeremy Waldron attempts to reconcile this with the fact that Locke seems to have been perfectly aware that an atheist does indeed have, or at any rate can think that he has, an account of why men should keep their promises.[45] In the *Essay Concerning Human Understanding*, Locke notes that a Hobbesian is true to his word out of fear of the Leviathan (ECHU I.3.5). Waldron suggests, though admits that he must speculate at this point, that the problem lies in the fact that the great Leviathan functions only if men keep their promises, i.e., if they believe in God. Still, as he notes, this would not justify the prosecution of the occasional individual, for the majority who do believe would keep the Leviathan working well enough that he would have his reason to be trustworthy. Nor does this reconstruction of Locke's thought explain why certain polytheists should not also be excluded from toleration: polytropic Odysseus may have been problematic for the Greek gentleman, but it is precisely that sort of difficulty which makes Homer's gods ill-suited to certain styles of politics.[46] In the end, Waldron intimates, it seems that the atheist is somehow to be converted by the threat of sanctions (but cf. LCT 69 [27]; ET 155–56).

However problematic this resolution may be, it fails to account for something else that Locke says in the very same breath of the *Essay Concerning*

Human Understanding as his remark about the Hobbesian's promise-keeping. It turns out that, in Locke's mind, the pagan philosophers did indeed have a reason for keeping their word that did not rely upon the idea of a god. It instead relied upon the goodness of virtue for its own sake, rewarded externally or not. Attentiveness to this statement might lead us to expect Locke to restrict himself in the *Letter Concerning Toleration* to saying that an atheist cannot be trusted or relied upon to keep his promises, as distinguished from it being unreasonable that an atheist should think himself bound to do so. The former phrasing would leave the door open to there being a valid, if aristocratically subtle, reason to be true to one's word. This expectation is not met.

Instead, Locke says in his condemnation of atheists that the taking away of God, even only in thought, dissolves all (LCT 135 [51]). This sounds very much like a statement that, absent the fear of a legislating and retributing power, everything is permitted, nothing forbidden (cf. RC 245). That is, from this it appears that the problem is not that atheists actually are unreliable subjects, but rather that they ought not be reliable subjects. An honest atheist is confused, or rather an atheist who is honest out of more than just policy is confused. Locke's argument against tolerating atheists seems to be that Carneades was right about justice![47] But if this is what Locke was thinking, then idolaters should not be tolerated, either, since from a Christian perspective, *their* gods certainly will not punish them for breaking their vows, while the God who might do so is not going to refrain from punishing them anyway—so they too *should* not feel bound by their oaths. But wait, is not a clear-sighted atheist as nonexistent as an atheist claims God is, if we take Locke's statements about natural theology seriously (cf. RC 238)? How can he be worried about clear-sighted atheists?

Some scholars have speculated that Locke demands religious toleration out of a concern for epistemological fallibility: since we cannot know which god is the true one, or how it demands to be worshipped, we cannot impose one faith on all by political power; since we know that atheism is incorrect, however, it may be suppressed. This is urged by Greg Forster, for example.[48] Yet we can know with the same certainty that polytheism is wrong, at least if we can accept that the wise among the pagans discovered the one god when they sought him (cf. RC 238).

More problematic, however, is that this is not the argument which Locke makes. It seems, on this reading, that the real arguments for the conclusions of the *Letter Concerning Toleration* are contained in the *Essay Concerning Human Understanding* and the *Reasonableness of Christianity*; they would not even be hinted at in the *Letter* itself. This is about as plausible as Alex Tuckness's thesis that Locke's political views are best discovered in the *Third Letter For Toleration*, evidence from the *Two Treatises* contrary to his reading notwithstanding.[49] Atheism in the *Letter* does pose some difficulties for the Straussian interpretation of Locke, but this is no excuse for ignoring the greater, even insurmountable problems with the alternatives, nor for engaging in flights of fancy when it comes to explaining what Locke wrote.

What, then, are we left with? The argument against toleration for atheism falls apart on the basis of arguments which Locke had already written down in the *Essay Concerning Human Understanding* and did not change before publishing it (or in any subsequent edition). It is not an issue in Locke's short essay on atheism.[50] It also contradicts the independence and self-sufficiency of politics from theology, an independence which forms the basis of toleration throughout the *Letter*. These are facts, and the only question for us concerns their significance.

Extending toleration to idolaters proved necessary in order to delegitimate bad arguments that some religious practices are simply beyond the pale of tolerability. There is no similar rhetorical payoff for tolerating atheists, and not solely because they have no rituals as such. Only a particular sort of Christian will be persuaded to accept Locke's theological reforms or to cease (for all practical purposes) from viewing politics as a part of God's law for human beings, namely, the sort zealots often decry as lukewarm Christians; one who would move them, however, must be circumspect in how he presents himself, both his foundations and his goal. The principle of toleration is not limited to the inoffensively familiar, but what rhetoric can accomplish, or could have accomplished in Locke's situation, probably is. Locke had to be artful in his acknowledgment that the separation of church and state, effectually if not in principle, elevates the latter over the former (cf. LCT 127–31 [48–49]): the further from religious skepticism the advocate of such a thing appears, the better. And who knows what will be possible once those respectable, traditional, conservative, family-oriented pagans are less foreign? They should, at any rate, be more comprehensible to the religious mainstream than a clear-sighted atheist. As far as sympathy for those poor atheists goes, they can be trusted to get along on their own, whether such measures are required indefinitely or simply in the meantime. It is quite plausible, if not certain, that these thoughts were in Locke's mind, as well.

I will close this discussion of the *Letter Concerning Toleration* by noting a peculiar feature which is obscured in Popple's translation because of his manner of handling *dices* and *quaeris*. It may be important or unimportant depending on how much you make of such things. It involves the central item of a series, and not much of my argument will be lost if those who are impatient with that sort of analysis skip to the next section.

The one place where Locke indicates his addressee's participation with "You ask" rather than "You will say," even though several of the addressee's statements have actually been questions, happens also to be the most important question in the *Two Treatises of Government.*

> You ask: What if the magistrate believes that what he commands [contrary to the conscience of the private person] lies within his power and is of benefit to the commonwealth, but his subjects believe the contrary? Who shall be judge between them? I answer: God alone; for there is no judge upon earth between the legislator and the people. (LCT 129 [49]; cf. TT II 21, II 168, II 241)

This is, incidentally, the central of a series of five statements attributed to the addressee.

There are twenty-six occasions in which Locke indicates that he attributes a position to his addressee. There is, however, also one occasion—and to the best of my knowledge, after repeated searches, only one occasion—in which Locke raises and answers an objection against toleration without prefacing it with "you will say" or "you ask." Ironically, Popple turns it into an indicated interjection: he translates, "But (some will say) let men at least profess that they believe" (cf. LCT 121 [46]). Locke's response, without the indication of an "I respond," is that no magistrate who demanded this understands salvation, for he would have the dissenter lie to both God and man for the sake of his soul. There are thirteen indicated interjections on the one side of this, and thirteen on the other.[51]

The demand that is made here without being attributed to the addressee—that if belief does not lie within the scope of our will, then let a man at least *profess* that he believes the orthodoxy—is infinitely objectionable only to someone who believes that professions of faith bear upon one's eternal misery or felicity. That is, the central of the twenty-seven statements in the *Letter Concerning Toleration* that are not in the author's voice just happens to be what an atheist would take from its teaching regarding the toleration of atheism. I believe that this is Locke's advice to atheists reading the *Letter* under circumstances similar to his own, and that what is debatable is whether chance or intention is responsible for its placement in the center of a series.

Justifying the Commonwealth

As I indicated at the close of chapter 4, the Lockean commonwealth cannot be explained by his sincere desire for peace: timidity, if thought through, counsels submission, not revolution. The man who took peace as a moral imperative, with ever increasing consistency, was Hobbes, not Locke. He might have objected that Locke did not succeed in purging all vestiges of vainglory from his opinions. Be that as it may, Locke does not reveal to us the ultimate ground for his political prescriptions. I do not mean simply the question of why Locke's politics are secular, but why, given secularism, *these* are the politics that he recommends.

But, we might ask, is it not the state of nature? True, we could say, Locke may have written his account of it such that it revealed the world he wanted it to, but can we not see that world? That is, doesn't he justify his politics on a sort of realism, on an understanding of how nature really is? If this is the case, then we might not be at a total loss as to why he advocated a particular form of politics. The Lockean commonwealth would stand or fall with his account of the world. So, for example, prerogative is hardly justifiable if there is no flux. If law can actually govern human beings perfectly, then there is no need for extralegal action. If Locke had cleaved to the theology attributed to him by Carl Schmitt, he would have written a very different book.

It is one thing, however, to describe reality; it is quite another to say what the proper reaction to that reality is. An awareness of imminent mortality can lead to both Bacchanalias and valetudinarianism. Locke, moreover, was by no means the only person to have seen the world as he did. As I mentioned in chapter 3, his objection to the rule of law (namely, flux) differs from Aristotle's, but the latter was by no means ignorant of that facet of life. Nor can it be said that the latter just failed to understand the place of force in the world.[52] And yet who could be more different in his reaction to the world than Locke is from Aristotle? It is Locke's reasons for the propriety of his reaction that are absent from the *Two Treatises*. We can, however, say something about his view of the world. We are able to detect what he was reacting to. Locke certainly cannot be mistaken for an optimist.

In attacking Filmer, Locke had questioned his use of the phrase "*By the Appointment of God*": "I wish he had told us here what he meant *by God's Appointment*. For whatsoever Providence orders, or the Law of Nature directs, or positive Revelation declares, may be said to be *by God's Appointment*" (TT I 16). This division of "*God's Appointment*" into Providence, the law of nature, and positive Revelation is Locke's, not Filmer's. "*God's Appointment*" may be what He has caused (Providence), the dictates of reason (the law of nature), what He has commanded (positive Revelation), or some mixture of these.

Yet while the law of nature "obliges every one" (TT II 6), and divine commandment should certainly be heeded, Providence is of absolutely no moral worth whatsoever. It is only what God has caused to happen and may not be good for the individual or the community. "If any one will say, that what happens in Providence to be preserved, God is careful to preserve as a thing therefore to be esteemed by Men as necessary or useful, 'tis a peculiar Propriety of Speech, which every one will not think fit to imitate" (TT I

147). For example, God brought about the subjection of Edom to Israel, or foretold that He would do so, but that does not constitute any "declaration of the Right of Inheritance to Dominion" on Israel's part (TT I 118; cf. TT I 48). He brought it about that women "should ordinarily" be subject to their husbands, but they need not submit to this any more than to the pangs of labor, should they be able to avoid either (TT I 47). Providence simply does not oblige. One is not immoral for opposing it, as these examples show.

Now this facet of Locke's argument certainly has repercussions for what he means by the law of nature. It does not sit well with the so-called Workmanship argument's being a good foundation of that law, for example (cf. II 6).[53] Yet we should not allow this to blind us to how Locke has redefined Providence. After all, Roger Williams did not mean for the name of his New England settlement to be a synonym for Fortune, or worse. He instead called it Providence because he saw the hand of a *beneficent* God at work, whereas Locke's Providence is not even so much the handiwork of a merely omnipotent God as it is at best a misleading indicator of God's will, assuming that God is just.[54]

Thomas Pangle has rightly identified *food* as the core of Providence's delinquency.[55] A part of his point is that Locke suggests that the Christian God also evinces through His commandments an outright hostility toward man. The law of nature permits one to hunt deer for food (cf. TT II 30), and it is an "Eternal Rule to all Men" (TT II 135). Yet Locke had earlier argued that God did not grant man permission to eat meat until the time of Noah (TT I 39), and the law of nature was certainly operative before the deluge (cf. TT II 11, II 57). God prefers the shepherd to the farmer, meaning that human labor can in no way be the source of our nourishment, which in turn requires a bounty of readily gatherable foodstuffs.

And it is regarding this crucial fact, which alone can rescue the beneficence of a God who commands these things, that Locke equivocates: "*God has given us all things richly*," he says, quoting Paul's First Letter to Timothy, and there is a "plenty of natural provisions" (TT II 31); man found that God had given him "more than he knew what to do with" (TT II 34). Yet the reason why man began to toil in the fields rather than simply gather acorns and other fruits of the earth was "the penury of his Condition" (TT II 32); "Nature and the Earth furnished only the almost worthless Materials" (TT II 43).

In fact, we can take the bare existence of farms as sufficient proof that what God has provided for through his Providence is instead the punishment of Adam: "cursed is the ground for thy sake; in sorrow shalt thou eat of it all the days of thy life; thorns also and thistles shall it bring forth to thee; and thou shalt eat the herb of the field; in the sweat of thy face shalt thou eat bread" (Gen. 3:17–19). Locke says that it is *human* labor that accounts for nine tenths of the value any item has to a human being (TT II 37, II 40). And then humanity gives itself ninety-nine percent of its commodities, only one percent coming from nature (TT II 40). And then nature in its generosity provides less than a penny on the dollar, one thousandth of what we can call our own (TT II 43). "And a King of a large and fruitful Territory there [in America], feeds, lodges, and is clad worse than a day Labourer in *England*" (TT II 41).

If the ground surrendered its cornucopia willingly, we could say that the law of nature was indeed a law of peace. One could acquire a private title to goods appropriated from the common storehouse of nature by mixing one's labor with them, for there would be enough and as good left for another (cf. TT II 27, II 33). After all, anyone who contested your ownership of something that they could just as easily acquire by doing the exact same thing as you did must wish you some unreasonable ill. Perhaps they want it just for the pleasure of taking it from you. Alternatively, they may be simply too lazy or too averse to manual labor to follow in your industrious footsteps. If that is the case, then their purpose may not be the heady rush of dominion over a conscious life, but they do see nothing wrong with treating you as their slave, bending your labor to their advantage without your consent. And as you cannot but be expected to resist this, you are justified in treating anyone who would do this as, well, not the sort person who thinks through the consequences of their actions. They may be punished as any wild beast.

The problem arises when the ground's cornucopia must be wrested from its miserly grip. The permission to appropriate from the common stores does not depend on leaving enough and as good for another, only the exclusive title to what one has taken. The right of appropriation instead comes from our desires. As Locke retells the story of Genesis in the *First Treatise* (TT I 86), God made man and planted in him a strong desire for preservation, just as he had done with the other animals. He also provided the means to that preservation. This is because God did not intend for man to perish. Therefore, Locke continues, God spoke to man: "Be fruitful and multiply, and replenish the earth, and subdue it: and have dominion over the fish of the sea, and over the fowl of the air, and over every living thing that moveth upon the earth. . . . Behold, I have given you every herb bearing seed, which is upon the face of the earth, and every tree, in the which is the fruit of a tree yielding seed; to you it shall be for meat" (Gen. 1:28–29). Locke is resistant to these words having been literally spoken, however, preferring them to have instead been immediately understood by man in a Hobbesian manner. Whereas animals understand this divine grant to eat food by their sense and instinct, Locke says in this same passage, humans do so by their sense and reason.

> For the desire, strong desire of Preserving his Life and Being having been Planted in him, as a Principle of Action by God himself, Reason, *which was the Voice of God in him*, could not but teach him and assure him, that pursuing that natural Inclination he had to preserve his Being, he followed the Will of his Maker. (TT I 86)

Two sections later, Locke calls this "the first and strongest desire" implanted in man (TT I 88). Because man must eat, because his desire is for his own preservation, we know he must have a right to eat, and a right that he can act upon: the voice of reason tells man that all the world is his to enjoy before he ever finds confirmation for this in Paul's First Letter to Timothy (cf. TT II 31, 1 Tim. 6:17).

Yet respecting another's appropriation does not make sense when one's own preservation *does* come into competition (cf. TT II 6). This is not to say that there is no law of nature in the state of nature. Nothing like the medieval natural law can be said to exist there, of course, but what Locke has redefined to be the law of nature does exist even when nature is a barren waste. The problem, however, is that rights under that law must be said to conflict, or to impose no corresponding duty on another. This is not the sole source of the state of nature's being, for almost all intents and purposes, a state of war—there is also the depravity of some human beings to be accounted for—but it does deflate the rationalist pretension that all strife is the result of unreasonable, and thus unenlightened, claims of right.[56]

Everywhere Locke sees that the stronger carries the day, whether it be with justice or without, and the good man can find no support or succor except in his own arms and those of his confederates. Nature is similarly content to let the righteous starve, freeze, or be eaten along with the wicked. Irrational man-shaped beasts make war upon their neighbors for imagined slights and the thrill of dominion, convinced of their rationality and justice. Those willing to work for their own survival and allow others to do the same, moreover, would not even be able to carve out a separate peace for themselves had they not rejected Providence as a guide regarding right.

Given the dolorous vision of man's place in the world I have just extracted from the *Two Treatises*, it bears noting how radically Carl Schmitt misinterpreted Locke. He mistook the inanities of a certain strand of thought in the nineteenth and twentieth centuries to be indicative of an entire tradition and everyone within it. This seems to have been a consequence of his belief that, "All significant concepts of the modern theory of the state are secularized theological concepts," and that the belief that lay at the root of liberalism was deism:

> This theology and metaphysics rejected not only the transgression of the laws of nature through an exception brought about by direct intervention, as is found in the idea of a miracle, but also the sovereign's direct intervention in a valid legal order. The rationalism of the Enlightenment rejected the exception in every form.[57]

Locke was for him in turn the "father of the liberal *Rechtsstaat*."[58] Schmitt overlooked entirely the experience of a rational man within an *irrational* world that lies at the root of Locke's political doctrine and that makes preservation, comfort, and a stability *willed* onto an unwilling world the primary and definitive purpose of politics.

Schmitt's conceptual categories are in fact a hindrance to the analysis of Locke's thought. To Schmitt, liberalism is the attempt to neutralize and depoliticize the political, i.e., the fundamental division of human beings into friend and enemy, an attempt which he saw as necessary for any form of individualism.[59] Yet turning to Locke, the core of a commonwealth is the decision to break from the rest of mankind, i.e., to *invent* what Schmitt says is the essence of the political precisely in order to serve liberal ends.[60]

It is because Schmitt had in his mind what liberalism must be that he could not see Locke's liberalism for what it was. His Locke set down the principles of right as the sole consideration of any significance in his system, alongside a corresponding and equally foundational belief in the utter inconsequentiality of the bare facts regarding actual force.[61] This Locke was compelled, against himself, to admit a place for a concern with exigent circumstances; it is no surprise that Schmitt agrees with those interpreters who argue that prerogative is authoritatively reviewed by the legislature. As though Locke had not written one word about revolution, Schmitt wryly observes that, regarding prerogative, "it seems Locke did not see a problem of particular political importance."[62] For Schmitt Locke's dilemma reaches its breaking point with the federative power, i.e., in the commonwealth's contact with the Other, the Stranger, relations with which must be left entirely beyond law. At last, Locke is brought back around to the futility of his endeavor: "The responsibility of doing whatever is demanded under the circumstances for the [public] interest, combined with corresponding powers to represent the state's authority, is certainly the characteristic content of a *commissio*."[63]

Locke's defense is not simply that he in fact understood what Schmitt says he did not and could not have (a point to which I shall return shortly). It is not that he knew the bare facts of actual force to be of supreme importance. Rather, it is that, seeing these things, he is not at all led back to the *commissio*: the prince who bases his actions on prerogative rather than law does not represent the state's authority. Indeed, Schmitt's state does not exist for

Locke: there is nothing that "is in the decisive case the ultimate authority" or "possesses the monopoly on politics."[64] Schmitt's error regarding Locke goes beyond a matter of historiography; rather his conceptual categories cannot even explain Locke once the historiographical error is corrected.

Schmitt was unable to come to terms with Locke because he saw in liberalism the subterranean triumph of deism. It might perhaps have been that Schmitt could not imagine that a political theory that did not demand of men that they give themselves wholly over to the community could not also conceive of the world as a battleground: individualism made sense to him only as the rejection of the necessity for committed conflict. The relation between flux and religion that I explored in chapter 3, the hostility of Providence described above—these were irreconcilable with limited government of any sort, in his mind. This is not to say that there is no quasi-theological manifestation of Locke's moral hopes hiding in the back of his secular politics, only that it is not deism.

Political society comes into being because of the effectual rule of force. That there are unjust men who would violate the law of nature, which is to say irrational men who would violate the law of reason, makes necessary the natural power of each individual to execute that law. This is not, however, a solution to the problem of injustice in the state of nature. Each man has the power to execute the law of nature, but in attempting to do so men often do the exact opposite: they violate it (TT II 13, II 124–6). It is the frequently unjust exercise of natural executive power that makes the state of nature unendurable. The only "government" that may be said to exist there is that of natural executive power; when this is misused, it becomes the "government" of unjust force (cf. TT II 6, II 38). Such a government, either through wickedness or misapplication of the law of nature, is indistinguishable from the rule of injustice. The just rule of force (i.e., force ruling according to justice), on the other hand, requires the impartiality of political society.

Political society must be more than simply impartial, however. A tyrant can after all have a simple rule for all of his subject-slaves, treating each equally as his property, but this is not political society (TT II 93). Rather, it must also be the sort of thing to which a rational creature could freely give his consent, and this requires that it be ruled by law.

Yet because the world is in a state of constant flux, the rule of law is insufficient. If man would have the benefits of political society, he must permit the legitimacy of prerogative. In order to have justice, he must risk injustice; peace, war; society, anarchy. Just when it seems that there is an alternative to rule according to will, human nature reenters the scene to render arbitrary power necessary.

The world is not outright hostile to man, however: it is not friendly, but neither is it simply an enemy. After all, were it simply hostile, man's prospects would be less than bleak. A hostile world would *inexorably* oppose all his designs, and only some other-worldly power could rescue him from starvation, beasts of prey, or even spontaneous combustion. Compared with the possibilities, the world appears blessedly indifferent to his well-being. It provides, if unintentionally, the tools and materials which allow humanity to rectify its failures in almost every other respect: nature is no more an enemy than is the wheat that falls before man's scythe. Relief is possible in this world, so long as one learns to work within this world. The ground can be rendered provident rather than stingy by subduing it. Political society, moreover, can largely render life endurable: it can stand tall before the might of injustice, provide an arena in which the reformation of nature can bear real fruit, and deal with the world's unpredictability. So long as we are willing "to conquer and to bind nature," as Francis Bacon put it,[65] we can render possible those conditions in which reasonable people can live together, needing to worry only about the unreasonable. Men must change the way they live together, though, adopting and accepting rules for the development of property under *positive* law, if this great project "for the relief and benefit of man's condition"[66] is to take place. In Locke's formulation, "The great and *chief end* therefore, of Mens uniting into Commonwealths, and putting themselves under Government, *is the Preservation of their Property*" (TT II 124).[67]

Since all of this requires working within the world, however, these problems cannot ever be totally overcome. Those entrusted with the force of the community may abuse that trust. Crops can fail for reasons that are apparent only after the famine has begun. But the best way to deal with nature can in principle be determined. Locke believes that he has determined it. His solution is premised upon a total overthrow of the reigning political doctrines. The people must be emboldened such that they actually demand the Lockean commonwealth: only the latter can really protect them against a world so detrimental to their survival. They must be so emboldened, in fact, that they risk that very survival. They will accept rulers, for self-rule is the essence of the state of nature, but they themselves will be the judge of them. They will maintain the balance between prerogative and legislative supremacy.

The commonwealth is supported, in the end, by nothing other than the threat of popular violence. It is the latter that keeps officials in line, passing and enforcing only those laws consistent with legislative power. When, however, the rule of law eventual fails, society's only recourse lies in extralegality, and popular resistance is the only check against its misuse. Everything hinges on the credible threat of revolution. The people must by some means or another never forget the Lockean doctrine, equivocations and all.

This is of course not the most that one could hope for; greater hopes are in effect demands that the world be an impossibly different place, in Locke's view.[68] Accordingly, he would argue that this is the most that one could rationally hope for. The ideal order may rest on a delicate balance between law and flexibility, obligation and prudence, the phlegmatic and the choleric, but the ideal balance can be determined. Once brought about, there is nothing wrong with such an order, Locke argues. This is an order that need never be abandoned. Revolution is needed to sustain it, not to introduce a better one. The problem of justice is soluble. Thus, the political problem itself is soluble, even if its actualization requires some legerdemain with the logic. Man is not simply a hostage of chance.

Conclusion

The *Two Treatises of Government* was written and published in order to change England; Locke's purpose was to make it more like the Lockean commonwealth I have described in this book. The *Treatises* was not conceived of as a means to win votes for this or that policy in Parliament but rather as what we would recognize as propagandistic political theory. Locke's ambition was to legislate for England just as assuredly as Homer had laid down the law to ancient Greece, i.e., by influencing and even molding how men saw themselves and their relation to the world around them.

Some scholars might perhaps object that no one could have had so encompassing an ambition, but the plain and declared existence of such men suggests more that it is they who lack similar ambitions, not mankind the capacity for such audacity. Perhaps it might be urged in the place of this objection that such a grand design would require so inflated a sense of importance as to verge on the megalomaniacal, but the fact that some men have indeed exercised such an influence on the world shows that we cannot pooh-pooh Locke for this reason either.

Now given the fact that the Lockean commonwealth has very little if anything to say about our big-versus-small government debates—it is "limited government" to the extent that formal politics is no longer to be the architectonic art—there is some question about Locke's relation to rights-based liberalism. There is even some suggestion that Locke might be more "republican" in his outlook. I may perhaps have added fuel to the latter contention's furnace by my radical portrayal of the Lockean commonwealth.

It would certainly be unfair to say that Locke is opposed to "politics" per se, in the way that Carl Schmitt saw liberalism to be an attempt to do away with the political altogether. Locke would no doubt look upon the fact that most of us are citizens but once every four years when we vote for president, and many not even that much, with some alarm; the ignorance and herdlike willingness to be led wherever the most polished piper marches that characterizes public opinion could hardly be what Locke desired from the Baconian conquest of nature. Schmitt saw the depoliticization of life go hand in hand with the "liberal" insistence upon legalism, and as Locke was a critic of the latter, it should not surprise us that he would have been no close friend of the former.

Yet for however much the Lockean commonwealth demands more political participation and engagement than we have exhibited, even of the informal variety; for however much it must occasionally call upon genuine civic virtue; it would be wrong to see in it a meaningful civic republicanism. After all, these things are needed for the defense of decidedly liberal principles. There is no warm communitarian underbelly to the Lockean commonwealth. The extent of our partnership in a coercive system, or at least our joint interest in overseeing that system, is not set by any inclination we might have to joint participation in anything. We do, it is true, have social instincts according to Locke, a "love . . . of Society" (TT II 101), but it is only the satisfaction of our material, private needs that is of concern to the government. It is only the character of our private needs, and not whatever might be implied by our being by nature political animals, that is of concern to politics.

And here we have a bit of a problem. For what is to be defended is an essentially bourgeois way of life, an essentially bourgeois economic project. Yet the civic way of life—ministerial and hence subordinate to the former—that the Lockean commonwealth relies upon also demands an active, engaged populous willing to transcend its private concerns. Locke seems a bit divorced from reality when he implies that a day laborer will have to judge whether James II's suspension of the religious penal laws was as justified as the seemingly similar suspension by Charles II.

If Locke really does intend his revolution to sink down into the common consciousness of every Englishman, then we must certainly wonder at his sobriety. Of course, a revolution accomplished by means of propaganda is almost by necessity limited in its scope to those who have the leisure for reading and engagement in politically interesting activities. Any influence that is to be hoped for beyond this group must be mediated by popularizers and sermonizers of various stripes. This is never a pristine form of communication. This raises the very serious question of how successful such a revolution can be.

Locke's plan for the reformation of England and English principles requires more than the engagement of the people politically. They must be engaged in support of the Lockean commonwealth. They must be engaged for the sake of religious toleration, which means that they must support a government that does not care what you think religiously, which is almost by definition a secular government. So, for example, it is not enough for the people to glean from the popularizers of Locke's doctrine a kind of latitudinarian support for religious toleration of the inoffensively familiar, the same latitudinarianism to which Locke forcefully refrained from appealing in the *Letter Concerning Toleration*. They cannot be inclined to interpret the law in light of necessity rather than declare an act illegal but justified. They must think their principles worth killing for when they are, and at all other times think it better to avoid a quarrel.

I think that the largest hurdle that Locke faces in the revolution by rhetoric which he attempts results from a decision he made. He wanted discretionary acts to be so susceptible to public scrutiny that he permitted very little government action to have obligatory force: the definition of what counts as a law is very narrow for Locke, excluding the sorts of standards or balancing tests that characterize so much of Anglo-American jurisprudence. As a result, there is a radical disjuncture between ordinary and extraordinary politics in the Lockean commonwealth. It may be difficult—recent trends in the United States might even suggest that it is impossible, over the long term—to reconcile the common people to secular government, but we can at least identify the sort of people that such a project endeavors to bring about. Yet the fact that Locke so violently wrenches acts of prerogative from the sphere of ordinary, legal politics, the fact that there really are two separate modes of governance, means that the people must almost have multiple personalities, as well. This problem is not that the sort of citizen that Locke would have you be is difficult to bring about, but that he would have you in fact exhibit two different species of citizenship, or be both subject and citizen in their turn.

Put another way, Locke both does and does not want to celebrate bourgeois morality. The Lockean commonwealth certainly inclines one toward a way of life that Rousseau would later criticize as bourgeois, that Tocqueville was to call democratic, and that we are now in the habit of referring to as mass society. Yet it cannot survive if its members do not possess something powerful within them that may well be irreconcilable with that way of life. The resolution cannot lie in some class of rational or enviably educated individuals who, calling themselves aristocrats or elites, will do yeoman's service to their middle-class masters; if anything, the product of *Some Thoughts Concerning Education* will be a decent, defanged milksop of a gentleman, of no danger to the commonwealth's constitutional order, and so also of restricted utility.[1]

My concern is in a sense Tocquevillean: the laws in the United States functioned well because of the *mœurs* of the American citizens, but those same *mœurs* were in some tension with the social and economic conditions that must prevail in a democracy. We were living on borrowed time. Tocqueville sought to make the French better by making them jealous of the Americans, praising us for the virtues we ought to have had; which is to say, for virtues which we did not actually possess. The Lockean commonwealth requires something like Tocqueville's nineteenth-century Americans, a fictional people who even in fantasy had bleak prospects for sustaining themselves.

I am not suggesting that such a thing is impossible, only that it is exceedingly unlikely. I do, however, suspect that such a society would be incredibly unstable. After all, the people are not enlightened to this way of life as superior—or these ways of life as superior, each in its turn—but are rather inspired. Locke does not have a satisfying account for the truth of what he encourages. So even if he were able to instill the sort of mood he desires, another philosopher or theorist or scribbler could come along, armed with nothing more than a more powerful rhetoric, and alter that political mood. Locke does not stand at the beginning of the modern project to remake politics with popularized "philosophy," but he also could not stand at the end of that project.

In any case, what does it mean for Locke to encourage men—even if in practice only well-situated men—to be more active in politics, or (more properly) to have more confidence in their own right to influence politics or to make political judgments without deferring to miter or crown?

What I have argued is that this comes down, in the end, to accepting Locke's definition of politics. This is to say, Locke encourages men to have a regard for a secular understanding of politics, or politics as we now understand it, i.e., as a sphere distinct from religion. Of course, since religion is a part of society, the separation of political theory from theology entails the separation of state and society. Locke may not have sired this distinction, but he embraced it like an adoptive father. What Locke does in publishing the *Two Treatises* is to get men to understand by the word *politics* what we understand by that word. Locke's reorientation so that men draw their claim to formal, recognized political power from the right of the people translates to secular government because the right of the "people" is itself secular. That right involves the defense of their this-worldly properties, and government exists for the preservation and increase of no other kind of good.

Locke's emphasis on privately held secular goods in politics could not but add importance to the question of legalism, which is why its ambivalent nature is so great a theme in the *Two Treatises*. If I may make one final jab at Robert Ferguson and the other pamphleteers of Locke's day, they were not compelled to confront the adequacy of government by mechanistic application of the law because they did not have any grand vision of politics, even if their immediate political goals should have required them to think more deeply about why their propaganda ought to be convincing. It was Locke who did this, and for this reason he is of enduring philosophic interest. The answers he came to by serious consideration of the political things compelled him to address the problem of legalism.

Quirks of biography and history are responsible for the *Two Treatises of Government*, but those *Treatises* are nevertheless of enduring interest to us. Biography and history conspired to make John Locke a philosopher, conspired to make the *Two Treatises* the political work of a philosopher. And in the end, it is this last fact that is the reason that we continue to read it with more than antiquarian interest. We may have adopted a different solution to the problem of legalism—we allow for far more discretion under the law than Locke does in order to reduce the disjuncture between ordinary and extraordinary politics, and have settled upon checks and balances as the preferred means of rendering that increased discretion safe[2]—but that problem is just as central in our democratic republic as it is in the Lockean commonwealth. For ours is a modified form of that commonwealth.

Notes

Introduction

1. See Peter Laslett, "The Gentry of Kent in 1640," *Cambridge Historical Journal* 9, no. 2 (1948): 148–64, esp. 159–60.

2. See Peter Laslett's introduction to *Two Treatises of Government*, by John Locke, ed. Peter Laslett, student ed. (1960; repr. Cambridge: Cambridge University Press, 1988), 37–38.

3. This is especially extreme as Peter Laslett's work suggests that Locke actually left a draft of the *Two Treatises* with Tyrell under the cover name *De Morbo Gallico* (though Laslett proposes that Tyrell did not know what he possessed) and that Locke at the very least told him that he was the author between August 1691 and August 1692. Locke's ire might be understandable, as Tyrell would therefore be betraying an intimate secret rather than just pushing a friend to admit what most intelligent people apparently already knew or suspected, but we might wonder at the proportion between Locke's response and Tyrell's crime; cf. Laslett's discussion of "*De Morbo Gallico*" in Introduction to *Two Treatises of Government*, 62–64; Richard Cox, *Locke on War and Peace* (Oxford: Clarendon Press, 1960), 12–14. On the relationship between Locke and the *Political Aphorisms*, see Richard Ashcraft and M. M. Goldsmith, "Locke, Revolution Principles, and the Formation of Whig Ideology," *Historical Journal* 26, no. 4 (December 1983): 773–800; cf. Michael Zuckert, *Natural Rights and the New Republicanism* (Princeton, NJ: Princeton University Press, 1994), 289–91.

4. Peter Laslett's suggestion, that it is impossible to maintain "that the original conception of the book was to justify a revolution which had already been consummated," seems supported only by the fact that Locke did not conceive of the book to justify the revolution consummated in 1688–89; Laslett, "The English Revolution and Locke's 'Two Treatises of Government'," *Cambridge Historical Journal* 12, no. 1 (March 1956): 41; cf. Richard Ashcraft, "Revolutionary Politics and Locke's *Two Treatises of Government*," *Political Theory* 8, no. 4 (November 1980): 429–85. See J. R. Milton, "Dating Locke's *Second Treatise*," *History of Political Thought* 16, no. 3 (Autumn 1995): 356–90, esp. 384–85.

5. See, for example, Christopher Anderson, "Safe Enough in his Honesty and Prudence," *History of Political Thought* 13, no. 4 (Winter 1992): 605–30; Robert

Faulkner, "The First Liberal Democrat," *Review of Politics* 63, no. 1 (Winter 2001): 5–39; J. W. Gough, *John Locke's Political Philosophy*, revised ed. (Oxford: Clarendon Press, 1956); Peter Josephson, *The Great Art of Government* (Lawrence: University Press of Kansas, 2002); Harvey C. Mansfield, *Taming the Prince* (1989; repr. Baltimore: Johns Hopkins University Press, 1993); Martin Seliger, *The Liberal Politics of John Locke* (New York: Praeger, 1969).

6. See Greg Forster, *John Locke's Politics of Moral Consensus* (Cambridge: Cambridge University Press, 2005), esp. 218–58; Ruth Grant, *John Locke's Liberalism* (Chicago: University of Chicago Press, 1987); Kirstie McClure, *Judging Rights* (Ithaca, NY: Cornell University Press, 1996); A. John Simmons, *The Lockean Theory of Rights* (Princeton, NJ: Princeton University Press, 1992); Simmons, *On the Edge of Anarchy* (Princeton, NJ: Princeton University Press, 1993); Alex Tuckness, *Locke and the Legislative Point of View* (Princeton, NJ: Princeton University Press, 2002). I nonetheless think that it is important that Locke begins with a focus on authority, and never entirely abandons the importance of authority in at least the less magnificent spheres of politics.

7. What I mean by the relationship among consent, authority, and obligation is spelled out at greater length in chapter 2.

8. Ferguson, *A Brief Justification of the Prince of Orange's Descent into England* (London, 1689; EEBO, Wing F733).

9. See, e.g., Ashcraft, "Revolutionary Politics," esp. 456–58.

10. Ferguson, *A Brief Justification*, 8.

11. Ferguson, *A Brief Justification*, 13.

12. See Zuckert, *Natural Rights and the New Republicanism*, 101–49.

13. See Blackstone, *Commentaries on the Laws of England*, I 161–62.

14. Coke, *Reports*, vol. 12, 63ff.

15. Pocock, "The Myth of John Locke and the Obsession with Liberalism," in *John Locke*, by J. G. A. Pocock and Richard Ashcraft (Los Angeles: William Andrews Clark Memorial Library, 1980), 6.

1. The Condition of Man without Government

1. See Thomas Pangle, *The Spirit of Modern Republicanism* (Chicago: University of Chicago Press, 1988), 246; Martin Seliger, *The Liberal Politics of John Locke* (New York: Praeger, 1969), 83–85.

2. Simmons, "Locke's State of Nature," *Political Theory* 17, no. 3 (August 1989): 449–70; *On the Edge of Anarchy* (Princeton, NJ: Princeton University Press, 1993), 13–23.

3. See Michael Zuckert, *Natural Rights and the New Republicanism* (Princeton, NJ: Princeton University Press, 1994), 222.

4. See A. John Simmons, *The Lockean Theory of Rights* (Princeton, NJ: Princeton University Press, 1992), 26–46; Zuckert, *Natural Rights and the New Republicanism*, 209–10. I would maintain that this element of vindictiveness toward the irrational retains some force in Locke's thought, even after the transcendent version of natural law has also been shown to be untenable. Cf. Simmons, *On the Edge of Anarchy*, 45–46.

5. Cf. Grant, *John Locke's Liberalism* (Chicago: University of Chicago Press, 1987), 128–29.

6. Thomas Pangle suggests that the law of nature also changes regarding the so-called enough and as good proviso regarding acquisition in the state of nature; *Spirit of Modern Republicanism*, 164ff.; cf. TT II 27, II 33, II 35. I do not think that this proviso is ever slackened: one may claim a natural right to goods only if it has been respected. It is instead positive law alone that permits one to own property within civil society (cf. TT II 45, II 120), and so respect for that property is a function of having consented to that society.

7. Alex Tuckness attempts to make this obligation instead flow from obedience to God; see "The Coherence of a Mind," *Journal of the History of Philosophy* 37, no. 1 (January 1999): 73–90. Essential to his reasoning on this matter is his statement, "God would not have made a creation that he did not want preserved as much as possible" (84). Locke explicitly denies that this is true; cf. TT I 147; Leo Strauss, *Natural Right and History* (Chicago: University of Chicago Press, 1953), 228. Other scholars attempt to render the obligation to all mankind primary, and consequently reduce self-preservation to a mere corollary of this more general duty; cf. Seliger, *Liberal Politics*, 62–66; Simmons, *Lockean Theory of Rights*, 59–67, 336–52. This reverses the plain reading of §6 of the *Second Treatise*, sits awkwardly with the preference for one's own preservation that is also commanded (why not instead save the one best able to benefit the community?), and does not account for Locke's description of the right in the *First Treatise* or his hedonism.

8. See Pangle, *Spirit of Modern Republicanism*, 143–44, 306–7n2; Zuckert, *Natural Rights and the New Republicanism*, 271. One has a duty to yield (some) of one's surplus because the needy have a right to it; they do not have a right to it because one has a duty. Moreover, their right and one's duty disappear in the absence of a surplus—mere inequality is insufficient to generate either.

9. Thomas Pangle sees this as a revision of the natural right of inheritance on Locke's part; *Spirit of Modern Republicanism*, 232–43.

10. Govert den Hartogh grapples with this point, but does not resolve it. See "Tully's Locke," *Political Theory* 18, no. 4 (November 1990): 663.

11. Coby, "The Law of Nature in Locke's *Second Treatise*," *Review of Politics* 49, no. 1 (Winter 1987): 10–11.

12. Cf. *Paraphrase and Notes on the Epistles of St. Paul*, reprinted in *The Works of John Locke in Nine Volumes*, 12th ed., vol. VII (London: Rivington, 1824; Online Library of Liberty [oll.libertyfund.org]), 292–93.

13. See Luther, "Secular Authority: To What Extant It Should Be Obeyed," reprinted in *Selections from His Writings*, ed. John Dillenberger (New York: Anchor Books, 1962), 366–67.

14. On the problems that arise from Locke's saying that man was not given permission to eat meat until after the flood, even though there is a natural right to hunt deer for food (TT II 30), see Pangle, *Spirit of Modern Republicanism*, 141–51, 158–71; Zuckert, *Natural Rights and the New Republicanism*, 259–64.

15. Martin Seliger insists that Locke's use of the Bible is largely unexceptionable, although his arguments require the claim that Straussian interpreters, for example, *attribute* man's permission to punish criminals to self-preservation, when according to Seliger Locke has in reality already justified this permission on the basis that we are all the workmanship of God; Seliger, *Liberal Politics*, 56–58. This seems at odds with the plain meaning of TT II 11.

16. Ruth Grant asserts the opposite, saying that "natural executive power, as Locke understands it, is the logical consequence of a situation where each has a duty to respect the rights of his equals;" *John Locke's Liberalism*, 91. She does not, however, explain the train of logic that leads to this consequence.

17. See Strauss, *Natural Right and History*, 222–23.

18. For the argument that follows, I am indebted to A. John Simmons, "Locke and the Right to Punish," *Philosophy and Public Affairs* 17, no. 3 (August 1989): 449–70. Simmons argues that the reasons provided in TT II 7 and II 8 actually boil down to the right to preserve all mankind. As this right will not account for the full executive power (it will at most allow one to punish *dangerous* criminals, not petty thieves), and as it is only implied in the text, Simmons discounts it. He therefore moves to the argument from political necessity, which I sketch in the main body of the text. Simmons raises a good point that this argument undercuts most of what Locke says, for the power to punish aliens can be based on tacit consent rather than on natural executive power (cf. TT II 119), or else it also provides a power to punish *subjects* without *their* consent. Before closing this footnote, however, it bears remarking that Simmons says that the first argument offered, described above, must transform itself into the right to preserve all mankind because he believes Locke to be serious that God's unknown and often contemptuously ignored sanctions for violations of the law of nature in the next life suffice to make it a true law.

19. On this shift, see Peter Josephson, *The Great Art of Government* (Lawrence: University Press of Kansas, 2002), 75–78; Pangle, *Spirit of Modern Republicanism*, 132; Zuckert, *Natural Rights and the New Republicanism*, 222.

20. This point is made by George Windstrup, "Locke on Suicide," *Political Theory* 8, no. 2 (May 1980): 169–82. See also Gary D. Glenn, "Inalienable Rights and Locke's

Argument for Limited Government," *Journal of Politics* 46, no. 1 (February 1984): 80–105; Grant, *John Locke's Liberalism*, 66–71; Willmoore Kendall, *John Locke and the Doctrine of Majority Rule* (1941; repr. Urbana: University of Illinois Press, 1965), 85–86.

21. This will change with the advent of political society. This is naturally arbitrary power; politically arbitrary power and how it relates to the former will be discussed in chapter 2.

22. This quotation refers to an absolute monarch, but Locke states in no uncertain terms that such a "government" is simply one form of the state of nature. Therefore, this belongs among the inconveniences of that state, at least in one of its instantiations.

23. For other accounts of this problem, see Richard Cox, *Locke on War and Peace* (Oxford: Clarendon Press, 1960), 45–105; Josephson, *Great Art of Government*, 69–85; Pangle, *Spirit of Modern Republicanism*, 131–33, 244–51; Seliger, *Liberal Politics*, 82–106; Simmons, *On the Edge of Anarchy*, 13–33; Strauss, *Natural Right and History*, 224–26; Zuckert, *Natural Rights and the New Republicanism*.

24. Simmons, "Locke's State of Nature."

25. Cf. Simmons, "Locke's State of Nature," 455.

26. See Josephson, *Great Art of Government*, 72–85.

27. Simmons adds a third means by which punishment might be unjust in order to avoid the conclusion that a marauding band that just happens to fall upon a murderer, or a rational sadist who punishes precisely as the guilty deserve in order to satisfy his lust for the knife, are not guilty for the latter's death: the act must be intended as punishment; "Locke and the Right to Punish." This appears to be stretching Locke's argument, especially regarding the rational sadist, so long as he is careful to apply the right punishment to the right person. Simmons is clear that he is applying a Kantian standard of morality; it seems less plausible for this to be Locke's standard, but cf. *Lockean Theory*, 36–46.

28. See Kirstie McClure, *Judging Rights* (Ithaca, NY: Cornell University Press, 1996), esp. 156–87. Philip Vogt instead suggests that the "Golden Age" to which Locke refers is not premonetary, but rather prelapsarian, i.e., the condition of Adam in the Garden of Eden. Seeing as Locke speaks of peoples and governors in that state, it is certainly difficult to imagine it applying to Adam, Eve, and whatever children they had at that time. See Vogt, "Locke, Eden, and the Two States of Nature," *Journal of the History of Philosophy* 35, no. 4 (October 1997): 523–44; cf. Robert Markley, "Land Enough in the World," *South Atlantic Quarterly* 98, no. 4 (Fall 1999): 717–37.

29. Martin Seliger goes so far as to say that the Golden Age (cf. TT II 111) was actually an improvement on the moral state of man before the existence of government: man without government is a moral reprobate before the Golden Age comes about, let alone once it ceases. See "Locke's Natural Law and the Foundation of Politics," *Journal of the History of Ideas* 24, no. 3 (July–September 1963): 337–54;

cf. Ruth W. Grant, "Locke's Political Anthropology and Lockean Individualism," *Journal of Politics* 50, no. 1 (February 1988): 42–63; Pangle, *Spirit of Modern Republicanism*, 249–51.

30. That Locke considered man to be a predator is apparent from his discussion of conjugal relations (cf. TT II 80).

31. *The Declaration of James Duke of Monmouth* (1685; EEBO, Wing M2429), 8.

32. Locke's use of Jephthah is problematic for his doctrines of conquest and parental power. He is Locke's paradigm of disputes regarding justice that cannot be settled peacefully (cf. TT II 21, II 176, II 221). "*The Lord the Judge* (says he) *be Judge this day between the Children of* Israel, *and the Children of* Ammon, *Judg.* 11. 27. and then Prosecuting, and relying on his *appeal*, he leads out his Army to Battle" (TT II 21). Yet Locke's entire doctrine of conquest denies that victory in war grants any right to the possession of the land of the sort that Jephthah claims, even when the victor is just; see Strauss, *Natural Right and History*; Cox, *Locke on War and Peace*; Pangle, *Spirit of Modern Republicanism*; Michael Zuckert, *Launching Liberalism* (Lawrence: University of Kansas Press, 2002).

In using the story of Jephthah in this way, Locke almost, although not quite, has the precedent of Hugo Grotius; cf. *The Rights of War and Peace*, ed. Richard Tuck, 3 vol. (Indianapolis: Liberty Fund, 2005), I.2.2 (p. 186), II.15.9.5 (p. 830), III.6.7.1 (p. 1325). Yet this would not be the aspect of the Jephthah tale that resonated most with Locke's readers or that they were the most familiar with. The main reference to Jephthah in contemporary literature involved the vow he made that, "whatsoever cometh forth of the doors of my house to meet me, when I return in peace from the children of Ammon, shall surely be the LORD's, and I will offer it up for a burnt offering" (Jud. 11:31); cf. Isaac Barrow, *Several Sermons Against Evil-Speaking* (London, 1678; EEBO, Wing B959), 110; William Bates, *The Great Duty of Resignation to the Divine Will in Afflictions* (London, 1684; EEBO, Wing B1111), 78–9; Edward Buckler, *A Buckler Against the Fear of Death* (London, 1640; EEBO, STC (2nd ed.) 4008.5), Part II, Section 5, Meditation 4.

As things turned out, it was Jephthah's daughter that ran out to welcome him back. There was some dispute in Locke's day as to whether Jephthah fulfilled this vow as he had promised or rather by committing his daughter to a nunnery; see John Lightfoot, *The Harmony of the Foure Evangelists* (London, 1644; EEBO, Wing L2058), 46; *The works of the Reverend and learned John Lightfoot* (London, 1684; EEBO L2051), 1215–22. I have found one place where "daughters of *Jephtha*" was actually used as a synonym for nuns; cf. Archibald Campbell, *Instructions to a Son* (London, 1661; EEBO, Wing A3657), 40. Yet, Locke's doctrine of paternal power cannot be reconciled with Jephthah's right to dispose of his daughter, however he might have fulfilled that vow.

33. For Locke's repudiation of a Filmer-esque Providence, see John Dunn, *The Political Thought of John Locke* (Cambridge: Cambridge University Press, 1969), 121, 153ff.

34. Hooker, *Laws of the Ecclesiastical Polity*, Bk. VIII, Ch. 2, §5.

35. Cf. Pasquale Pasquino, "Hobbes, Religion, and Rational Choice," *Pacific Philosophical Quarterly* 82 (2001): 406–19. Vainglory is why one might endure so bad a state, not the sole cause of its misery. It must, therefore, attain a moral stature of its own, as must whatever works against it, namely, fear. Hobbes does create a new morality from the state of nature, where fear is virtuous and pride vicious, but this is certainly something of a thin morality. Cf. Leo Strauss, *The Political Philosophy of Hobbes*, trans. Elsa M. Sinclair (1936; repr. Chicago: University of Chicago Press, 1952).

36. Several scholars take this to actually be the case. This view can be seen, to varying degrees, in Richard Ashcraft, "Locke's State of Nature," *American Political Science Review* 62, no. 3 (September 1968): 898–915; John Kilcullen, "Locke on Political Obligation," *Review of Politics* 45, no. 3 (July 1983): 323–44; Simmons, *On the Edge of Anarchy*, 26–33; John W. Yolton, "Locke on the Law of Nature," *The Philosophical Review* 67, no. 4 (October 1958): 477–98.

37. Ruth Grant goes too far in saying that "Locke is not concerned to show that men may be naturally peaceful. Rather, he is concerned to show that the condition of men under government may be warlike;" *John Locke's Liberalism*, 72. I take Locke to have had both concerns.

38. Hobbes, *Leviathan* XIII.8.

39. Robert Goldwin shows why Locke is able to redefine war in this way while still leaving it as a very real possibility for the state of nature: the opposite of the state of war is not the state of nature but the state of peace, just as the opposite of the state of nature is not the state of war but political society; see "Locke's State of Nature in Political Society," *Western Political Quarterly* 29, no. 1 (March 1976): 126–35; and "John Locke" in *History of Political Philosophy*, ed. Leo Strauss and Joseph Cropsey, 3d ed. (Chicago: University of Chicago Press, 1987): 476–512.

40. See Strauss, *Natural Right and History*, 226–31.

41. Cf. Hobbes, *De Cive* II.2; *Leviathan* XIV.4ff.

42. See Josephson, *Great Art of Government*, 3, 56–66.

2. *The Rule of Law*

1. Shklar, *Legalism* (Cambridge, MA: Harvard University Press, 1964), 1.

2. Carl Schmitt, *Die Diktatur*, 5th ed. (Berlin: Dunker & Humblot, 1989), 40–42; *Political Theology*, trans. George Schwab (Chicago: University of Chicago Press, 1985), 13–14; *Crisis of Parliamentary Democracy*, trans. Ellen Kennedy (Cambridge: MIT Press, 1985), 42; *Legality and Legitimacy*, trans. Jeffery Seitzer (Durham, NC: Duke University Press, 2004), 99. Schmitt's appraisal is shared by Kirstie

McClure, *Judging Rights* (Ithaca, NY: Cornell University Press, 1996); Alex Tuckness, *Locke and the Legislative Point of View* (Princeton, NJ: Princeton University Press, 1994). While Ruth Grant does not argue that Locke is a legalist, she does implicitly agree with Schmitt that Locke set down the principles of right as the sole premise in his political theory; see Grant, *John Locke's Liberalism* (Chicago: University of Chicago Press, 1987).

3. The relationship among consent, obligation, and authority is contrasted with one's private judgment regarding politics below.

4. Zuckert, *Natural Rights and the New Republicanism* (Princeton, NJ: Princeton University Press, 1994), 248.

5. I bring this up again in chapter 5.

6. See Thomas Pangle, *The Spirit of Modern Republicanism* (Chicago: University of Chicago Press, 1988), 211–12.

7. Some scholars attempt to draw from tacit consent an obligation to the law greater than what is owed by transient resident aliens; see C. B. Macpherson, *The Political Theory of Possessive Individualism* (Oxford: Clarendon Press, 1962); A. John Simmons, *On the Edge of Anarchy* (Princeton, NJ: Princeton University Press, 1993), 80–90. This is rebutted in Peter Josephson, *The Great Art of Government* (Lawrence: University Press of Kansas, 2002).

8. Cf. A. John Simmons' discussion of what consent is; *On the Edge of Anarchy*, 69–70.

9. Italics added.

10. Italics added.

11. See Grant, *John Locke's Liberalism*, 110–4, 135; Pangle, *Spirit of Modern Republicanism*, 247. Peter Josephson asserts to the contrary that consent *can* be withdrawn, i.e., that a member of the commonwealth may reclaim the two surrendered natural powers without being correct that government is dissolved; *Great Art of Government*, 279–80. This relies upon his reinterpretation of express consent as a sentiment of *amour de la patrie* (156–60), a reinterpretation prepared by his narrowing the distance between tacit and express consent, a "subject" and a "member" of the commonwealth (148–56). Yet Locke's initial mention of "member" in the *Two Treatises* (the word does not occur in the *First*) is to link it with obligations born of promises (TT II 14); the second instance of it proclaims that all who are not members of political society are in the state of nature (TT II 15). Whatever problems arise from Locke's doctrine of consent, they cannot be resolved by extracting it from an argument concerned with authority and the suspension of private judgment. The impermissibility of withdrawing consent once given is crucial if some acts of purported revolution can be considered wrong, i.e., there must be some way to say that an authority still stands despite some malcontented individuals' refusal to recognize it.

12. Cf. *Leviathan* XVI.1–8, 13–15; XVII.5, 7; XXI.5, 11–16.

13. Ruth Grant makes this the sole reason that unanimity is not required; *John Locke's Liberalism*, 115–19. This does not, however, explain why Locke does not rest his argument here but instead moves on to questions of practicality. The problem of majority rule is also discussed in Simmons, *On the Edge of Anarchy*, 90–98.

14. Kendall's argument is also addressed in J. W. Gough, *John Locke's Political Philosophy*, revised ed. (Oxford: Clarendon Press, 1956), 24–46; Josephson, *Great Art of Government*, 126–39; Macpherson, *Possessive Individualism*, 195–96; Martin Seliger, *The Liberal Politics of John Locke* (New York: Praeger, 1969), 75–81.

15. Kendall, *John Locke and the Doctrine of Majority Rule* (1941; repr. Urbana: University of Illinois Press, 1965), 112.

16. Kendall, *John Locke*, 134. I will leave aside the fact that this latent premise denies that the majority is the source of a judgment's being ethically right: were the latter the case, this would be a corollary, not a premise.

17. Kendall, *John Locke*, 134n12.

18. That is, among those who live like beasts. Peter Laslett remarks that this passage proclaims "the essential rightness of 'Natural Man' and reads almost like Rousseau, the Rousseau of the *Discours sur l'Inégalité*;" see his note to §58 in John Locke, *Two Treatises of Government*, ed. Laslett (Cambridge: Cambridge University Press: 1988), 182n. This is contested, rightly, by Nathan Tarcov, who argues that the numerous (unfavorable) comparisons between men and lions, wolves, etc., suggest that the "irrational untaught Inhabitants" are wild animals; see *Locke's Education for Liberty* (Chicago: University of Chicago Press, 1984), 69. Locke's rhetoric here asks whether it would be better to live as beasts: it does not, *pace* Laslett, conclude in the goodness of natural man but does raise it as a possibility.

19. It is noteworthy that even this disparity between adults and children does not give one individual authority over another on account of superior rationality: parental power is a shared power, and so never, or rarely ever, the possession of a single individual. Cf. TT I 48, II 52–53; Pangle, *Spirit of Modern Republicanism*, 233–55.

20. Cf. *Essay Concerning Human Understanding*, IV.17; *Of the Conduct of the Understanding*, §3. Reason as Locke uses it in the *Two Treatises* seems to encompass discernment, judgment, and wit, in addition to reason. Peter Josephson argues that Locke does not see this as an authentic form of reason, but one that will be respected anyway since people might still have good habits, or listen to someone else who actually does have reason, or some other justification which he alludes to without mentioning; *Great Art of Government*, 56–66.

21. See Simmons, "Inalienable Rights and Locke's *Treatises*," *Philosophy and Public Affairs* 12, no. 3 (Summer 1983): 175–204; *On the Edge of Anarchy*, 101–46. This fact seems a sufficient answer to Willmoore Kendall's observation that a man *can* sign these rights over to society since Locke never speaks of "inalienable" rights; see *John Locke*, 68–74. Ruth Grant demonstrates how the nonpossession of

such a right need not derive from man's ownership by God; see *John Locke's Liberalism*, 68–71.

22. Reprinted in *State Tracts*, vol. II (London, 1692; EEBO, Wing S5331): 23–26.

23. I discussed this in chapter 1. Martin Seliger allows for only the first of these definitions of arbitrary power; see *Liberal Politics*, 246–47.

24. Ruth Grant presents them as two different definitions unified by an element of unreasonableness; see *John Locke's Liberalism*, 72–73. A. John Simmons also attempts to define both absolute and arbitrary; see *On the Edge of Anarchy*, 54–55.

25. I omit chance as a reasonable explanation: the *First Treatise* amply demonstrates that the word *sovereign* was a part of Locke's active vocabulary. Jonas Proast noted that the *Letter Concerning Toleration* called rulers "magistrates" rather than "sovereigns;" *The Argument of the Letter Concerning Toleration Briefly Consider'd and Answer'd* (Oxford, 1690; EEBO Wing P3538), 16. Locke himself draws attention to this point in his reply, emphasizing that it is Proast (not himself) who thinks it proper to call them "sovereigns" (2LCT 77). Locke silently concedes the battle in his subsequent exchanges.

26. See Richard Cox, *Locke on War and Peace* (Oxford: Clarendon Press, 1960). Cox is followed by Seliger, *Liberal Politics*, 325–27.

27. For excellent discussions of this, see Grant, *John Locke's Liberalism*, 72–78; John T. Scott, "The Sovereignless State and Locke's Language of Obligation," *American Political Science Review* 94, no. 3 (September 2000): 547–61.

28. Locke's argument in this section is that the ability to make war is no mark of sovereignty, unless we will say that every captain or planter is a sovereign, an absolute king. It is true, he continues, that in political society only the supreme power may make war and peace, but not everyone with a similar power need be in political society. I mention this because one might say that Locke here uses *supreme power* and *sovereign* synonymously. Yet this would mean that he also used *supreme power* and *absolute king* synonymously, which seems bizarre. The passage does make sense, however, if we keep *supreme power* and *sovereign* distinct: only the supreme power in society can make war, whether or not that power is an absolute monarch, but the ability to make war is no sign of supreme power (e.g., in the state of nature) or of absolute kingship (e.g., in political society).

29. Robert Filmer, *Patriarcha and Other Writings*, ed. Johann P. Sommerville (Cambridge: Cambridge University Press, 1991), 146.

30. Filmer, *Patriarcha and Other Writings*, 161.

31. Jean Bodin, *Six Books of the Commonwealth*, Bk. 1, Ch. 10; excerpted in Jean Bodin, *On Sovereignty*, ed. and trans. Julian H. Franklin (Cambridge: Cambridge University Press, 1992), 56.

32. Bodin, *Six Books*, Bk. 1, Ch. 10; excerpted in *On Sovereignty*, 49.

33. See also Richard Ashcraft, "Locke's State of Nature," *American Political Science Review* 62, no. 3 (September 1968): 898–915; and Charles Tarlton, "A Rope of Sand," *The Historical Journal* 21, no. 1 (1978): 43–73.

34. Ruth Grant insists that promises do hold in the face of threats to preservation, even though she recognizes that no one may consent to slavery, for those promises would not forfeit one's right to life; see *John Locke's Liberalism*, 66–72, 94, 131–32. This distinction seems tenuous: if someone has a right to endanger my life, and that right implies a duty on my part to permit my life to be endangered, it seems that my right to life is forfeit; see Gary Glenn, "Inalienable Rights and Locke's Argument for Limited Government," *Journal of Politics* 46, no. 1 (February 1984): 80–105. Grant's response to this relies on rights' always implying duties, which is not always the case in the *Two Treatises*.

35. See Simmons, *On the Edge of Anarchy*, 72–79.

36. See John Dunn, *The Political Thought of John Locke* (Cambridge: Cambridge University Press, 1969), esp. 130ff.

37. See Scott, "The Sovereignless State and Locke's Language of Obligation."

38. See Pangle, *Spirit of Modern Republicanism*, 270–71.

39. Peter Josephson argues that Locke's doctrine of consent is instead intended to inculcate a regard for individual rights and a sense of liberal patriotism; *Great Art of Government*, 134–39, 148–65. This understates the emphatic relationship between consent and authority, the question being how any individual can have an obligation to obey in the absence of a divinely-ordained ruler (cf. TT II 1). The general tenor of Locke's discussion is why individuals should sacrifice for a community which they do *not* love; his arguments, even in Josephson's reading, fail to establish the reasonableness of such a love, moreover. If a doctrine of consent does indeed produce a prejudice in the majority that it must respect individual rights, and a sentiment in the individual that he is a part of something larger than himself, then this would have to be appended to or replace Locke's presentation.

40. See Jonathan Scott, "The Law of War," *History of Political Thought* 13, no. 4 (Winter 1992): 565–85.

41. Locke holds open the possibility that such a one's will *is* better than that of others, even if its superiority cannot be verified. It is for this reason that we must interpret "arbitrary" here in its political sense of "without positive law": a will that is "naturally" arbitrary—unguided by the law of nature—can never be "better."

42. Italics added.

43. See H. L. A. Hart, *The Concept of Law*, 2d ed., ed. Penelope Bulloch and Joseph Raz (Oxford: Clarendon Press, 1994); Hans Kelsen, *General Theory of Law and State* (Cambridge, MA: Harvard University Press, 1949); Kelsen, *Pure Theory of Law*, 2d ed., trans. Max Knight (Berkeley and Los Angeles: University of California Press, 1967); Joseph Raz, *The Authority of Law* (Oxford: Clarendon Press,

1979). George Thomas remarks that the difficulty some scholars (like myself) have in seeing how prerogative brings necessity within the compass of lawful government, rather than its highlighting the tension between law and necessity, arises from "a narrowly positivistic conception of law;" "As Far as Republican Principles Will Admit," *Presidential Studies Quarterly* 30, no. 3 (September 2000): 540. This is precisely Locke's conception of law, however.

44. Ronald Dworkin, *Law's Empire* (Cambridge, MA: Belknap Press of Harvard University, 1986).

45. See Locke, "Selecting the Grand Jury," in *Political Essays*, ed. Mark Goldie (Cambridge: Cambridge University Press, 1997): 283–87. For the support given to the Stuart kings by the courts, see Zuckert, *Natural Rights and the New Republicanism*, 51–52, 57.

46. See, e.g., Antonin Scalia, "Originalism: The Lesser Evil," *University of Cincinnati Law Review* 57 (1989): 849–65; Scalia, *A Matter of Interpretation*, ed. Amy Gutmann (Princeton, NJ: Princeton University Press, 1997).

47. See Frederic S. Burin, "The Theory of the Rule of Law and the Structure of the Constitutional State," *American University Law Review* 15, no. 3 (June 1966): 313–40; and Harvey Mansfield, *Taming the Prince* (1989; repr. Baltimore: Johns Hopkins University Press, 1993), 186, 200.

48. Mansfield, *Taming the Prince*, 188.

49. Cf. Ferguson, *A Brief Justification of the Prince of Orange's Descent into England* (London, 1689; EEBO, Wing F733); and *Political Aphorisms: or, the True Maxims of Government Displayed* (London, 1690; EEBO, Wing [2nd. ed.] H917E).

3. Prerogative and the Limits of Legislative Supremacy

1. I am using *lawful* here to refer to positive law. Ruth Grant notes that all government is "lawful" according to the law of nature, else it would be no government at all; prerogative is thus the "lawful" violation of positive law; see *John Locke's Liberalism* (Chicago: University of Chicago Press, 1987), 142. As the adoption of Locke's terminology in this respect would serve more to obscure his thought than to reveal it, at least to modern readers, I will equate lawful government with the *Rechtsstaat* and not with just any legitimate regime.

2. *Ex Parte Milligan*, 71 U.S. (4 Wall.) 2, 121 (1866).

3. Cf. George Thomas, "As Far As Republican Principles Will Admit," *Presidential Studies Quarterly* 30, no. 3 (September 2000): 534–52.

4. Cf. Thomas Pangle, *The Spirit of Modern Republicanism* (Chicago: University of Chicago Press, 1988), 257.

5. Given the scorn heaped upon Straussian interpreters of Locke by some initiates into the Cambridge method of historiography, it is almost fitting that Locke's remoteness from his contemporaries regarding prerogative has been overlooked. David Resnick interprets Locke as having spoken of prerogative only to erode it; "Locke and the Rejection of the Ancient Constitution," *Political Theory* 12, no. 1 (February 1984): 97–114. A. H. MacLean, in arguing that all of the essential characteristics of Locke's *Second Treatise* are present in George Lawson's *Politica Sacra & Civilis*, omits any mentions of prerogative as one of those essential characteristics, instead noting the absolute character of legislative supremacy; "George Lawson and John Locke," *Cambridge Historical Journal* 9, no. 1 (1947): 69–77. Richard Ashcraft and M. M. Goldsmith do the same thing with an anonymous pamphlet entitled *Political Aphorisms*; "Locke, Revolution Principles, and the Formation of Whig Ideology," *Historical Journal* 26, no.4 (1983): 773–800.

One could read Richard Ashcraft's works on Locke and be left with no inkling that something odd is going on with prerogative: Ashcraft sees it relating only to the calling of Parliaments, and there he leaves it with almost no discretionary authority at all! He quotes and paraphrases Locke's words, but does not comment upon them; see *Revolutionary Politics and Locke's "Two Treatises of Government"* (Princeton, NJ: Princeton University Press, 1986), 237–39, cf. 111–12, 320–21; *Locke's "Two Treatises of Government"* (London: Allen & Unwin, 1987), 190–91.

Charles Tarlton also makes it seem as though Locke and the Tories had the same definition of prerogative. According to him, the Whig argument copied by Locke promised that Charles II would be secure in many of his prerogatives if only he acceded to the exclusion of his brother James from the line of succession; see "The Exclusion Controversy, Pamphleteering, and Locke's *Two Treatises*," *Historical Journal* 24, no. 1 (1981): 49–68; and "The Rulers Now on Earth," *Historical Journal* 28, no. 2 (1985): 279–98. How this can be reconciled with Locke's words is uncertain.

6. Reprinted in *State Tracts*, vol II (London, 1692; EEBO, Wing S5331), 271–72.

7. Reprinted in *State Tracts*, vol. II: 223.

8. Ferguson, *A Brief Justification of the Prince of Orange's Descent into England* (London, 1689; EEBO, Wing F733), 8.

9. [Shaftesbury?], *A Letter from a Person of Quality, to His Friend in the Country* (1675; EEBO, Wing [2nd ed.] S2897aA), 4; italics reversed.

10. With regard to a supposed dispensing power, William's declaration of the reasons for which he came into England states that "tho the King may pardon the Punishment that a Transgressor has incurred, and to which he is condemned, as in the cases of *Treason* or *Felony*; yet it cannot be with any colour of Reason inferred from thence, that the King can entirely Suspend the Execution of those Laws, relating to *Treason* or *Felony*: Unless it is pretended that he is cloathed with a Despotick and Arbitrary Power, and that the Lives, Liberties, Honors,

and Estates of the Subjects, depend wholly on his good Will and Pleasure" (*State Tracts*, vol. II, 420).

11. Locke's participation in drafting the *Letter from a Person of Quality, to His Friend in the Country* is the subject of some disagreement. I agree with Richard Ashcraft that, as with the *Fundamental Constitutions of Carolina*, it is sensible to see Shaftesbury as the author, with Locke working as his assistant; see *Revolutionary Politics*, esp. 120–23. In any event, the views I just quoted from it are explicitly attributed to Shaftesbury, and we cannot say with certainty the extent to which Locke shared in them in 1675.

12. Richard Ashcraft would seem to disagree, at least implicitly. He treats Locke's discussion of "flux" as nothing more than a rhetorical riposte to those Tories who suggested that Parliament could not possibly speak for the people; if it is not truly representative on account of the rotten boroughs, Ashcraft's Locke answers, this is the king's fault, for it is his prerogative to redraw the electoral districts; see *Revolutionary Politics*, 237–39. This diminution of the flux's importance follows upon Ashcraft's neglect of prerogative in general.

13. Thomas Pangle includes "passion" among the causes of society's recalcitrance to rule by law, not just emergency; *Spirit of Modern Republicanism*, 255–56. This seems to rely upon his linking of law and reason as that which governs an unruly society.

14. John Dunn, *The Political Thought of John Locke* (Cambridge: Cambridge University Press, 1969), 153.

15. Dunn, *Political Thought of John Locke*, 153.

16. Pasquino, "Locke on King's Prerogative," *Political Theory* 26, no. 2 (April 1998): 198–208.

17. Mansfield, *Taming the Prince* (1989; repr. Baltimore: Johns Hopkins University Press, 1993).

18. McClure, *Judging Rights* (Ithaca, NY: Cornell University Press, 1996).

19. Jeremy Waldron, by contrast, is almost entirely silent on the theological implications of prerogative: it arises only to be dismissed, to show that the existence of a 'wise and god-like prince' does not violate the equality that, according to Waldron, Locke saw as decisive; see *God, Locke, and Equality* (Cambridge: Cambridge University Press, 2002), 135, 140.

20. Mansfield, *Taming the Prince*, 203. See Christopher Anderson, "Safe Enough in his Honesty and Prudence," *History of Political Thought* 13, no. 4 (Winter 1992): 621; Pasquino, "Locke on King's Prerogative," 202; Thomas, "As Far As Republican Principles Will Admit," 538.

21. Cf. the earlier discussion of the word *arbitrary* in chapter 2.

22. Simmons, *The Lockean Theory of Rights* (Princeton, NJ: Princeton University Press, 1992), 46–59.

23. Cf. *Vieth v. Jubelirer*, 541 U.S. 267 (2004).

24. See Robert Filmer, "Patriarcha," in *Patriarcha and Other Writings*, ed. Johann P. Sommerville, (Cambridge: Cambridge University Press, 1991), esp. 44–5.

25. See Samuel Rutherford, *Lex Rex: The Law and the Prince* (London, 1644; EEBO, Wing R2386), 218ff.; Anon., *Vox Populi: Or the Peoples Claim to their Parliament's Sitting*, reprinted in *State Tracts*, vol. II: 219–24, 219; Johnson, Untitled, reprinted in *State Tracts*, vol II: 271–72; Ferguson, *Brief Justification*.

26. Fatovic, "Constitutionalism and Contingency," *History of Political Thought* 25, no. 2 (Summer 2004): 276–97, 285.

27. Benjamin Kleinerman seems to miss this when he suggests that Locke favored setting the times for assembling the legislature in the original constitution; according to Kleinerman, Locke felt that leaving this to the executive's discretion was the mark of a poorly ordered commonwealth. See Kleinerman, "Can the Prince Really Be Tamed?," *American Political Science Review* 101, no. 2 (May 2007): 209–22, 218–19. Richard Ashcraft also seems to indicate that Locke preferred settling the times of election in the constitution, at least when he was discussing the government of Virginia; see "Political Theory and Political Reform," *Western Political Quarterly* 22, no. 4 (December 1969): 742–58; *Locke's "Two Treatises of Government,"* 188–89.

28. See Peter Josephson, *The Great Art of Government* (Lawrence: University Press of Kansas, 2002), 226–27. In an earlier presentation of this argument, I was too extreme in denying any place for constitutional provisions; see Ross J. Corbett, "The Extraconstitutionality of Lockean Prerogative," *Review of Politics* 68, no. 3 (Summer 2006): 428–48, esp. 437–38.

29. Cf. *De legibus* III.iii; see also John Bellamie, *A Iustification of "The City Remonstrance" and Its Vindication* (London, 1646; EEBO, Wing B1814), 34; Thomas Hobbes, *Elements of Law*, ch. 28, §1; Rutherford, *Lex Rex*, 218ff.; and Algernon Sidney, *Discourses Concerning Government* (London, 1698; EEBO Wing S3761), 90, 252.

30. Robert Faulkner attempts to address this difficulty as well but is forced to understate the limits that government by consent places on the use of political power; see Faulkner, "The First Liberal Democrat," *Review of Politics* 63, no. 1 (Winter 2001): 12–4.

31. Grant, *John Locke's Liberalism*, 144–45. She takes Locke to be entirely serious about this reform's being a restoration rather than an alteration of the legislative. Yet the problem of the rotten boroughs arises only because the people did *not* actually establish the "restored" system: they may have desired to have a fair and proportional representation but they really just distributed knights and burgesses in perpetuity according to then-current population patterns (or to drop Locke's conceit, the English kings did so).

32. The fact that the old legislature has been corrupted is deemphasized by Peter Josephson, who consequently argues that this use of prerogative goes against

even the will of the people, and therefore that reason or prudence may temporarily elevate itself above government by consent so long as the people are eventually brought around to the prince's view of their welfare; *Great Art of Government*, 233. On my reading, such extraconstitutional reform can be justified only if the will of the people is not actually expressed through their legislators, and so is not an example of a prince's being wiser than his people.

33. See, e.g., Faulkner, "First Liberal Democrat;" Grant, *John Locke's Liberalism*, 83–88; Kleinerman, "Can the Prince Really Be Tamed?"; Thomas Langston and Michael Lind, "John Locke and the Limits of Presidential Prerogative," *Polity* 24, no. 1 (Fall 1991): 49–68; David Weaver, "Leadership, Locke, and the Federalist," *American Journal of Political Science* 41, no. 2 (April 1997): 420–46, esp. 426, 430, 433–35.

34. This is only a problem if consent implies more than bare acquiescence, or if government by consent means something more than a submissive population. This is denied by Robert Faulkner, "First Liberal Democrat," 13; see also Martin Seliger, "Locke's Theory of Revolutionary Action," *Western Political Quarterly* 16, no. 3 (September 1963): 548–68; *The Liberal Politics of John Locke* (New York: Praeger, 1969). But as discussed before, every people has submitted to those that rule them (cf. TT I 43; Charles Tarlton, "A Rope of Sand," *The Historical Journal* 21, no. 1 [March 1978]: 56–59). A normatively interesting consensual government demands a bit more (cf. TT II 186). Otherwise, every government would be legitimate: Locke would not be the correction of Hobbes on Hobbesian principles that many scholars see him as—he would *be* Hobbes, albeit with better spin.

35. Ruth Grant silently replaces this example with breaking into a person's home to save a child from a fire; *John Locke's Liberalism*, 84. The situation Locke actually describes is far more problematic for the view of rights Grant attributes to him.

36. A. John Simmons argues that this would be morally unacceptable from within a Lockean framework; it is therefore a powerful piece of evidence against his having captured the essence of Locke's moral theory; see *Lockean Theory of Rights*, 54.

37. This possibility comes the closest to supporting Josephson's characterization of prerogative as representing reason, as opposed to popular consent or the will of the people, in pursuing the public good; *Great Art of Government*, 230–43.

38. This is noted by Ruth Grant, but she goes on to remark that "Locke refers to prerogative power as discretionary rather than arbitrary," which is false; see *John Locke's Liberalism*, 72–3.

39. See Grant, *John Locke's Liberalism*, 84–5; Langston and Lind, "John Locke and the Limits of Presidential Prerogative," esp. 59–60.

40. See Weaver, "Leadership, Locke, and the Federalist;" Faulkner, "First Liberal Democrat."

41. Cox, *Locke on War and Peace* (Oxford: Clarendon Press, 1960), esp. 128–30. See also Fatovic, "Constitutionalism and Contingency," esp. 280–87; Faulkner, "First Liberal Democrat," esp. 29–36; Kleinerman, "Can the Prince Really Be Tamed?"; Seliger, *Liberal Politics*, 339–49; Thomas, "As Far As Republican Principles Will Admit." Sean Mattie calls prerogative both "executive power" and a "natural power;" see "Prerogative and the Rule of Law in John Locke and the Lincoln Presidency," *Review of Politics* 67, no. 1 (Winter 2005): 77–111, esp. 86. Thomas Pangle tacitly includes prerogative under executive power; *Spirit of Modern Republicanism*, 255–57. It can at times appear that Harvey Mansfield also interprets Locke as blending prerogative and executive power. He is clear, however, that what Locke expands is the power available to the executive, not his definition of executive power per se: "Executive *power* is subordinate, but the executive *person* may not be;" *Taming the Prince*, 201. It is instructive to contrast Mansfield's procedure with Cox's. Cox melts the federative, executive, and prerogative powers together, going so far as to quote passages concerning one to make a point about another; cf. *Locke on War and Peace*, 127. Mansfield also depicts Locke's discussion of the federative power as the entering wedge in the argument for broad extralegal discretion. Yet even if the "practical alliance . . . observed between the executive and federative powers . . . overrides their theoretical distinctness," they do remain theoretically distinct for Mansfield; *Taming the Prince*, 201. It is this distinction between executive power and prerogative that permits the modern executive to have the "formal weakness" that, when contrasted with its "informal strength," accounts for its ambivalence.

42. William King's *The State of the Protestants of Ireland* (London, 1691; EEBO, Wing K538) explicitly states just this; cf. 67–68. Langston and Lind rely on this fact for their assertion that the Constitution does not grant the President any "antilegal prerogative" above that of any other citizen; "John Locke and the Limits of Presidential Prerogative," 59–60, 66. See also Grant, *John Locke's Liberalism*, 84–85.

43. See Grant, *John Locke's Liberalism*, 84.

44. See Grant, *John Locke's Liberalism*, 170.

45. Cox, *Locke on War and Peace*.

46. This is noticed, and variously addressed, by Josephson, *Great Art of Government*, 279–80; Pangle, *Spirit of Modern Republicanism*, 247–49.

47. See Cox, *Locke on War and Peace*, 42–44, 94–104.

48. For example, Ruth Grant is explicit that this is a form of political society; "Locke's Political Anthropology and Lockean Individualism," *Journal of Politics* 50, no. 1 (February 1988): 42–63. Martin Seliger implies that it is a form of political society; *Liberal Politics*, 209–63. Harvey Mansfield denies that it is so; *Taming the Prince*, 199.

49. John Dunn notes that acquiescence and consent differ, the latter being stronger than the former, yet is driven to say that one *must* acquiesce in prerogative; see "Consent in the Political Theory of John Locke," *The Historical Journal* 10, no. 2

(1967): 180. Since this is a matter of private judgment in Dunn's analysis, however, it is not really political obligation. Robert Faulkner sees the two as identical, mostly because he does not see consent as a positive act; see "The First Liberal Democrat." How it then produces obligation is absent from his account, though Faulkner does try to sidestep this issue by emphasizing the representative nature of Locke's government (in the parliamentary rather than Hobbesian sense of representation), suggesting that having representation alone implies consenting to what the other representatives decide for you. This easily falls into the account given by Jacqueline Stevens: "consent does not refer to an individual's consent, but rather to the consent of the majority;" see Stevens, "The Reasonableness of John Locke's Majority," *Political Theory* 24, no. 3 (August 1996): 436. How such a majority then arises, such societies not existing by nature, then, remains mysterious.

Martin Seliger, arguing that Locke made acquiescence into consent, therefore sees the people as in practice consenting to arbitrary power when they acquiesce to prerogative, something expressly forbidden by Locke; see "Locke's Theory of Revolutionary Action;" *Liberal Politics*, esp. 219–30.

50. Italics added.

51. See Josephson, *Great Art of Government*, 236, 240.

52. Cf. Hart, *The Concept of Law*, 2d ed. (Oxford: Clarendon Press, 1994).

53. This shift is not followed by Ruth Grant in *John Locke's Liberalism*. She recognizes that prerogative cannot possess a political status, and that one should not consider government dissolved when prerogative is exercised, but does not recognize the significance of these facts with regard to the essence of legitimate government.

54. Reprinted in *State Tracts*, vol. II: 25.

55. *State Tracts*, vol. II, 224.

56. [Shaftesbury?], *A Letter from a Person of Quality, to His Friend in the Country*, 5 (italics reversed).

57. Martin Seliger argues that these passages are an "overstatement," and are reformulated later on; *Liberal Politics*, 244–50.

58. For an exploration of why man might be obligated to obey God, see Simmons, *Lockean Theory of Rights*, 26–36. A less satisfactory argument is asserted by Greg Forster, *John's Locke's Politics of Moral Consensus* (Cambridge: Cambridge University Press, 2005), 167–93.

59. A. John Simmons instead concludes that Locke rejects the entire argument that godlike princes have any title to authority because Locke does not advocate absolute monarchy; *Lockean Theory of Rights*, 29n39.

60. Locke added this passage in his hand-corrected copy of the 3d edition; see Richard Cox's note in Locke, *Second Treatise of Government*, ed. Richard Cox (Wheeling, IL: Harlan Davidson, 1982), 27n5.

61. David Weaver finds this implausible; see "Leadership, Locke, and the Federalist." Martin Seliger sees prerogative as remedying the defects of basing legitimate government on the threat of popular revolution, such revolution never actually occurring in practice; consequently, he sees nothing but emigration or secession to check the prince; see "Locke's Theory of Revolutionary Action."

62. Martin Seliger takes this in fact to be the case: "Nothing is indicated to contradict the conclusion that the moment the people desist from active resistance, they must be supposed to have consented to the acceptance of a conqueror or usurper by a politically articulate minority;" see "Locke's Theory of Revolutionary Action," 553. Cf. TT Pref., I 121, II 176, II 192.

4. Resistance, Revolution, and the Limits of Politics

1. See, e.g., Peter Laslett's introduction to *Two Treatises of Government*, by John Locke, ed. Peter Laslett, student edition (1960; repr. Cambridge: Cambridge University Press, 1988); Richard Ashcraft, *Revolutionary Politics and Locke's "Two Treatises of Government"* (Princeton, NJ: Princeton University Press, 1986).

2. This is dealt with at greater length in chapter 5.

3. Tully, "Political Freedom," *Journal of Philosophy* 87, no. 10 (October 1990): 519.

4. Italics added.

5. See A. John Simmons, *On the Edge of Anarchy* (Princeton, NJ: Princeton University Press, 1993), 172–75.

6. While Locke does seem to suggest that political society simply precludes the state of war altogether (TT II 227), he must be taken here to mean that it precludes the *continuation* of that state (cf. II 21): "*Force without Right, upon a Man's Person, makes a State of War*, both where there is, and is not, a common Judge" (TT II 19). The alternative to this reading is that Locke switches to Hobbes's definition of war. It was his earlier refusal to do so that allowed him to say that the state of nature was not a state of war (see chapter 1). Cf. II 227, where the dissolution of government begins the state of war, not the state of nature. I shall not pursue this possibility further.

7. Ruth Grant takes this to be the case with all instances of conquest; *John Locke's Liberalism* (Chicago: University of Chicago Press, 1987), 147–48.

8. Cf. Hobbes, *Leviathan* XXIX.23.

9. See Grant, *John Locke's Liberalism*, 145n55, and context.

10. This is possible only if the problem of scarcity has been overcome: competition is the one rational cause of war, for Locke; cf. Thomas Pangle, *The Spirit of Modern Republicanism* (Chicago: University of Chicago Press, 1988), 244–45. A.

John Simmons wants to avoid the conclusion that this constitutes a state of nature; *On the Edge of Anarchy*, 167–77.

11. See Grant, *John Locke's Liberalism*, 101–10, 146–55; Grant, "Locke's Political Anthropology and Lockean Individualism," *Journal of Politics* 50, no. 1 (February 1998): 42–63; Peter Josephson, *The Great Art of Government* (Lawrence: University Press of Kansas, 2002), 135; Pangle, *Spirit of Modern Republicanism*, 246; Martin Seliger, *The Liberal Politics of John Locke* (New York: Praeger, 1969), 107–38; Leo Strauss, *Natural Right and History* (Chicago: University of Chicago Press, 1953), 232 & n. 100; Nathan Tarcov, "Locke's *Second Treatise* and 'The Best Fence Against Rebellion'," *Review of Politics* 43, no. 2 (April 1981): 198–217. My analysis differs from that of Tarcov in that society also survives when the legislative has already been altered, not just when the people suspect a design to alter it. This is because I do not consider society to be the establishment of a common judge but rather the intention to establish that judge by renouncing one's obligations to all the rest of mankind. I take the difference between the second and third modes of dissolution to serve a rhetorical purpose, therefore: in both society persists, but men are in the state of nature; the second is the entering wedge that makes the third more palatable.

12. Hobbes, *Leviathan* XXI.11–17.

13. Ruth Grant attempts to explain the lack of an exception for prerogative in II 202 by noting that prerogative is not necessarily a transgression of law (since it is permissible by the law of nature), or that Locke does not have to state the exception every time he states the rule; *John Locke's Liberalism*, 141–42. The first explanation does not seem compatible with the statement's context, where what is spoken of is positive law. The second is also unlikely, given Locke's attention to detail and correction of subsequent editions of the *Two Treatises.*

14. A. John Simmons recognizes that Locke's arguments tend toward this tense conclusion, but attempts to save him from it; *On the Edge of Anarchy*, 178–92.

15. See Josephson, *Great Art of Government*, 134–39, 163–65.

16. Peter Josephson states that "The people tend to be conservative in their judgments; others must innovate;" *Great Art of Government*, 137; cf. Thomas Pangle, "Executive Energy and Popular Spirit in Lockean Constitutionalism," *Presidential Studies Quarterly* 17, no. 2 (Spring 1987): 253–65. Locke's solution, however, seems to be that the people must become less conservative, less pliant to the means Pangle and Josephson suggest a prudent prince will employ, not to reserve a special right for the farsighted minority.

17. *Luther v. Borden*, 48 U.S. (7 How.) 1, 43 (1849).

18. See Josephson, *Great Art of Government*, 202–3. Ruth Grant gives a different reading of these problems, one that mutes the role of the appeal to Heaven as a judge of right; see *John Locke's Liberalism*, 162–78.

19. I discuss this again in chapter 6.

20. Bodleian MS Locke e. 18, fo. 2v–3v; reprinted as "On Allegiance and the Revolution," in John Locke, *Political Essays*, ed. Mark Goldie, 306–13 (Cambridge: Cambridge University Press, 1997).

21. Charles Tarlton sees this as the main part of Locke's strategy; see "A Rope of Sand," *Historical Journal* 21, no. 1 (1978): 43–73.

22. Peter Laslett disagrees, noting that Locke parted ways with Sidney and Tyrell in refusing to call Filmer a Hobbesian; introduction to *Two Treatises*, 71.

23. Seliger, "Locke's Theory of Revolutionary Action," *Western Political Quarterly* 16, no. 3 (September 1963): 567.

24. Cf. Hobbes, *Leviathan* XX.1–2, XXI.1–10.

25. Strauss, *Natural Right and History*, 220–221.

26. For what sense can be made of Locke's foundations, see Pangle, *Spirit of Modern Republicanism*, esp. 205–7.

5. The Lockean Commonwealth

1. As a number of scholars have pointed out, this is true to an extent even in otherwise legitimate societies: every individual, upon coming to the age of majority, is in a state of nature until he accedes to the social compact; see Peter Josephson, *The Great Art of Government* (Lawrence: University Press of Kansas, 2002), 124–26; Michael Zuckert, *Natural Rights and the New Republicanism* (Princeton, NJ: Princeton University Press, 1994), 18. Ruth Grant is resistant to these implications of Locke's doctrine; see *John Locke's Liberalism* (Chicago: University of Chicago Press, 1987), 125–26; cf. Martin Seliger, *The Liberal Politics of John Locke* (New York: Praeger, 1969), 82–138.

2. See Thomas Pangle, *The Spirit of Modern Republicanism* (Chicago: University of Chicago, 1988), 139, 172–83, 240–43, 249–51.

3. I mean this in a different spirit from Thomas Pangle's criticism of Harvey Mansfield, who had argued that the state of nature forms the foundation of Locke's criticism of the biblical God in the *First Treatise*; see Mansfield, "On the Political Character of Property in Locke," in *Powers, Possessions and Freedom*, ed. Alkis Kontos, 23–38 (Toronto: University of Toronto Press, 1979). Pangle argued instead that this criticism is what allows Locke to begin from the state of nature; see Pangle, *Spirit of Modern Republicanism*, 307n4. I mean instead the debate that might go on between Locke and Aristotle, or Rousseau, or Nietzsche.

4. Seliger, *Liberal Politics*, 32–33.

5. See Jeremy Waldron, "Is the Rule of Law an Essentially Contested Concept (In Florida)?," *Law and Philosophy* 21, no. 2 (March 2002): 137–64. A good survey of contemporary debates on the subject can be found in Frederic S. Burin, "The Theory

of the Rule of Law and the Structure of the Constitutional State," *American University Law Review* 15, no. 3 (June 1966): 313–40; Judith N. Shklar, "Political Theory and the Rule of Law," chap. 2 in *Political Thought and Political Thinkers* (Chicago: University of Chicago Press, 1998); and Natalie Stoljar, "Interpretation, Indeterminacy and Authority," *Journal of Political Philosophy* 11, no. 4 (2003): 470–98. See also the vol. 36 in the *Nomos* series, *The Rule of Law*, ed. Ian Shapiro (New York: New York University Press, 1994).

6. See Robert Ferguson, *A Brief Justification of the Prince of Orange's Descent into England* (London, 1689; EEBO, Wing F733).

7. On the objectives of the Rye House Plotters, see Richard Ashcraft, *Revolutionary Politics and Locke's "Two Treatises of Government"* (Princeton, NJ: Princeton University Press, 1986), 393.

8. See Robert Faulkner, "The First Liberal Democrat," *Review of Politics* 63, no. 1 (Winter 2001): 5–39; Josephson, *Great Art of Government*, esp. 205–29; C. B. Macpherson, *The Political Theory of Possessive Individualism* (Oxford: Clarendon Press, 1962); Seliger, *Liberal Politics*; Neil Wood, *John Locke and Agrarian Capitalism* (Berkeley and Los Angeles: University of California Press, 1984). Locke's failure to set down a specific constitution is noted by Grant, *John Locke's Liberalism*, 88–98, 200; Pangle, *Spirit of Modern Republicanism*, 255; A. John Simmons, *On the Edge of Anarchy* (Princeton, NJ: Princeton University Press, 1993), 94–98.

9. On the relationship between the divine right of kings and the Stuart monarchs, see Zuckert, *Natural Rights and the New Republicanism*, 30–43.

10. Cf. Robert Filmer, *Freeholder's Grand Inquest*, in *Patriarcha, and Other Writings*, ed. Johann P. Sommerville (Cambridge: Cambridge University Press, 1991).

11. I discuss this at greater length at the beginning of chapter 6.

12. See George Thomas, "As Far As Republican Principles Will Admit," *Presidential Studies Quarterly* 30, no. 3 (September 2000): 534–52, esp. 542–44. An alternative reading of this problem is presented by Grant, *John Locke's Liberalism*, 176–77.

13. Fatovic, "Constitutionalism and Contingency," *History of Political Thought* 25, no. 2 (Summer 2004): 296.

14. This is denied by Grant, *John Locke's Liberalism*, esp. 66–67, 172–74; A. John Simmons, *The Lockean Theory of Rights* (Princeton, NJ: Princeton University Press, 1992), 51–52. At a minimum, such an asymmetry is in fact present regarding a rightful slaveholder and his slaves; see Zuckert, *Natural Rights and the New Republicanism*, 241–42; but cf. Zuckert's discussion of property, 277–78.

15. I discussed this at somewhat greater length in chapter 3.

16. Article I, Section 1.

17. There can be little doubt as to whether a bill has become a law but we frequently contest whether the president is authorized to employ the military forces of

the United States; cf. Clinton's bombing of Serb forces in Kosovo and George W. Bush's invasion of Iraq.

18. See Josephson, *Great Art of Government*; Benjamin A. Kleinerman, "Can the Prince Really Be Tamed?" *American Political Science Review* 101, no. 2 (May 2007): 209–22; Thomas Pangle, "Executive Energy and Popular Spirit in Lockean Constitutionalism," *Presidential Studies Quarterly* 17, no. 2 (Spring 1987): 253–65; Pangle, *Spirit of Modern Republicanism*, 257.

19. Benjamin Kleinerman does not see the people as having learned this lesson. As a matter of historical fact he is probably right, but Locke's history cannot be taken as an indication of what he thought historically true; see Kleinerman, "Can the Prince Really Be Tamed?," esp. 211–12.

20. See Kleinerman, "Can the Prince Really Be Tamed?," esp. 213–15. George Thomas disagrees; see "As Far as Republican Principles Will Admit," 535n2.

21. Robert Faulkner and Peter Josephson disagree, preferring a more "discreet" exercise of prerogative and a cabinet-style executive in order better to hide such discretion; see Faulkner, "The First Liberal Democrat;" Josephson, *Great Art of Government*, 240, 344n22.

22. Not an unreasonable expectation: Tocqueville claims that Americans are all Cartesians without having even heard of Descartes; *Democracy in America*, trans. Harvey C. Mansfield and Delba Wilthrop (Chicago: University of Chicago Press, 2000): vol. II, part 1, ch. 1. Locke would no doubt approve wholeheartedly were Englishmen similarly Lockean.

23. Alexander Hamilton, James Madison, and John Jay, *The Federalist Papers*, ed. Clinton Rossiter (New York: Mentor Books, 1999), No. 51, p. 290.

24. Cf. Winston Churchill, *Marlborough: His Life and Times*, Vol. I (1933; repr. Chicago: University of Chicago Press, 2002), 224. Churchill is far less hagiographic on pp. 205–6.

25. See Josephson, *Great Art of Government*, 108–16, 211–12; Pangle, *Spirit of Modern Republicanism*, 172–76; David Resnick, "Locke and the Rejection of the Ancient Constitution," *Political Theory* 12, no. 1 (January 1984): 97–114. This is denied in Greg Forster, *John Locke's Politics of Moral Consensus* (Cambridge: Cambridge University Press, 2005); and Seliger, *Liberal Politics*, 54–55, 230–37. I address Forster's reading in chapter 6.

26. See Josephson, *Great Art of Government*, 102–8.

27. A piteous account of who was slaughtered or sold into slavery, and why, is contained in Churchill, *Marlborough*, I: 197–200.

28. C. B. Macpherson suggests that Locke would have exempted the lifestyle of a bourgeois capitalist from the effects of a life lived without significant leisure; see *Theory of Possessive Individualism*, 222–29.

29. Cf. Pangle, *Spirit of Modern Republicanism*, 189–97.

30. For the view that this is what Machiavelli did consciously, for example, see Leo Strauss, *Thoughts on Machiavelli* (1958; repr. Chicago: University of Chicago Press, 1978); cf. Harvey C. Mansfield, *Machiavelli's New Modes and Orders* (1979; repr. Chicago: University of Chicago Press, 2001); *Machiavelli's Virtue* (Chicago: University of Chicago Press, 1996).

31. Josephson, *Great Art of Government*, 282. For an attempt to explain what might have motivated Locke to provide such a public doctrine, see Pangle, *Spirit of Modern Republicanism*, 203–4.

32. For a moderately different treatment of this issue, see Pangle, *Spirit of Modern Republicanism*, 262–75. I do not think that Locke intends to point toward the philosopher, nor am I as concerned with highlighting Locke's deficient presentation or understanding of that human type.

33. Italics added.

34. Cf. Zuckert, *Natural Rights and the New Republicanism*, 241–42.

35. This half of what Locke teaches is emphasized by Grant, *John Locke's Liberalism*, esp. 40–8, 92–3, 192–7.

36. Patrick Riley, arguing mostly from the *Essay Concerning Human Understanding* rather than from the *Two Treatises*, also notes this tension, though he judges it to be a *progression* from liberty as a matter of will to liberty as reason; see "Locke on 'Voluntary Agreement' and Political Power," *Western Political Quarterly* 29, no. 1 (March 1976): 136–45.

37. Cf. Steven Forde, "What Does Locke Expect Us to Know?" *Review of Politics* 68, no. 2 (May 2006): 232–58.

38. See Robert A. Goldwin, "John Locke," in *History of Political Philosophy*, ed. Leo Strauss and Joseph Cropsey, 3d ed. (Chicago: University of Chicago Press, 1987), 506.

6. *Justifying Secular Politics*

1. Cf. Thomas Pangle, *The Spirit of Modern Republicanism* (Chicago: University of Chicago, 1988), 138–39.

2. John Locke, *Two Treatises of Government*, ed. Peter Laslett, student ed. (Cambridge: Cambridge University Press, 1988), 187n; see also Michael Zuckert, *Natural Rights and the New Republicanism* (Princeton, NJ: Princeton University Press, 1994), 39–49.

3. Luther, *The Large Catechism*, Part I, The Fourth Commandment, §141.

4. Lawson, *Politica Sacra & Civilis* (London, 1660; EEBO, Wing L710), 12, 45–46. It is all the more ironic, then, that Laslett follows A. H. Maclean in his

argument that "virtually every characteristic argument of the second of Locke's treatises *Of Government* had been advanced thirty years previously" by George Lawson; Maclean, "George Lawson and John Locke," *Cambridge Historical Journal* 9, no. 1 (March 1947): 71. I am uncertain how this thesis is plausible, given that Lawson's government is an aspect of God's authority, not man's natural executive power, and has no room for religious toleration of any kind; see Lawson, *Politica Sacra & Civilis*, esp. 7, 38. The only way in which Locke *does* seem to follow Lawson is to place the right of resistance with the people rather than with Parliament; see Ruth Grant, *John Locke's Liberalism* (Chicago: University of Chicago Press, 1987), 108.

5. Calvin, *Institutes of the Christian Religion*, Bk. II, Ch. 8, §35.

6. Reprinted in *State Tracts*, vol. II (London, 1692; EEBO, Wing S5331), 271.

7. *Paraphrase and Notes on the Epistles of St. Paul,* reprinted in *The Works of John Locke in Nine Volumes,* 12th ed., Vol. VII (London: Rivington, 1824; Online Library of Liberty [oll.libertyfund.org]), 405n†.

8. Proast, *A Third Letter Concerning Toleration* (Oxford: L. Lichfield, 1691; EEBO, Wing P3539), 62.

9. See Philip Abrams's introduction to *Two Tracts on Government*, by John Locke (Cambridge: Cambridge University Press, 1967).

10. For more on these topics, see Abrams's introduction to *Two Tracts*; Ingrid Creppell, "Locke on Toleration," *Political Theory* 24, no. 2 (May 1996): 200–40; J. W. Gough, "The Development of Locke's Belief in Toleration," in *A Letter Concerning Toleration in Focus*, by John Locke, ed. John Horton and Susan Mendus, 57–77 (New York: Routledge, 1991); Robert P. Kraynak, "John Locke: From Absolutism to Toleration," *American Political Science Review* 74, no. 1 (March 1980): 53–69.

11. Greg Forster's entire reinvention of Locke's political philosophy aims at denying this one point; *John Locke's Politics of Moral Consensus* (Cambridge: Cambridge University Press, 2005). This aim warrants refuting his book. His argument is that Locke sought to overcome the destructive sectarianism of his day by appealing to a baseline of morality upon which all men, regardless of sect, could agree. Politics would be guided by this baseline, not the various other opinions about which we could not be as certain. This baseline is provided, moreover, only by a religious foundation, not a secular one. Forster's evidence for this is limited to the fact that it would make Locke's politics work, and be an answer to the implicit nihilism of modern liberal theory, and be the answer which Forster himself desires. In order for Forster's interpretation to succeed, then, it must somehow make sense of Locke's texts. I will leave aside the fact that, like most reconstructions of Locke's thought, it makes Locke into one of the worst expositors of his own ideas who has ever lived; Forster is clear that he attributes no esoteric intention to Locke's vagueness. Rather, he must show that Locke's law of nature differs not only from the Hobbesian variety but also from the transcendent natural law variety; it must instead be of the immanent, medieval variety—to form the basis of a consensus, most men must actually know it. While it might be blotted out from an individual's heart here and there,

or even if most nations together fail in some particular regard, the consensus of all nations would be indicative of this law.

Forster's attribution of this position to Locke relies upon finding a distinction between the common consent of a nation and the universal consent of all mankind in TT I 88 so at odds with the plain meaning of that passage that his ability to discern it there can be explained only by his hope to find it somewhere—a hope born of his belief that it would be a solution to, rather than a denial of, the problem of moral pluralism for everyone to recognize that we are all under the authority of God, even if that God is only that of Christianity Lite; cf. *Moral Consensus*, 194–217, esp. 208–10. Forster's reading is especially bizarre given what Locke says about an impartial survey of "the Nations of the World," the means by which "their Governments, Religions, and Manners [are] brought in and continued amongst them," and the "but little Reverence for the Practices which are in use and credit amongst Men" which such a survey must produce (TT I 58). For a greater discussion of Locke's judgment on custom, see chapter 5.

12. Proast, *The Argument of the Letter Concerning Toleration Briefly Consider'd and Answer'd* (Oxford, 1690; EEBO, Wing P3538), 26.

13. This is in large part due to the fact that Proast fails to discern the argument in the *Letter* that does not rely on Locke's being correct about theology; see *Argument of the Letter*, 3–4. Their debate therefore centers on what is best for the propagation of Christianity and whether the Bible commands or even permits the use of civil power in advancing it. As Locke's second, third, and fourth letters concerning toleration are largely attacks on Proast's novel system, I shall not discuss them thematically.

14. Thomas Long objects that this ignores the plain meaning of Romans 13:3: that God *has* appointed governors so that we may live Christian lives; see *The Letter for Toleration Decipher'd* (London: Freeman Collins, 1689; EEBO, Wing L2973), 3. Proast is more liberal in his objection, noting that Locke's argument for this is circular and devoid of Christian charity; *Argument of the Letter*, 17–21. Locke's response does not deny the second charge, but instead accuses Proast of a parallel circularity (2LCT 116–23). Proast points to charity again and proceeds to demonstrate precisely how Locke begs the question; *Third Letter*, 32, 56–57.

15. Proast's refutation of the *Letter* is mistaken in that he thinks the inability to bring about religious reflection and subsequent conversion by force is an essential premise of Locke's argument for toleration; see *Argument of the Letter*. Greg Forster takes this to be almost the sole purpose of the *Letter*: it is "actually a theological work about salvation, disguised as a work of political theory;" *Moral Consensus*, 162. Locke emphatically denies that this is so (2LCT 67). Indeed, his attack on Proast's vision of force causing men to hearken to argument assumes that force actually *can* sway belief (2LCT 76–8).

16. Thomas Pangle seems to criticize Locke for not recognizing that this, rather than Locke's "physician's critique of the biblical God," is the core of the theologico-political problem; see Pangle, *Spirit of Modern Republicanism*, 147–9.

17. See also Pangle, *Spirit of Modern Republicanism*, 134–35, 151–81; Nathan Tarcov, *Locke's Education for Liberty* (Chicago: University of Chicago Press, 1984), 57–66.

18. Martin Seliger, *The Liberal Politics of John Locke* (New York: Praeger, 1969), 58.

19. Cf. Calvin, *Institutes of the Christian Religion*, Bk. IV, Ch. 20.

20. Long's opinion of the scriptural sources and sentiments to which Locke appeals is that they are the ruses of a Devil attempting to appear "as an Angel of Light[:] these are but baits to cover the hook and invite the Licentious Readers to swallow it the more greedily. It is a greater wonder, that any Person of common Apprehension should not discern the impostures;" *The Letter Decipher'd*, 4–5.

21. Jeremy Waldron disagrees; see *God, Locke, and Equality* (Cambridge: Cambridge University Press, 2002), 224, 230–31, 236–40.

22. "The Congress finds and declares that the Communist Party of the United States, although purportedly a political party, is in fact an instrumentality of a conspiracy to overthrow the Government of the United States. . . . Therefore, the Communist Party should be outlawed." 50 U.S.C. §841.

23. Quoted in Markus Fischer, "Machiavelli's Political Psychology," *Review of Politics* 59, no. 4 (Autumn 1997): 799; from Machiavelli, *The Chief Works and Others*, trans. Allan Gilbert (Durham, NC: Duke University Press, 1965), Familiar Letter #225, p. 1010.

24. Locke employs a similar rhetorical strategy in addressing the objections of Jonas Proast: because Proast admits that the magistrate's use of force may drive men away from the true religion, if used poorly, the magistrate must be denied the ability to use it at all (2LCT 69–72), whereas Proast was arguing only that it is not unjust for a true Christian prince to employ that force well; cf. Proast, *Argument of the Letter*, 4–17; *Third Letter*, 27–30.

25. Proast, *Argument of the Letter*, 2. Locke's response to the suggestion that he places trade and commerce above "other considerations" is peculiar. If Proast does not mean "above *religion*," Locke says, then he cannot fathom why he would make that suggestion. Locke's parallel statement is not, however, that if Proast *did* mean religion, his insinuation is very uncharitable. Rather, Locke says, "*if you do not know* that the author of the letter places the advancement of trade above religion, your insinuation is very uncharitable" (2LCT 63; italics added).

26. Long, *The Letter Decipher'd*, 2.

27. Proast, *Third Letter*, esp. 27–30, 61–62, 73–76.

28. Proast, *Third Letter*, 62. In *Questions Concerning the Law of Nature*, Locke does make the worship, or rather the "public worship" of the or a deity, or just of "divinity," obligatory, but he makes it a very conditional duty without specifying the conditions (cf. NL X 95).

29. See Raymond Klibansky's preface to *Epistola de Tolerantia—A Letter on Toleration*, by John Locke, trans. J. W. Gough (Oxford: Clarendon Press, 1968), xviii–xxvi.

30. Popple is much better at translating *respondeo*, but again not perfect. In Locke's Latin, there is no *respondeo* without a preceding *dices* or *quaeris*, though the converse is not true.

31. Popple translates this as "the" true church, but this would suggest that Locke believed there to be only one; see J. W. Gough, Introduction and Notes to *Epistola de Tolerantia*, 156n1.

32. Proast, *Argument of the Letter*, 1. Greg Forster misses this when he says that toleration is a specifically Christian duty; *Moral Consensus*, 161.

32. "Hints" may be too strong for *indicasse*, though it is preferred by both Popple and Gough in their translations. There is an element of actual indication or information in *indico* that is absent from, say, *subindico* or *innuo*.

34. Klibansky prefers this to Limborch's own interpretation as stated in a letter to Lady Masham in 1705, which replaced the initials which refer to his name with *Libertatis Amantem*, Friend of Liberty. His reasons for this are sound. See Klibansky, Preface to *Epistola de Tolerantia*, xviii–xix.

35. Popple translates both *adiaphora* and *indifferentes* as "indifferent things," thus obscuring the fact that Locke denies the existence of *adiaphora* and speaks in his own voice only of *indifferentes*.

36. But cf. *Employment Division v. Smith*, 494 U.S. 872 (1990).

37. See Ashcraft, *Revolutionary Politics and Locke's "Two Treatises of Government"* (Princeton, NJ: Princeton University Press, 1986), 498–99. Greg Forster takes Ashcraft to be referring to the opening charges that those who persecute tolerate "fornication, deceit, malice, and other vices, which according to the Apostle (Rom. i) so plainly smell of paganism," and "*adultery, fornication, uncleanness, lasciviousness, idolatry, and the like*;" Forster, *Moral Consensus*, 161, 292n63; cf. LCT 61–62 [24].

38. See Proast, *Argument of the Letter*, 1–2: "And all that he requires of any, to qualify them for the benefit of Toleration he endeavours to promote, is onely, That they be not *Atheists*; That they hold no *Opinions contrary to Civil Society*; and, That they *own and teach the Duty of tolerating all men in matters of meer Religion*."

39. Waldron, *God, Locke, and Equality*, 218–23.

40. Cf. *Church of Lukumi Babalu Aye v. Hialeah*, 508 U.S. 520 (1993).

41. J. R. Milton, "Locke's Life and Times," in *The Cambridge Companion to Locke*, ed. Vere Chappell, 5–25 (Cambridge: Cambridge University Press, 1994), 7.

42. For example, "Speech at Columbus, Ohio, September 16, 1859," in *Speeches and Writings, 1859–1865*, ed. Don E. Fehrenbacher (New York: Literary Classics of the United States, 1989), esp. 32–36.

43. *De Cive* XIV.19 (but cf. the reason given there with XV.2); appendix to the Latin edition of *Leviathan* II.35–38.

44. Cf. Pangle, *Spirit of Modern Republicanism*, 214.

45. Waldron, *God, Locke, and Equality*, 223–35.

46. Cf. Plato, *Lesser Hippias* and *Republic*, Books. II–III; Laurence Lampert, "Socrates' Defense of Polytropic Odysseus," *Review of Politics* 64, no. 2 (Spring 2002): 231–59.

47. Cf. Cicero, *De re publica*, Bk. III. Locke discusses Carneades in NL XI 105ff.; see Zuckert, *Natural Rights and the New Republicanism*, 211–15. See my discussion of the *Reasonableness of Christianity* in conjunction with the value of custom in chapter 5. I cannot be certain that Locke is able to avoid Carneades' conclusion, or even that he fully desired to. Thomas Pangle's remark that the *Reasonableness* "teaches that revelation, whether of Moses or of Christ, does not alter or enhance either the fundamental provisions of morality or the nature of obligation," seems an exaggeration; see Pangle, *Spirit of Modern Republicanism*, 154–55. Pangle draws this conclusion from a passage where Locke asserts that there is a law of nature, knowable by reason, in order to justify God's punishment of Adam, yet this is something that Pangle had earlier argued was unjust on Locke's premises (143–47). The effect of God's not punishing Adam, "in any point," Locke says, would be that "government and order are at an end; and there can be no bounds set to the lawless exorbitancy of unconfined man" (RC 14). The fact that Locke thought reason sufficient to discover nature's God and its "enforcement of the rational law without any assistance from Scripture," as Pangle says (155; cf. 149–51), does not alter Locke's assertions that this extrinsic enforcement is essential to morality's choiceworthiness. It is true that, both here in the *Reasonableness* and in the *Essay Concerning Human Understanding*, Locke repeats that reason cannot know that there is another life, while the rewards and sanctions of morality belong to that other life (ECHU II.28.6, II.28.8, IV.18.7; RC 245). It is impossible to square these arguments with his statement that there is "a Law, knowable by the light of Nature, *i.e.* without the help of positive Revelation" (ECHU I.3.13); still, to the extent that this affirmation of a natural law is present in the *Reasonableness*, it expresses itself only as the knowledge that there is one God who punishes in the next life: those who did not see the utility of morality "might have argued . . . and concluded, That because the good were most of them ill-treated here, there was another place where they should meet with better usage" (RC 245). Yet this is precisely what is knowable only by revelation! Whether we accept that Locke was confused here, or instead prefer that even this whole business about *nature's* God's being the font of morality is a sort of intellectual trap to shroud his moral teaching from the resolutely pious, he would still either let slip or teach the truth of moral nihilism. Given Locke's hedonism, we would have to say that reward and punishment, temporal or sempiternal, are precisely what is needed for there to be a moral law of any kind, a point which Pangle endorses (189–97, but cf. 201–4, 209), and so the revelation of the biblical God would in fact have to alter the fundamental provisions of morality. Whether Locke actually desired to teach this is another matter entirely.

48. Forster, *Moral Consensus*, esp. 112, 160–65; see also Sam Black, "Toleration and the Skeptical Inquirer in Locke," *Canadian Journal of Philosophy* 28, no. 4 (December 1998): 473–504; J. Judd Owen, "Locke's Case for Religious Toleration," *Journal of Politics* 69, no. 1 (February 2007): 156–68.

49. Tuckness, *Locke and the Legislative Point of View* (Princeton, NJ: Princeton University Press, 2002).

50. MS Locke, f. 1, pp. 367–70; reprinted in Locke, *Political Essays*, ed. Mark Goldie (Cambridge: Cambridge University Press, 1997), 245–6.

51. There are no interjections in the postscript, so even if that was added later it would not alter this calculation. On the composition of the *Letter Concerning Toleration*, see Klibansky, Preface to *Epistola de Tolerantia*, ix–x.

52. Aristotle never, after all, ceases to remind that military power is needed for any regime, no matter how just; cf. *Politics* 1283a16–23, 1291a23–28, 1309b14–17, 1325b10–13, 1328b4–8; see Robert C. Bartlett, "The 'Realism' of Classical Political Science," *American Journal of Political Science* 38, no. 2 (May 1994): 381–402. While regimes might be justified by the sort of multitude present in each, it is the distribution of military capacity that explains why the various regimes come into being; cf. *Politics* 1289b37, 1293a11–34, 1296b16–18, 1297b13–28, 1321a4–22.

53. This argument is put forward in Kirstie McClure, *Judging Rights* (Ithaca, NY: Cornell University Press, 1996), 27–101; James Tully, *A Discourse on Property* (Cambridge: Cambridge University Press, 1980). Its shortcomings are elucidated by Peter Josephson, *The Great Art of Government* (Lawrence: University Press of Kansas, 2002), 33–44, 92–96; Zuckert, *Natural Rights and the New Republicanism*, 217–19, 238–46, 259–75.

54. Cf. Pangle, *Spirit of Modern Republicanism*, 144–45.

55. Pangle, *Spirit of Modern Republicanism*, 141–51, 158–71; see also Zuckert, *Natural Rights and the New Republicanism*, 259–64.

56. See Pangle, *Spirit of Modern Republicanism*, 170–71. In order for Michael Zuckert to find a real property right in the absence of plenty, he must adopt a proto-Kantian, analytical argument; see *Natural Rights and the New Republicanism*, 275–86; *Launching Liberalism* (Lawrence: University Press of Kansas, 2002), 169–200; cf. James R. Stoner, Jr., "Was Leo Strauss Wrong about John Locke?," *Review of Politics* 66, no. 4 (Fall 2004): 553–63; Zuckert, "Perhaps He Was," *Review of Politics* 66, no. 4 (Fall 2004): 565–69; Stoner, "Not So . . . ," *Review of Politics* 66, no. 4 (Fall 2004): 571–73. A proto-Kantian Locke is also advocated by A. John Simmons, *The Lockean Theory of Rights* (Princeton, NJ: Princeton University Press, 1992), 36–46.

57. Schmitt, *Political Theology*, trans. George Schwab (Chicago: University of Chicago Press, 2005), 36–37. Kirstie McClure's interpretation of Locke's theology bears much in common with what Schmitt attributes to liberalism; see *Judging Rights*, esp. 27–39, 45–52.

58. Schmitt, *Legality and Legitimacy*, trans. Jeffrey Seitzer (Durham, NC: Duke University Press, 2004), 99; cf. *Political Theology*, 13–14; *Die Diktatur*, 5th ed. (Berlin: Duncker & Humblot, 1989), 40–42.

59. Schmitt, *The Concept of the Political*, expanded ed., trans. George Scwab (Chicago: University of Chicago Press, 2007), esp. 69–79.

60. This would elevate the importance of the federative power and is what makes Richard Cox's reading plausible; see *Locke on War and Peace* (Oxford: Clarendon Press, 1960). In chapter 3, I argued why society's initial emphasis on the federative power was mistaken, in Locke's view; my point here is merely that the distinction between friend and enemy is not absent from Locke's commonwealth. See also Josephson, *Great Art of Government*, 182–85.

61. For this and what follows, see Schmitt, *Die Diktatur*, 40–42.

62. Schmitt, *Die Diktatur*, 42.

63. Schmitt, *Die Diktatur*, 42.

64. Schmitt, *Concept of the Political*, 20, 22.

65. *vincitur et constingitur natura*. See *Instauratio Magna*, distributio operis.

66. *hominum statum levandem et juvandum*. See *Novum Organum* I.73, I.81; cf. *The Advancement of Learning*, Bk. I, V.11. For Locke's indebtedness to Bacon regarding his epistemology, see *On the Conduct of the Understanding*, §1; Pangle, *Spirit of Modern Republicanism*, 166–68.

67. See Pangle, *Spirit of Modern Republicanism*, 168–71; Zuckert, *Natural Rights and the New Republicanism*, 264–6.

68. See Ruth Grant, *John Locke's Liberalism*, 176–79, 202–5.

Conclusion

1. Cf. Thomas Pangle, *The Spirit of Modern Republicanism* (Chicago: University of Chicago Press, 1988), 215–29, esp. 225–27. Peter Josephson is far more sanguine about the Lockean commonwealth's prospects, concluding only with an awareness of what must be sacrificed for its invention; he sees Locke's educational regimen as sufficient to a liberal polity because he focuses far more on the rulers' prudence in governing the people than on the people's armed vigilance of their rulers; *The Great Art of Government* (Lawrence: University Press of Kansas, 2002), esp. 243–60, 277–82; cf. Christopher Anderson, "Safe Enough in his Honesty and Prudence," *History of Political Thought* 13, no. 4 (Winter 1992): 605–30; Harvey C. Mansfield, "The Right of Revolution," *Daedalus* 105, no. 4 (Fall 1976): 151–62; Pangle, "Executive Energy and Popular Spirit in Lockean Constitutionalism," *Presidential Studies Quarterly* 17, no. 2 (Spring 1987): 253–65. Robert Horwitz, too, focuses on the education more of a class of responsible leaders than of extemporary colonels charged

with mustering shopkeepers into a militia; "John Locke and the Preservation of Liberty," in *The Moral Foundations of the American Republic*, ed. Horwitz, 129–56 (Charlottesville: University Press of Virginia, 1977).

2. For the development of the modern executive, see Harvey Mansfield, *Taming the Prince* (1989; repr. Baltimore: Johns Hopkins University Press, 1993). How my thesis in this book fits within that framework is something I shall have to leave for another occasion.

Bibliography

Abrams, Philip. Introduction to *Two Tracts on Government*, by John Locke. Cambridge: Cambridge University Press, 1967.

Anderson, Christopher. "'Safe Enough in his Honesty and Prudence': The Ordinary Conduct of Government in the Thought of John Locke." *History of Political Thought* 13, no. 4 (Winter 1992): 605–30.

Aristotle. *The Politics.* Translated by Carnes Lord. Chicago: University of Chicago Press, 1984.

Ashcraft, Richard. "Locke's State of Nature: Historical Fact or Moral Fiction?" *American Political Science Review* 62, no. 3 (September 1968): 898–915.

———. "Political Theory and Political Reform." *Western Political Quarterly* 22, no. 4 (December 1969): 742–58.

———. "Revolutionary Politics and Locke's *Two Treatises of Government.*" *Political Theory* 8, no. 4 (November 1980): 429–85.

———. *Revolutionary Politics and Locke's "Two Treatises of Government."* Princeton, NJ: Princeton University Press, 1986.

———. *Locke's "Two Treatises of Government."* London: Allen & Unwin, 1987.

Ashcraft, Richard, and M. M. Goldsmith. "Locke, Revolution Principles, and the Formation of Whig Ideology." *Historical Journal* 26, no. 4 (December 1983): 773–800.

Bacon, Francis. *Instauratio Magna.* London, 1620. Reprint, Early English Books Online (eebo.chadwyck.com), STC (2nd. ed.) 1163.

———. *Of the proficience and aduancement of learning, diuine and humane.* London, 1605. Reprint, Early English Books Online (eebo.chadwyck.com), STC (2nd. ed.) 1164.

Barrow, Isaac. *Several Sermons Against Evil-Speaking.* London, 1678. Reprint, Early English Books Online (eebo.chadwyck.com),Wing B959.

Bartlett, Robert C. "The 'Realism' of Classical Political Science." *American Journal of Political Science* 38, no. 2 (May 1994): 381–402.

Bates, William. *The Great Duty of Resignation to the Divine Will in Afflictions Enforced from the Example of Our Suffering Saviour.* London, 1684. Reprint, Early English Books Online (eebo.chadwyck.com),Wing B1111.

Bellamie, John. *A Iustification of "The City Remonstrance" and its Vindication. Or, An Answer to a Book written by Mr. J. P. Entituled, The City Remonstrance Remonstrated. Wherein the frequent Falsifyings of the said Mr. J. P. are discovered, the many Charges by him laid upon the Remonstrance and its Vindicator, disproved, and the parity and agreement of the Remonstrance (especially in those particulars so much condemned by him) with the Propositions, Declarations, Remonstrances, and Votes, of both or either House of Parliament manifested.* London, 1646. Reprint, Early English Books Online (eebo.chadwyck.com), Wing B1814.

Black, Sam. "Toleration and the Skeptical Inquirer in Locke." *Canadian Journal of Philosophy* 28, no. 4 (December 1998): 473–504.

Blackstone, William. *Commentaries on the Laws of England.* 4 vols. 1765–69. Reprint in 2 vol., Clark, NJ: The Lawbook Exchange, Ltd., 2003.

Bodin, Jean. *On Sovereignty.* Translated by Julian H. Franklin. Cambridge: Cambridge University Press, 1992.

Buckler, Edward. *A Buckler Against the Fear of Death; or, Pious and Profitable Observations, Meditations, and Consolations.* London, 1640. Reprint, Early English Books Online (eebo.chadwyck.com), STC (2nd ed.) 4008.5.

Burin, Frederic S. "The Theory of the Rule of Law and the Structure of the Constitutional State." *American University Law Review* 15, no. 3 (June 1966): 313–40.

Calvin, John. *Institutes of the Christian Religion.* Edited by John T. McNeill. Translated by Ford Lewis Battles. Two Volumes. Philadelphia: Westminster Press, 1960.

Campbell, Archibald. *Instructions to a Son by Archibald, late Marquis of Argyl; written in the time of his confinement.* London, 1661. Reprint, Early English Books Online (eebo.chadwyck.com), Wing A3657.

Chappell, Vere, editor. *The Cambridge Companion to Locke.* Cambridge: Cambridge University Press, 1994.

Churchill, Winston. *Marlborough: His Life and Times*. Volume I. Chicago: University of Chicago Press, 2002. First published 1933 by George G. Harrap & Co.

Cicero, Marcus Tullius. *On the Commonwealth and On the Laws*. Edited by James E. G. Zetzel. Cambridge: Cambridge University Press, 1999.

Coby, Patrick. "The Law of Nature in Locke's *Second Treatise*." *Review of Politics* 49, no. 1 (Winter 1987): 3–28.

Coke, Edward. *The Selected Writings of Sir Edward Coke*. 3 vols. Edited by Steven Sheppard. Indianapolis: Liberty Fund, 2003.

Corbett, Ross J. "The Extraconstitutionality of Lockean Prerogative." *Review of Politics* 68, no. 3 (Summer 2006): 428–48.

Cox, Richard. *Locke on War and Peace*. Oxford: Clarendon Press, 1960.

Creppell, Ingrid. "Locke on Toleration." *Political Theory* 24, no. 2 (May 1996): 200–40.

Declaration of His Highness William Henry (by the Grace of God) Prince of Orange, &c. Of the Reasons Inducing Him to appear in Arms in the Kingdom of England, for the Preserving of the Protestant Religion, and Restoring the Laws and Liberties of England, Scotland and Ireland. Reprinted in *State Tracts* . . . , 420–25.

Dunn, John. "Consent in the Political Theory of John Locke." *The Historical Journal* 10, no. 2 (1967): 153–82 .

———. *The Political Thought of John Locke: An Historical Account of the Argument of the "Two Treatises of Government."* Cambridge: Cambridge University Press, 1969.

Dworkin, Ronald. *Law's Empire*. Cambridge, MA: Belknap Press of Harvard University, 1986.

Fatovic, Clement. "Constitutionalism and Contingency: Locke's Theory of Prerogative." *History of Political Thought* 25, no. 2 (Summer 2004): 276–97.

Faulkner, Robert. "The First Liberal Democrat: Locke's Popular Government." *Review of Politics* 63, no. 1 (Winter 2001): 5–39.

[Ferguson, Robert]. *A Brief Justification of the Prince of Orange's Descent into England, And of the Kingdoms Late Recourse to Arms. with A Modest Disquisition of what may Become the Wisdom and Justice of the Ensuing Convention in their Disposal of the Crown*. London, 1689. Reprint, Early English Books Online (eebo.chadwyck.com), Wing F733.

Filmer, Robert. *Patriarcha and Other Writings*. Edited by Johann P. Sommerville. Cambridge: Cambridge University Press, 1991.

Fischer, Markus. "Machiavelli's Political Psychology." *Review of Politics* 59, no. 4 (Autumn 1997): 789–829.

Forde, Steven. "Natural Law, Theology, and Morality in Locke." *American Journal of Political Science* 45, no. 2 (April 2001): 396–409.

———. "What Does Locke Expect Us to Know?" *Review of Politics* 68, no. 2 (May 2006): 232–58.

Forster, Greg. *John Locke's Politics of Moral Consensus*. Cambridge: Cambridge University Press, 2005.

Glenn, Gary. "Inalienable Rights and Locke's Argument for Limited Government." *Journal of Politics* 46, no. 1 (February 1984): 80–105.

Goldwin, Robert. "Locke's State of Nature in Political Society." *Western Political Quarterly* 29, no. 1 (March 1976): 126–35.

———. "John Locke." In *History of Political Philosophy*, edited by Leo Strauss and Joseph Cropsey, 476–512. Third Edition. Chicago: University of Chicago Press, 1987.

Gough, J. W. *John Locke's Political Philosophy*. Revised edition. Oxford: Clarendon Press, 1956.

———. Introduction and Notes to *Epistola de Tolerantia—A Letter on Toleration*, by John Locke. Edited by Raymond Klibansky. Translated by J. W. Gough. Oxford: Clarendon Press, 1968.

———. "The Development of Locke's Belief in Toleration." In *A Letter Concerning Toleration in Focus*, by John Locke. Edited by John Horton and Susan Mendus. New York: Routledge, 1991.

Grant, Ruth W. *John Locke's Liberalism*. Chicago: University of Chicago Press, 1987.

———. "Locke's Political Anthropology and Lockean Individualism." *Journal of Politics* 50, no. 1 (February 1988): 42–63.

Grotius, Hugo. *The Rights of War and Peace*. Edited by Richard Tuck. 3 volumes. Indianapolis: Liberty Fund, 2005.

Hamilton, Alexander, James Madison, and John Jay. *The Federalist Papers*. Edited by Clinton Rossiter. New York: Mentor Books, 1999.

Hart, H. L. A. *The Concept of Law*. 2d ed. Edited by Penelope Bulloch and Joseph Raz. Oxford: Clarendon Press, 1994. First edition 1961.

den Hartogh, Govert. "Tully's Locke." *Political Theory* 18, no. 4 (November 1990): 656–72.

Hobbes, Thomas. *Leviathan, with selected variants from the Latin edition of 1668*. Edited by Edwin Curley. Indianapolis: Hackett Publishing Company, 1994.

———. *Elements of Law, Natural and Politic*. Edited by J. C. A. Gaskin. Oxford: Oxford University Press, 1994.

———. *On the Citizen*. Edited by Richard Tuck and Michael Silverthorne. Cambridge: Cambridge University Press, 1998. Originally published as *De Cive*.

Hooker, Richard. *Of the Laws of Ecclesiastical Polity*. Edited by Georges Edelen, et al. 4 Volumes. Cambridge, MA: Belknap Press, 1977–82.

Horwitz, Robert. "John Locke and the Preservation of Liberty." In *The Moral Foundations of the American Republic*, edited by Robert Horwitz, 129–56. Charlottesville: University Press of Virginia, 1977.

———. Introduction to *Questions Concerning the Law of Nature*, by John Locke. Edited and translated by Robert Horwitz, Jenny Strauss Clay, and Diskin Clay. Ithaca, NY: Cornell University Press, 1990.

Josephson, Peter. *The Great Art of Government: Locke's Use of Consent*. Lawrence: University Press of Kansas, 2002.

Kelsen, Hans. *General Theory of Law and State*. Cambridge, MA: Harvard University Press, 1949. Originally published as *Allgemeine Staatslehre* (1925).

———. *Pure Theory of Law*. 2nd ed. Translated by Max Knight. Berkeley and Los Angeles: University of California Press, 1967. Originally published as *Reine Rechtslehre* (1960). First edition 1934.

Kendall, Wilmoore. *John Locke and the Doctrine of Majority Rule*. Urbana: University of Illinois Press, 1965. First published 1941.

Kilcullen, John. "Locke on Political Obligation." *Review of Politics* 45, no. 3 (July 1983): 323–44.

King, William. *The State of the Protestants of Ireland Under the late King James's Government; in which Their Carriage towards him is justified, and the absolute Necessity of their endeavouring to be free from his Government, and of submitting to their present Majesties is demonstrated*. London, 1691. Reprint, Early English Books Online (eebo.chadwyck.com), Wing K538.

Kleinerman, Benjamin A. "Can the Prince Really Be Tamed? Executive Prerogative, Popular Apathy, and the Constitutional Frame in Locke's *Second Treatise*." *American Political Science Review* 101, no. 2 (May 2007): 209–22.

Klibansky, Raymond. Preface to *Epistola de Tolerantia—A Letter on Toleration*, by John Locke. Edited by Raymond Klibansky. Translated by J. W. Gough. Oxford: Clarendon Press, 1968.

Kraynak, Robert P. "John Locke: From Absolutism to Toleration." *American Political Science Review* 74, no. 1 (March 1980): 53–69.

Lampert, Laurence. "Socrates' Defense of Polytropic Odysseus: Lying and Wrong-doing in Plato's *Lesser Hippias*." *Review of Politics* 64, no. 2 (Spring 2002): 231–59.

Langston, Thomas and Michael Lind. "John Locke and the Limits of Presidential Prerogative." *Polity* 24, no. 1 (Fall 1991): 49–68.

Laslett, Peter. "The Gentry of Kent in 1640." *Cambridge Historical Journal* 9, no. 2 (1948): 148–64.

———. "The English Revolution and Locke's *Two Treatises of Government*." *Cambridge Historical Journal* 12, no. 1 (March 1956): 40–55.

———. Introduction to *Two Treatises of Government*, by John Locke. Edited by Peter Laslett. Student edition. Cambridge: Cambridge University Press, 1988. First published 1960.

Lawson, George. *Politica Sacra & Civilis: or, A Modell of Civil and Eclesiasticall Government. wherein, Besides the positive Doctrine concerning State and Church in general, are debated the principall Controversies of the times. concerning The Constitution of the State and Church of England, tending to Righteousness, Truth and Peace.* London, 1660. Reprint, Early English Books Online (eebo.chadwyck.com), Wing L710.

Lightfoot, John. *The Harmony of the Foure Evangelists: Among themselves, and with the Old Testament.* London, 1644. Reprint, Early English Books Online (eebo.chadwyck.com),Wing L2058.

———. *The works of the Reverend and learned John Lightfoot D. D., late Master of Katherine Hall in Cambridge such as were, and such as never before were printed.* London, 1684. Reprint, Early English Books Online (eebo.chadwyck.com), Wing L2051.

Lincoln, Abraham. *Speeches and Writings, 1859–1865.* Edited by Don E. Fehrenbacher. New York: Literary Classics of the United States, 1989.

Lloyd, William. *A Discourse of God's Ways of Disposing of Kingdoms*. London, 1691. Reprint, Early English Books Online (eebo.chadwyck.com), Wing L2679.

Locke, John. *The Works of John Locke in Nine Volumes*. 12th edition. London: Rivington, 1824. Reprint, Online Library of Liberty (oll.libertyfund.org).

———. *Essays on the Law of Nature and associated writings*. Edited by W. von Leyden. Oxford: Clarendon Press, 1988. First published 1954.

———. *The Reasonableness of Christianity*. Edited by George W. Ewing. Washington, DC: Regnery Gateway, 1965.

———. *Two Tracts on Government*. Edited by Philip Abrams. Cambridge: Cambridge University Press, 1967.

———. *Epistola de Tolerantia—A Letter on Toleration*. Edited by Raymond Klibansky. Translated by J. W. Gough. Oxford: Clarendon Press, 1968.

———. *An Essay Concerning Human Understanding*. Edited by Peter H. Nidditch. Oxford: Clarendon Press, 1975.

———. *Second Treatise of Government*. Edited by Richard Cox. Wheeling, IL: Harlan Davidson, 1982.

———. *A Letter Concerning Toleration*. Translated by William Popple. Edited by James Tully. Indianapolis: Hackett Publishing Company, 1983.

———. *Two Treatises of Government*. Edited by Peter Laslett. Student edition. Cambridge: Cambridge University Press, 1988.

———. *Questions Concerning the Law of Nature*. Edited and translated by Robert Horwitz, Jenny Strauss Clay, and Diskin Clay. Ithaca, NY: Cornell University Press, 1990.

———. *A Letter Concerning Toleration in Focus*. Edited by John Horton and Susan Mendus. New York: Routledge, 1991.

———. *Some Thoughts Concerning Education and Of the Conduct of the Understanding*. Edited by Ruth W. Grant and Nathan Tarcov. Indianapolis: Hackett Publishing Company, 1996.

———. *Political Essays*. Edited by Mark Goldie. Cambridge: Cambridge University Press, 1997.

Long, Thomas. *The Letter for Toleration Decipher'd, and the Absurdity and Impiety of an Absolute Toleration Demonstrated, by the Judgment of Presbyterians,*

Independents, and by Mr. Calvin, Mr. Baxter, and the Parliament, 1662. London: Freeman Collins, 1689. Reprint, Early English Books Online (eebo.chadwyck.com), Wing L2973.

Luther, Martin. *Selections from His Writings.* Edited by John Dillenberger. New York: Anchor Books, 1962.

———. *The Large Catechism.* Translated by F. Samuel Janzow. St. Louis: Concordia Publishing House, 1988.

Maclean, A. H. "George Lawson and John Locke." *The Cambridge Historical Journal* 9, no. 1 (March 1947): 69–77.

Macpherson, C. B. *The Political Theory of Possessive Individualism: Hobbes to Locke.* Oxford: Clarendon Press, 1962.

Mansfield, Harvey C., Jr. "The Right of Revolution." *Daedalus* 105, no. 4 (Fall 1976): 151–62.

———. "On the Political Character of Property in Locke." In *Powers, Possessions and Freedom*, edited by Alkis Kontos, 23–38. Toronto: University of Toronto Press, 1979.

———. *Machiavelli's New Modes and Orders: a Study of the Discourses on Livy.* Chicago: University of Chicago Press, 2001. First published 1979 by Cornell University Press.

———. *Taming the Prince: the Ambivalence of Modern Executive Power.* Baltimore: Johns Hopkins University Press, 1993. First published 1989 by The Free Press.

———. *Machiavelli's Virtue.* Chicago: University of Chicago Press, 1996.

Markley, Robert. "'Land Enough in the World': Locke's Golden Age and the Infinite Extention of 'Use'." *South Atlantic Quarterly* 98, no. 4 (Fall 1999): 717–37.

Mattie, Sean. "Prerogative and the Rule of Law in John Locke and the Lincoln Presidency." *Review of Politics* 67, no. 1 (Winter 2005): 77–111.

McClure, Kirstie. *Judging Rights: Lockean Politics and the Limits of Consent.* Ithaca, NY: Cornell University Press, 1996.

Milton, J. R. "Locke's Life and Times." In *The Cambridge Companion to Locke*, edited by Vere Chappell, 5–25. Cambridge: Cambridge University Press, 1994.

———. "Dating Locke's *Second Treatise*." *History of Political Thought* 16, no. 3 (Autumn 1995): 356–90.

Monmouth, James Scott, 1st Duke of. *The Declaration of James Duke of Monmouth, & The Noblemen, Gentlemen & others, now in Arms, for Defence & vindication of the Protestant Religion, & the Laws, Rights, & Privilieges of England, from the Invasion made upon them: & for Delivering the Kingdom from the Usurpation & Tyranny of James Duke of York.* 1685. Reprint, Early English Books Online (eebo.chadwyck.com), Wing M2429.

Of the Fundamental Laws or Politick Constitution of this Kingdom. Reprinted in *State Tracts . . .*, 22–26.

Owen, J. Judd. "Locke's Case for Religious Toleration: Its Neglected Foundation in the *Essay Concerning Human Understanding*." *Journal of Politics* 69, no. 1 (February 2007): 156–68.

Pangle, Thomas L. "Executive Energy and Popular Spirit in Lockean Constitutionalism." *Presidential Studies Quarterly* 17, no. 2 (Spring 1987): 253–65.

———. *The Spirit of Modern Republicanism: the Moral Vision of the American Founders and the Philosophy of John Locke.* Chicago: University of Chicago Press, 1988.

Pasquino, Pasquale. "Locke on King's Prerogative." *Political Theory* 26, no. 2 (April 1998): 198–208.

———. "Hobbes, Religion, and Rational Choice: Hobbes's Two Leviathans and the Fool." *Pacific Philosophical Quarterly* 82 (2001): 406–19.

The Republic of Plato. Translated by Allan Bloom. Second edition. New York: Basic Books, 1991. First edition 1968.

Plato. "Lesser Hippias." Translated by James Leake. In *The Roots of Political Philosophy: Ten Forgotten Socratic* Dialogues, edited by Thomas L. Pangle, 281–99. Ithaca, NY: Cornell University Press, 1987.

Pocock, J. G. A. "The Myth of John Locke and the Obsession with Liberalism." In *John Locke: Papers Read at a Clark Library Seminar, 10 December 1977*, by J. G. A. Pocock and Richard Ashcraft. Los Angeles: William Andrews Clark Memorial Library, 1980.

Political Aphorisms: or, the True Maxims of Government Displayed. London, 1690. Reprint, Early English Books Online (eebo.chadwyck.com), Wing (2nd. ed.) H917E.

Proast, Jonas. *The Argument of the Letter Concerning Toleration Briefly Consider'd and Answer'd.* Oxford, 1690. Reprint, Early English Books Online (eebo.chadwyck.com), Wing P3538.

———. *A Third Letter Concerning Toleration*. Oxford: L. Lichfield, 1691. Reprint, Early English Books Online (eebo.chadwyck.com), Wing P3539.

Raz, Joseph. *The Authority of Law*. Oxford: Clarendon Press, 1979.

Resnick, David. "Locke and the Rejection of the Ancient Constitution." *Political Theory* 12, no. 1 (February 1984): 97–114.

Riley, Patrick. "Locke on 'Voluntary Agreement' and Political Power." *Western Political Quarterly* 29, no. 1 (March 1976): 136–45.

Rutherford, Samuel. *Lex Rex: The Law and the Prince*. London, 1644. Reprint, Early English Books Online (eebo.chadwyck.com), Wing R2386.

Scalia, Antonin. "Originalism: The Lesser Evil." *University of Cincinnati Law Review* 57 (1989): 849–65.

———. *A Matter of Interpretation*. Edited by Amy Gutmann. Princeton, NJ: Princeton University Press, 1997.

Schmitt, Carl. *Die Diktatur.* 5th edition. Berlin: Dunker & Humblot, 1989. First published 1922.

———. *Political Theology: Four Chapters on the Concept of Sovereignty*. Translated by George Schwab. Chicago: University of Chicago Press, 1985. Originally published as *Politische Theologie: Vier Kapitel zur Lehre von der Souveränität* (1922, 2nd ed. 1934).

———. *The Crisis of Parliamentary Democracy*. Translated by Ellen Kennedy. Cambridge, MA: MIT Press, 1985. Originally published as *Die geistesgeschichtliche Lage des heutigen Parlamentarismus* (1923, 2nd ed. 1626).

———. *Legality and Legitimacy*. Translated by Jeffery Seitzer. Durham, NC: Duke University Press, 2004. Originally published as *Legalität und Legitimität* (1932).

———. *The Concept of the Political*. Expanded edition. Translated by George Schwab. Chicago: University of Chicago Press, 2007. Originally published as *Der Begriff des Politischen* (1927, 2nd ed. 1932).

Scott, John T. "The Sovereignless State and Locke's Language of Obligation." *American Political Science Review* 94, no. 3 (September 2000): 547–61.

Scott, Jonathan. "The Law of War: Grotius, Sidney, Locke and the Political Theory of Rebellion." *History of Political Thought* 13, no. 4 (Winter 1992): 565–85.

Seliger, Martin. "Locke's Natural Law and the Foundation of Politics." *Journal of the History of Ideas* 24, no. 3 (July–September 1963): 337–54.

———. "Locke's Theory of Revolutionary Action." *Western Political Quarterly* 16, no. 3 (September 1963): 548–68.

———. *The Liberal Politics of John Locke.* New York: Praeger, 1969.

[Shaftesbury, Anthony Ashley-Cooper, 1st Earl of ?]. *A Letter From a Person of Quality to His Friend in the Country.* 1675. Reprint, Early English Books Online (eebo.chadwyck.com), Wing (2nd. ed.) S2897aA.

Shapiro, Ian, ed. *The Rule of Law.* New York: New York University Press, 1994.

Shklar, Judith. *Legalism: Laws, Morals, and Political Trials.* Cambridge, MA: Harvard University Press, 1964.

———. "Political Theory and the Rule of Law." Chapter 2 in *Political Thought and Political Thinkers.* Chicago: University of Chicago Press, 1998.

Sidney, Algernon. *Discourses Concerning Government.* London, 1698. Reprint, Early English Books Online (eebo.chadwyck.com), Wing S3761.

Simmons, A. John. "Inalienable Rights and Locke's *Treatises.*" *Philosophy and Public Affairs* 12, no. 3 (Summer 1983): 175–204.

———. "Locke's State of Nature." *Political Theory* 17, no. 3 (August 1989): 449–70.

———. "Locke and the Right to Punish." *Philosophy and Public Affairs* 20, no. 4 (Autumn 1991): 311–49.

———. *The Lockean Theory of Rights.* Princeton, NJ: Princeton University Press, 1992.

———. *On the Edge of Anarchy.* Princeton, NJ: Princeton University Press, 1993.

State Tracts: Being a Farther Collection of Several Choice Treatises Relating to the Government From the Year 1660 to 1689. London, 1692. Reprint, Early English Books Online (eebo.chadwyck.com), Wing S5331.

Stevens, Jacqueline. "The Reasonableness of John Locke's Majority: Property Rights, Consent, and Resistance in the *Second Treatise.*" *Political Theory* 24, no. 3 (August 1996): 423–63.

Stoljar, Natalie. "Interpretation, Indeterminacy and Authority: Some Recent Controversies in the Philosophy of Law." *Journal of Political Philosophy* 11, no. 4 (2003): 470–98.

Stoner, James R., Jr. "Was Leo Strauss Wrong about John Locke?" *Review of Politics* 66, no. 4 (Fall 2004): 553–63.

———. "Not So . . ." *Review of Politics* 66, no. 4 (Fall 2004): 571–73.

Strauss, Leo. *The Political Philosophy of Hobbes: Its Basis and Its Genesis.* Translated by Elsa M. Sinclair. Chicago: University of Chicago Press, 1952. First published 1936 by Clarendon Press. Originally published as *Hobbes' politische Wissenschaft in ihrer Genesis* (1935).

———. *Natural Right and History.* Chicago: University of Chicago Press, 1953.

———. *Thoughts on Machiavelli.* Chicago: University of Chicago Press, 1978. First published 1958 by The Free Press.

———. *What is Political Philosophy? and Other Studies.* Chicago: University of Chicago Press, 1988. First published 1959 by The Free Press.

Tarcov, Nathan. "Locke's *Second Treatise* and 'The Best Fence Against Rebellion'." *Review of Politics* 43, no. 2 (April 1981): 198–217.

———. *Locke's Education for Liberty.* Chicago: University of Chicago Press, 1984.

Tarlton, Charles. "'A Rope of Sand': Interpreting Locke's *First Treatise of Government.*" *Historical Journal* 21, no. 1 (March 1978): 43–73.

———. "The Exclusion Controversy, Pamphleteering, and Locke's *Two Treatises.*" *Historical Journal* 24, no. 1 (March 1981): 49–68.

———. "'The Rulers Now on Earth': Locke's *Two Treatises* and the Revolution of 1688." *Historical Journal* 28, no. 2 (June 1985): 279–98.

Thomas, George. "'As Far As Republican Principles Will Admit': Presidential Prerogative and Constitutional Government." *Presidential Studies Quarterly* 30, no. 3 (September 2000): 534–52.

Tocqueville, Alexis de. *Democracy in America.* Translated by Harvey C. Mansfield, Jr., and Delba Winthrop. Chicago: University of Chicago Press, 2000.

Tuckness, Alex. "The Coherence of a Mind: John Locke and the Law of Nature." *Journal of the History of Philosophy* 37, no. 1 (January 1999): 73–90.

———. *Locke and the Legislative Point of View.* Princeton, NJ: Princeton University Press, 2002.

Tully, James. *A Discourse on Property: John Locke and His Adversaries.* Cambridge: Cambridge University Press, 1980.

———. "Political Freedom." *Journal of Philosophy* 87, no. 10 (October 1990): 517–23.

———. *An Approach to Political Philosophy: Locke in Contexts.* Cambridge: Cambridge University Press, 1993.

Vogt, Philip. "Locke, Eden, and the Two States of Nature." *Journal of the History of Philosophy* 35, no. 4 (October 1997): 523–44.

Vox Populi: Or, The Peoples Claim to their Parliament's Sitting, to Redress Grievances, and to provide for the Common Safety, by the known Laws and Constitutions of the Nation. 1681. Reprinted in *State Tracts . . .*, 219–24.

Waldron, Jeremy. "Is the Rule of Law an Essentially Contested Concept (In Florida)?" *Law and Philosophy* 21, no. 2 (March 2002): 137–64.

———. *God, Locke, and Equality: Christian Foundations in Locke's Political Thought.* Cambridge: Cambridge University Press, 2002.

Weaver, David R. "Leadership, Locke, and the Federalist." *American Journal of Political Science* 41, no. 2 (April 1997): 420–46.

Windstrup, George. "Locke on Suicide." *Political Theory* 8, no. 2 (May 1980): 169–82.

Wood, Neil. *John Locke and Agrarian Capitalism.* Berkeley and Los Angeles: University of California Press, 1984.

Yolton, John. "Locke on the Law of Nature." *Philosophical Review* 67, no. 4 (October 1958): 477–98.

Zuckert, Michael. *Natural Rights and the New Republicanism.* Princeton, NJ: Princeton University Press, 1994.

———. *Launching Liberalism.* Lawrence: University of Kansas Press, 2002.

———. "Perhaps He Was." *Review of Politics* 66, no. 4 (Fall 2004): 565–69.

Index

www.ingramcontent.com/pod-product-compliance
Lightning Source LLC
LaVergne TN
LVHW101626040926
847296LV00026B/110